The Secret History of Language

AF194436

What are the causes of language change? Where do words come from? Is modern technology and social media corrupting our language? Language change is just as relevant today as it ever was, yet the secrets of how and why it occurs remain tantalizingly out of reach to anyone without a background in linguistics. This book has the answers. Written by one of the leading experts in the field, it provides readers with an accessible account of language change, unraveling the processes and phenomena that have so far remained locked within academia. It explores a range of fascinating topics, such as whether language change is bad, whether change is different in some kinds of languages than others, and if television, AI, and modern technology have any impact on language change. Written in a lively and engaging way, it uncovers the marvels and mysteries of language change for anyone curious about this captivating field.

Lyle Campbell is Professor Emeritus at the University of Hawai'i Mānoa. His research specializations include historical linguistics, language documentation, American Indian languages, and typology. He has been awarded the Linguistic Society of America's Leonard Bloomfield Book Award twice, for *American Indian Languages* (Oxford University Press, 1997) and *Historical Syntax in Cross-Linguistic Perspective* (with Harris, Cambridge University Press, 1995).

The Secret History of Language

Language Change Unraveled

Lyle Campbell

University of Hawai'i, Mānoa

CAMBRIDGE
UNIVERSITY PRESS

CAMBRIDGE
UNIVERSITY PRESS

Shaftesbury Road, Cambridge CB2 8EA, United Kingdom

One Liberty Plaza, 20th Floor, New York, NY 10006, USA

477 Williamstown Road, Port Melbourne, VIC 3207, Australia

314–321, 3rd Floor, Plot 3, Splendor Forum, Jasola District Centre,
New Delhi – 110025, India

Cambridge University Press is part of Cambridge University Press & Assessment,
a department of the University of Cambridge.

We share the University's mission to contribute to society through the pursuit of
education, learning and research at the highest international levels of excellence.

www.cambridge.org
Information on this title: www.cambridge.org/9781009757966

DOI: 10.1017/9781009757959

First published 2026

A catalogue record for this publication is available from the British Library

Library of Congress Cataloging-in-Publication Data
Names: Campbell, Lyle author
Title: The secret history of language : language change unraveled / Lyle Campbell,
University of Hawai'i, Manoa.
Description: Cambridge, United Kingdom ; New York, NY : Cambridge University
Press, 2026. | Includes bibliographical references and index.
Identifiers: LCCN 2025052204 (print) | LCCN 2025052205 (ebook) |
ISBN 9781009757966 hardback | ISBN 9781009757997 paperback |
ISBN 9781009757959 ebook
Subjects: LCSH: Linguistic change
Classification: LCC P142 .C37 2026 (print) | LCC P142 (ebook)
LC record available at https://lccn.loc.gov/2025052204
LC ebook record available at https://lccn.loc.gov/2025052205

ISBN 978-1-009-75796-6 Hardback
ISBN 978-1-009-75799-7 Paperback

Contents

Figures

Maps

Tables

Preface

This book explores the history of languages and the kinds of changes that languages undergo. These changes can make languages seem mysterious. Their mysteries are unraveled, revealing the marvels lying behind them. The book is intended for a general audience. I greatly enjoyed writing it, and hope you enjoy reading it.

Terminology and Symbols

To describe, explain, and exemplify language changes, it is necessary to talk about sounds, parts of grammar, kinds of changes, and the classification of languages, and ordinarily that requires terminology and symbols that most people may not be familiar with. I have avoided technical terms wherever possible, and where they are needed, I have attempted to explain them in ways that make them clear to readers of all sorts. Many of these terms and symbols are defined where they are first encountered in the text, and the **Glossary** at the end of the book defines and explains most of them. Terms that can be found in the glossary are in boldface when first encountered in the text. Symbols for sounds and uncommon orthographic characters and for other conventions are explained in the **Symbol List** at the beginning of the book.

While the terminology and symbols can at times feel daunting, it helps to keep in mind that complete understanding of them is seldom crucial for understanding the point that is being discussed, and it is OK to skip on past things that are more difficult to interpret without missing much of consequence.

Examples

Most of the book's examples are drawn from English, although some are from other languages, too, when it serves the purpose. Relying primarily on English examples helps to make the concepts easier to follow for most readers. Often, multiple examples are presented to illustrate things under discussion, sometimes more examples than needed. Each example is interesting in its own right, but not every example is going to resonate in the same way with every reader, which is why the multiple examples are presented. Not everyone is going to want to read each example, either, so, once you have grasped the idea involved, you can feel free to skip over unneeded or less interesting examples and move on.

Acknowledgments

I am very grateful to Helen Barton and Isabel Collins of Cambridge University Press for their extensive work, invaluable recommendations, and constant encouragement. A special thanks, also, is due to Sue Browning, the copy-editor, for painstaking labor and effective feedback which much improved the book, and to David McCutcheon, the cartographer who created the maps in this book.

Notes on the Text

Symbol List

The following list of symbols that are used to represent sounds in a written form identifies what the symbols encountered in the book represent and how to interpret them. The symbols are listed in two parts, phonetic symbols and orthographic symbols.

Symbols that represent sounds that match letters of the English alphabet are not explained here, as they present no challenge for interpreting them – the sounds of *p, t, k, b, d, g* (as in **goat**, **goose**), *f, v,* s, *z, l, m, n, w,* and *h*. Symbols for sounds not found in the examples in the book are also not included. A good number of the examples in this book contain symbols that were used in the sources cited, and how to interpret the sounds represented by these symbols is explained here.

Phonetic Symbols

Some sources use symbols from the Americanist Phonetic Alphabet (APA), though most linguists prefer the International Phonetic Alphabet (IPA). Most of the symbols in the two transcription systems are the same except for a few consonants and some vowels. In the list here, where there is a difference between the two, both are given, first the APA symbol for the sound, followed by its IPA equivalent in parentheses.

The official names of phonetic symbols tell how they are articulated, though typically in Latinate technical terms rather than in everyday English words. In the list of phonetic symbols here, the official names are given (in case they may be helpful), but it is anticipated that most readers will pay those names little attention. The explanations and descriptions in common English after these phonetic names should be more useful.

The technical names include where the sound is produced in the mouth (called its "point of articulation") and how it is pronounced (called "manner of articulation"). It will help to define and describe some of the primary manners of articulation first, to avoid lots of repetition, and then list symbols for sounds according to their points of articulation.

Manners of Articulation

voiced Sounds with the vocal cords vibrating during their production, as in English *b, d, g, v*, "*zh*" ([ž], IPA [ʒ]), "*dh*" ([ð]), *r, l, m, n*, "*ng*" ([ŋ]), *w, y*, etc., and vowels.

voiceless Sounds produced without the vocal cords vibrating during their production, as with English *p, t, k, f, s*, "*sh*" ([š], IPA [ʃ]), "th" ([θ]), etc.

stop A consonant in whose articulation the flow of air in the vocal tract is completely blocked momentarily before it is suddenly released, as in the pronunciation of *p, t, k, b, d*, and *g* in English.

nasal Speech sounds in which air passes through the nose during their production. Nasal consonants, as in English *m, n*, and *ŋ* (the "ng" sound as in *sing*), are produced with the mouth closed, so air escapes solely through the nose. In nasalized vowels, the mouth is not closed and air passes through the nose and mouth at the same time.

fricative A speech sound where the airstream is not completely blocked, where the vocal tract is constricted to a narrow passage so that friction (turbulence) characterizes the sound, as in English *f, s*, "*sh*" ([š], IPA [ʃ]), *v, z*, "*zh*" ([ž], IPA [ʒ]), and "th" ([θ]) and "*dh*" ([ð]), etc.

affricate A consonant that combines a stop and a fricative, beginning in a stop that is released as a fricative. Though complex, an affricate is a single speech sound, as the "ch" sound ([č], IPA [tʃ]) in *chin* or the "dzh" sound ([ǰ], IPA [dʒ]) in *jam*.

approximant A consonant that is produced by constricting the vocal tract slightly, but not so much that it creates turbulence as in the case of fricatives. The approximants in English are *l, r, w*, and *y*.

aspirated A consonant whose articulation is released with a small puff of air, a brief burst of breath when the sound is produced. It is represented with a raised "h," as in English, *pie* [pʰai].

Points of Articulation

Consonants

bilabial   Sounds pronounced with closure or near closure of the two lips (for example, *p, b, m*).

p^y (IPA [p^j]) voiceless palatalized bilabial fricative – a *p* released with a short *y*-like sound. Palatalized consonants are produced with the blade or front of the tongue drawn up farther toward the roof of the mouth (hard palate) than in the pronunciation of their plain counterparts.

dental   Sounds pronounced with the tongue touching the upper teeth:

θ voiceless dental fricative; the "th" sound in *think, bath*. It is represented by a letter of the Greek alphabet called "theta."

ð voiced dental fricative; the "th" sound in *those, bathe*. Also a letter in Old English writing, called "eth."

alveolar   Sounds pronounced with the tongue placed on or near the alveolar ridge, the bony bump behind the upper teeth (for example, *t, d, n, s, z*).

ɫ voiceless lateral approximant – a kind of *l* that sounds like *l* whispered, like blowing through an *l*

ḷ syllabic *l*, an *l* that serves as the nucleus of a syllable that has no vowel, as in the final syllable of *bundle, people*

ṇ syllabic *n*, an *n* that serves as the nucleus of a syllable that has no vowel, as in the final syllable of *button*

ṛ syllabic *r*, an *r* that serves as the nucleus of a syllable that has no vowel

tl voiceless alveolar lateral affricate – a sound that combines a *t*-like sound released into a voiceless *l* (like *l* whispered, like blowing through an *l*)

t^y (IPA [t^j]) voiceless palatalized alveolar stop – a *t* released with a short *y*-like sound

alveopalatal   (palato-alveolar) Sounds produced with the blade or front of the tongue touching or very near to the front of the hard palate near the alveolar ridge, the bony bump behind the upper teeth:

š (IPA [ʃ]) voiceless alveopalatal fricative, as the "sh" sound of *ship, mash*

ž (IPA [ʒ]) voiced alveopalatal fricative, as the "zh" sound of *Asia, vision, beige* č (IPA [ʧ]) voiceless alveopalatal affricate, as the "ch" sound in of *chip*, *match*

ǰ (IPA [ʤ]) voiced alveopalatal affricate, as the "j" sound in *job*, *large*

palatal   Sounds articulated on or near the hard palate:

y (IPA [j])voiced palatal approximant, as in *year*, *young*, *beyond*. In this book, *y* is used consistently to represent this sound, except in some examples from Germanic languages where the letter *j* represents the *y* sound.

velar   Sounds produced with the back of the tongue on or very near the soft palate, as for example, the *k* sound of "c" or "k," as in *coat*, **kick**, the "g" sound in *goat*, log, or the "ng" sound in *sing*.

k^h voiceless aspirated velar stop. A *k*-like sound pronounced with a small puff of air when released, as for example the "k" sound in English *cot*, but not in *Scot* where the "k" sound is not aspirated.

k^w voiceless labialized velar stop, like the *qu* of **quick**, **equal**, sometimes written as *kw* in Indo-European sources

g^w voiced labialized velar stop, like the *gu* of **guava**, **guacamole**, sometimes written as *gw* in Indo-European sources

x voiceless velar fricative, as the sound of German "ch" in *Bach* and *Achtung* 'watch out!'

uvular   Sounds similar to sounds like *k* and *g*, but produced further towards the back of the mouth, involving the uvula, the small, fleshy tissue that hangs at the back of the soft palate.

q voiceless uvular stop (like *k* but pronounced further back in the mouth)

χ voiceless uvular fricative (like "ch" in *Bach* but pronounced further back in the mouth)

pharyngeal   Sounds produced with the root of the tongue pushed back toward the wall of the pharynx, the back of the throat.

ħ voiceless pharyngeal fricative, for example the sound in Arabic commonly transliterated as *ḥ*

glottal   Sounds located at the glottis, the part of the larynx that contains the vocal cords. The most common glottal sounds are glottal stop ([ʔ]) and *h*.

ʔ glottal stop, the sound when the vocal cords are briefly closed, as for example the sound in the pause between the two parts of *oh-oh*

Vowels

Vowels are voiced sounds that are distinguished according to the position of the tongue in the mouth.

front A vowel produced with the tongue towards the front of the mouth (for example, *i* in *feet* and *e* in *late*)

back A vowel produced with the tongue towards the back of the mouth (for example, *u* in *goose* and *o* as in the first part of the vowel of *boat* in North American English)

central A vowel produced in the central area of the mouth (for example, *ə*, the vowel of *but, rough*)

high A vowel produced with the tongue towards the roof of the mouth (for example, *i* in *feet* and *u* in *goose*)

low A vowel produced with the tongue towards the floor of the mouth (for example, *a* in *father*).

mid A vowel produced with the tongue in the middle of the mouth, neither high nor low (for example, *ɛ* as in *met, red*).

Vowel symbols seen in some of the examples in this book include:

ə Mid central vowel, as in **up, but, about, ugly**

æ Low front vowel, as the vowel in *bat, cap*. It is also a letter used in writing Old English, with this same phonetic value

ã Low back nasalized vowel. A nasalized vowel is pronounced with air flowing through both the nose and the mouth simultaneously, seen in this book in words from Portuguese and French. The *ã* represents a sound like *a* of *father* but nasalized, like the last vowel of English *salon* but stopping before the *n* is pronounced, or like English *song*, but without pronouncing the *ng* part and without rounding the lips.

õ Mid back nasalized vowel, something like the vowel of English *moan* and *known*, but stopping before the final *n* is pronounced

ɛ Mid open front vowel, as the vowel in *pet, bed*

ɪ High open front vowel, as the vowel in *pit, bid*

ɔ Mid open back vowel, as the vowel in *paw, bought, caught* (in English dialects that have not merged [ɔ] with [a])

ʊ High open back vowel, as the vowel in *book, put*.

Orthographic Symbols

α   The Greek letter "alpha"; it has the phonetic value of [a].

β   The Greek letter "beta"; it has the phonetic value of [b].

ä   Finnish letter that represents [æ], a voiced low front vowel. German and Swedish also use the letter ä, but its phonetic value there is closer to [ɛ], as in English *pet, ten*.

ą   A nasalized *a*, used to represent this sound in Proto-Germanic, a voiced low back nasalized vowel. The IPA equivalent for this sound is [ã].

å   A letter of the Swedish alphabet that represents a sound like [o].

ø   A letter used in Danish, Norwegian, and Faroese to represent a front rounded vowel, pronounced forward in the mouth in the position of [e] but with the lips rounded; [ø] is also the IPA symbol that represents this sound.

ç   A letter with the phonetic value of *s* used in French and Portuguese, called "*c* cedilla."

ġ   In Old English, *ġ* was pronounced [y] (as in *yes*). It represented *g* that was changing to *y* before front vowels.

ğ   A Turkish letter. It is silent or optionally pronounced as a weak *w* between round vowels or between a round vowel and *a* or *e*, as in the name of Turkish president Recep Tayyip *Erdoğan*, whose last name sounds like "urdowan." Turkish *yoğurt* 'yoghurt' sounds like [yo.urt], two syllables.

ḥ   Symbol used for transliteration of the Arabic voiceless pharyngeal fricative, IPA [ħ]. Pharyngeal sounds are produced with the root of the tongue pushed back toward the wall of the pharynx, the back of the throat.

k̂   Proto-Indo-European is <u>reconstructed</u> with what is called a series of palatal velars, *k̂, ĝ, ĝh*, pronounced more forward in the mouth than *k, g, gh*, respectively, towards the hard palate more than on the soft palate, as is the case for *k, g, gh*. The *k̂* is the sound from this series that mostly shows up in examples cited in this book.

kh   Symbol used for transliteration of the Arabic voiceless uvular fricative, IPA [χ] (like "ch" in *Bach*, but pronounced further back in the mouth).

ñ   A Spanish letter that represents a palatal nasal, a sound, similar to *ny* in English *canyon*.

ö   A letter used in Old Norse, German, Swedish, Icelandic, Finnish, Estonian, Turkish, Hungarian, and related languages. It represents what in the IPA is [ø], a voiced mid front rounded vowel. It is

	like "e" of *pet* pronounced with the lips rounded, like an *o* with the tongue moved to the front of the mouth.
þ	A runic letter used in Old English to write the "th" sound as in *think, bath,* called "thorn."
ṭ	Symbol for the transcription of "emphatic" *t* in Arabic and some other Semitic and Afroasiatic languages. The "emphatic" consonants of these languages are pharyngealized, meaning that the tongue is retracted toward the back of the throat during their articulation.
ü	A letter used in German, Swedish, Turkish, Hungarian, and a few other languages to represent the sound that in the IPA is [y], a voiced high front rounded vowel. It is like *i* pronounced with the lips rounded, like a *u* with the tongue moved to the front of the mouth.
ʼ	Symbol used to represent glottal stop ([ʔ]) in a number of languages, in particular in Indigenous languages of the Americas.
ʻ	The letter in Hawaiian, called *ʻokina,* that represents glottal stop ([ʔ]), as for example in *Hawaiʻi.*

Notations

Conventional notations used in presenting materials are the following.

★	An asterisk placed before a word or form indicates that it is reconstructed, inferred to have existed in the common ancestor language (proto-language) of a <u>language family</u> or in an earlier stage of a particular language. It usually signifies something reconstructed by the <u>comparative method</u> (see the Glossary).
>	means 'became, changed to'.
<	signifies 'came from, changed from'.
<...>	indicates that the material in the brackets is given exactly as found in the source, for example as written in some early manuscript.
[...]	square brackets indicate phonetic transcription; they represent the exact pronunciation of the sound, word, phrase, or whatever is enclosed in the brackets.
/.../	indicates that what is written between slashes represents contrastive sounds of a language, that is, sounds that can signal words that have different meanings (as *p* versus *t* in *pen/ten, pie/tie*). These are sounds that are recognized as the real speech sounds of the language by native speakers. The technical term for such a sound is "phoneme."

The diacritic of a bar over a vowel (for example, $\bar{a}$, $\bar{e}$, $\bar{\imath}$, $\bar{u}$) is called a "macron." It signifies vowel length, that the duration of the vowel with this diacritic is longer than a corresponding plain vowel lacking this diacritic.

About References

The sources of things cited are given in the text in the standard convention of author's last name followed by the year of publication and the page or pages of the cited material in parentheses. For example, "(Sapir 1933: 155)" references a work from the author Sapir, published in 1933, found on page 155. The full details for the reference are found by looking up the entry for Sapir's 1933 publication in the references at the end of this book. References cited from websites are given in footnotes. The etymologies are based on information from multiple sources, primarily from Online Etymological Dictionary (at www.etymonline.com), Watkins (2011), and Mallory and Adams (1997). Cases from these sources are given without further identification. For cases not based on these sources, references are provided in the text.

1 Language History
Past Offenses or Glorious Achievements?

Every living language, like the perspiring bodies of living creatures, is in perpetual motion and alteration; some words go off, and become obsolete; others are taken in, and by degrees grow into common use; or the same word is inverted to a new sense and notion, which in tract of time makes as observable a change in the air and features of a language as age makes in the lines and mien of a face.

(Richard Bentley [written 1698] cited in Orrery 1698: 186)

Introduction

Have you ever wondered where certain words come from? Have you sometimes wanted to know why your language has stuff that seems unusual or weird? Have you puzzled over the language's exceptions or oddities? Have you ever felt bothered by the changes some people make when they speak? If so, you are among masses of people whose interests and whose displeasures feed the many popular books, websites and blogs, newspaper columns, podcasts, media broadcasts, and magazine articles about the history of words and about "proper" grammar. That is, as unaware of it as most of us may be, there is extensive public interest in language change and language history. Nonetheless, modern education does not equip us well to satisfy the curiosity or to pursue the interest. We are poorly served by the proclamations of the pseudo-intellectual self-appointed language pundits and grammar police on these matters.

This book aims at filling the gap, at satisfying curiosity and providing fundamental understanding about how and why languages change. It is intended as a non-technical, accessible book for anyone with a natural curiosity about the history of language and language change. It is about "the secret history of language," secret only in the sense of it being mostly unknown outside of academic circles. The book unravels mysteries and reveals the marvels of language change and language history. Solving how and why a language changed in specific cases can be like detective work, exciting and satisfying, but without crimes.

In this first chapter, the stage is set by debunking some myths, common misconceptions about language and how it changes. The following often-asked questions all embody common myths – misconceptions – about language and language change.

1. Is language change bad? Is it corruption/degeneration/decay?
2. Is the cause of language change laziness, or even immorality, and, if not, what are its causes?
3a. Is change different in some kinds of languages than it is in other sorts of languages?
3b. Are some languages "primitive," and so therefore subject to different kinds of changes from the sorts of changes found in more "civilized" tongues?
4. Does language change affect written languages differently from unwritten ones?
5. Is social media or technology corrupting our language? What impact, if any, do social media, television, AI, and modern technology have on language change?
6. Does size matter? For example, is English a better language because it has a truly massive dictionary? Better put, where do words come from, and in what ways, if any, is English vocabulary special?
7. Can kinds of societies or cultures determine the kinds of features a language will have and the kinds of changes languages can undergo to bring these features about?

Myths about Languages and How They Change

Like many academic disciplines, linguistics has its foundations in the early 1800s. It had to contend with numerous myths (misconceptions) about language change and about the very nature of language itself as the field evolved into the scientific discipline it is today. The following are a few examples that illustrate the kinds of weird erroneous thinking that had to be dealt with. Many of these questions are confronted in discussion scattered throughout this book.

The "Primitive" Languages Myth

Are some languages "primitive" and therefore subject to different kinds of changes from those that take place in other kinds of languages? The answer is a resounding "no." There are no "primitive" languages. Claims of the following sorts were made.

[Speaking of the Puris of Brazil:] Their language is extremely poor . . . in today, tomorrow, and yesterday, they have but the word for day, the further meaning being expressed by signs. For to-day they say "day," and touch the head or point upwards; for to-morrow, "day," and point forward with the finger; and for yesterday also "day," pointing then backwards. (Pfeiffer 1852: 58. This claim was often cited and repeated.)

What shall we say, for instance . . . of the Yamparico, "who speaks a sort of gibberish like the growling of a dog" . . . ? Of the aborigines of Victoria, among whom new-born babes are killed and eaten by their parents and brothers, and who have no numerals beyond three? . . . Of the Fuegians, "whose language is an inarticulate clucking," and who kill and eat their old women before their dogs, because, as a Fuegian boy naïvely and candidly expressed it, "Doggies catch otters, old women no" . . . Of the negroes of New Guinea, who were seen springing from branch to branch of the trees like monkeys, gesticulating, screaming, and laughing? . . . Of the forest tribes of Malacca, who lisp their words, whose sound is like the noise of birds? . . . Of the wild Veddahs of Ceylon, who have gutturals and grimaces instead of language? (Farrar 1873: 39–40)

The same deficiency of abstract terms, that is, of words in which the subjective predominates over the objective element, marks many barbarous languages. The Malayans, for instance, have words to signify different sorts and parts of trees, but none to signify "tree" itself; while the Algonquin can localise special individual acts of loving, but cannot express the act regarded in the abstract . . . Similarly, the Cherokee possesses thirteen different verbs to denote particular kinds of "washing," but none to denote "washing" in a general sense. (Sayce 1875: 81)

Savages will have 20 independent words each expressing the act of cutting some particular thing, without having any name for the act of cutting in general; they will have as many to describe birds, fish and trees of different kinds, but no equivalents for the terms "bird", "fish", or "tree". (Payne 1899: 103)

Even to this day there are said to be some low tribes in South America whose spoken language is so imperfect that they cannot converse in the dark. (*Science Progress*, 1914, vol. 8: 524)

The common belief in the nineteenth and early twentieth centuries was that only European languages, the assumed languages of "civilization," were fully adequate. It was repeated over and over that "savages" or "barbarians" lacked true language. This claim was thought to be nearly self-evident because of the supposed poverty of their vocabulary, alleged lack of grammar, and presumed simple structure. Their languages were alternatively accused of lacking abstract, generic terms or of having only generic words, lacking specific terms – damned if you do, damned if you don't. In short, they were considered primitive, and primitive languages were assumed to have these "primitive" attributes.

All of these claims about so-called primitive languages are utterly false – today it is well established that there are no "primitive" languages. All languages are fully adequate for the communicative needs of the societies that speak them. No language is better or worse suited than any other for these purposes. Language scholars today support "linguistic relativity," that languages can differ on their own terms and should not be judged based on what is thought appropriate in some other language. In the words of the much-admired twentieth-century American linguist and anthropologist Edward Sapir:

The gift of speech and a well ordered language are characteristic of every known group of human beings ... The truth of the matter is that language is an essentially perfect means of expression and communication among every known people. (Sapir 1933: 155)

The Rapid Change Myth

Several myths relate to the "primitive language" fallacy, for example the claim that so-called primitive languages change really rapidly, far more rapidly than "civilized" ones. It was maintained, for example, that:

[The vocabulary of savages is] slippery and unstable as a dream. (Payne 1899: 89)

From 20 to 40 years is probably a liberal allotment for the average life of a very low savage language. (Payne 1899: 92)

[From Edward B. Tylor, a founding figure in anthropology as an academic discipline]: Indeed, anyone who will attend to how English words run together in talking may satisfy himself that his own language would undergo rapid changes like those of barbaric tongues, were it not for the schoolmaster and the printer, who insist on keeping our words fixed and separate. (Tylor 1881: 142)

[From Sir James George Frazer, prominent figure in early social anthropology, author of the hugely influential *The Golden Bough*]: The mint of words was in the hands of the old women of the tribe [Abipones of Argentina], and whatever term they stamped with their approval and put into circulation was immediately accepted without a murmur by high and low alike, and spread like wildfire through every camp and settlement of the tribe. You would be astonished ... to see how meekly the whole nation acquiesces in the decision of a withered old hag, and how completely the old familiar words fall instantly out of use and are never repeated either through force of habit or forgetfulness. In seven years ... the native word for jaguar was changed thrice, and the words for crocodile, thorn, and the slaughter of cattle underwent similar though less varied vicissitudes. (Frazer 1957: 335–346 [first published in 1890])

The early history of scientific linguistics and anthropology had to combat inane armchair pronouncements such as these. Now we know that, no, language change is not different in some kinds of languages from what it is in other kinds. The claim of really rapid change in so-called "primitive" languages is dead wrong. There are no "primitive," "savage," or "barbaric" languages.

The Great Eskimo Snow Hoax

You have probably heard it said that Eskimo has dozens or even hundreds of words for snow. This is also a myth. Let's take a look at it, called "the great Eskimo snow hoax" (Martin 1986, Pullum 1989). The claim is wrong, but it was not a purposeful attempt to deceive, though it does involve a colossal distortion and fundamental misunderstanding.

It started with Franz Boas, the founder of American linguistics and American anthropology. Boas (1911: 25–26) mentioned terms for snow in order to caution against superficial language comparisons. He had studied the "Eskimos" (that is, Inuit) on Baffin Island in his first field-work. He cited four Inuit words for snow: *aput* 'snow on the ground', *qana* 'falling snow', *piqsirpoq* 'drifting snow', and *qimusqsuq* 'a snow drift'. He compared them with English *river, lake, rain, brook*, where a different root is used for each of these different forms of water, as it is for different forms of snow in Inuit, although English might just as well derive these same concepts from phrases based on *water* as it does for kinds of snow, as in *snow drift* and *snow bank*. Boas' point was that Inuit, with its different roots for things involving snow, is like English with its different roots for things involving water, just a superficial fact about differences between languages. For example, English has cases with distinct roots that refer to essentially the same thing, as in *year* vs. *annual, father* vs. *paternal, baby* vs. *infant*, and on and on, where another language may have but a single root to convey these related concepts, a trivial fact about how languages can differ from one another.

From his reading of Boas' article, Benjamin Lee Whorf (1956: 216) claimed five 'snow' words in Eskimo (Inuit). From this, the idea got repeated over and over, with ever increasing numbers of Eskimo words for snow being claimed, now sometimes said to be hundreds or even thousands, and said to illustrate radically different world views, some-times linked with notions of environmental determinism affecting what one finds in a language's vocabulary. That, however, was not at all Boas' point.

One modern Eskimo (that is, Inuit) dictionary has only three roots for snow. In another variety of Inuit, linguists count about a dozen 'snow' words. But then, so what? In English skiers' snow terminology, snow words exceed this number by a large margin, and even common everyday English comes close, with its words *snow, blizzard, sleet, flurry, drift, slush, powder*, *flake*, and maybe also *avalanche*, *fall* (snowfall), *pack* (snowpack), *drift* (snowdrift), and so on.

The "Correct Language" Myth

Common misconceptions about language change don't just come from the past, but some are still with us even now, encountered with surprising frequency. An oft-heard outspoken opinion is that language change is bad. Versions of this claim are widespread on the internet, in newspaper columns, in various books by wannabe language pundits, in coffee shops, sometimes in classrooms, and in letters to the editor of newspapers and journals. David Crystal (pictured in Figure 1.1), a British linguist famous for his many achievements and publications, described masses of such letters of complaint in his 2009 book, *Just a Phrase I'm Going Through*. He wrote:

The producer asked me to go through all the letters [of complaint about language] that had been sent in to the BBC during the previous month or so. There were hundreds. I made my survey and produced a "top ten" of complaints. *Between you and I* was the Number 1 hate. And "hate" was the operative word ... People didn't just "dislike" usages such as split infinitives and intrusive *r*'s. They were "horrified", "appalled", "scandalized". (Crystal 2009: 197)

The popular attitude towards language change is predominantly negative. Changes in language are typically seen as corruption, decay, degeneration, or due to laziness. We read that English grammar is suffering deterioration that reflects social decay, linked with poor education and the sloppy language of the youth, that our language is being reduced

Figure 1.1 David Crystal.
Source: Photo by Steve Cray/*South China Morning Post* via Getty Images.

to a bare remnant of its former and rightful glory – described with droves of other words that express negative judgements.

Where Do Notions of Correct, Pure, Good Language and against Language Change Come From?

Such complaints and charges condemning changes in language have been made throughout history. Ranulf Higden (ca. 1280–ca. 1364), English Benedictine monk, wrote in Latin about harm to English. In John Trevisa's translation to English, Higden lamented that: "By intermingling and mixing, first with Danes and afterwards with Normans, in many people the language of the land is harmed, and some use strange inarticulate utterance, chattering, snarling, and harsh teeth-gnashing."[1]

Jonathan Swift (pictured in Figure 1.2) author of *Gulliver's Travels* and *A Modest Proposal*, attributed language decline to the "licentiousness which entered with the *Restoration* [1660], and from infecting our Religion and Morals, fell to corrupt our Language" (in his *A Proposal for Correcting, Improving and Ascertaining the English Tongue* [1711–1712]).

Figure 1.2 Jonathan Swift
Source: Wikimedia Commons.

[1] Cited by Crystal (2005).

Figure 1.3 The Brothers Grimm, Jacob (right) and Wilhelm (left)
Source: clu / DigitalVision Vectors / Getty Images.

The Brothers Grimm (pictured in Figure 1.3), well known for their role in fairytales but celebrated also for their important contributions to the development of historical linguistics, held that:

The farther back in time one can climb, the more beautiful and more perfect he finds the form of language, [while] the closer he comes to its present form, the more painful it is to him to find the power and adroitness of the language in decline and decay.[2] (Grimm and Grimm 1854: iii)

Jacob and Wilhelm Grimm's works on both fairytales and the history of the German language reflect their involvement in the German Romanticism movement with its promotion of German nationalism (see Chapter 5).

As Thomas Lounsbury, a nineteenth-century professor of Language and Literature at Yale University, put it:

There seems to have been in every period of the past, as there is now, a distinct apprehension in the minds of very many worthy persons that the English tongue is always in the condition of approaching collapse, and that arduous efforts must be put forth, and put forth persistently, in order to save it from destruction. (Lounsbury 1908: 2)

---

[2] Je weiter aufwärts er klimmen kann, desto schöner und vollkommner dünkt ihn die leibliche gestalt der sprache, je näher ihrer jetzigen fassung er tritt, desto weher thut ihm jene macht und gewandtheit der form in abnahme und verfall zu finden.

Is Language Change Good or Bad?

Versions of this question are frequent in public discourse of many sorts. As mentioned, the changes are often seen as various sorts of corruption and decay, sometimes even as perversions, and a threat to morality and even to national security. We read that language deterioration reflects social decay, that our language is embattled, being destroyed, reduced to an almost unrecognizable remnant of its former excellence. And the guilty parties who are to be blamed for the current bad state of language? They are variably reported to be the youth with their sloppy language use, laziness, parents, teachers, poor educational policies, the media, popular culture, modern technology, the internet, politicians, globalization, neglect of religion, moral decline, and America.

America is often deemed the culprit for ongoing degeneration of the English language. The American journalist Edwin Newman, for example, wrote *Strictly Speaking: Will America Be the Death of English?* (1974). British newspapers report complaints of the corrupting American influence in the UK pushing out traditional British pronunciations in words such as *adverTISEment* for *adVERTisement* and *paytriotic* for *patriotic*, and for *schedule* being pronounced now as "*skedule*" rather than "*shedule*." In Britain, *controversy* was earlier pronounced as *CONtroversy* and shifted only relatively recently for many speakers there to *conTROversy*. People in the UK complained of unfortunate American influence when they heard *conTROversy* on the radio, though it has never been pronounced with the stress on that syllable in America (Copping 2011).

The despondency over assumed language decay has even spawned poetry:

> Coin brassy words at will, debase the coinage;
> We're in an if-you-cannot-lick-them-join age,
> A slovenliness-provides-its-own-excuse age,
> Where usage overnight condones misusage,
> Farewell, farewell to my beloved language,
> Once English, now a vile orangutanguage.
> (Ogden Nash 1960. *Laments for a Dying Language*)

Concerns for the presumed negative effects of language change figured strongly in the motives for establishing language academies – to protect languages from decay and to foster their purity. French has the Académie Française, Spanish has the Real Academia Española, and German has the Rat für deutsche Rechtschreibung. English is one of the few major European languages that have no language academy attempting to protect them from unwanted change.

The distress of many notwithstanding, languages keep changing and the language of today is just as able to meet our communicative needs as the language of years long gone by. The changes taking place today that so distress purists and prescriptivists are the same in kind and character as past changes about which there was once much complaint when they were taking place but whose results today are held to have enriched the modern language. Languages are always changing, adapting to accommodate the needs and desires of their users. That is why new words are constantly being added (see Chapter 2). As users' needs and interests change, language change follows. Merriam-Webster added 690 new words to its dictionary in 2023, among them the likes of:

edgelord (noun, slang) 'someone who makes wildly dark and exaggerated statements (as on an internet forum) with the intent of shocking others'

simp (verb, informal) 'to show excessive devotion to or longing for someone or something'

smishing (noun) 'the practice of sending text messages to someone in order to trick the person into revealing personal or confidential information which can then be used for criminal purposes'

zhuzh (noun) 'a small improvement, adjustment, or addition that completes the overall look, taste, etc. of something'; (verb) 'to improve in flavor or appearance by way of a small improvement, adjustment, or addition' – often used with *up*[3]

The Cambridge Dictionary added a whopping 3,200 new words in 2024.

From an objective, scientific standpoint, language change is inherently neither good nor bad – it just is. So, where do notions of correct, pure, good language and against language change come from? They do not come from the languages themselves. Society can assign negative or positive value – stigma or prestige – to things in language for various non-linguistic reasons, which very often is the case with new or ongoing changes in language. Linguists aren't concerned with notions of "proper" or "correct" language; rather they analyze actual language usage. For them, nonstandard language is no better or worse than standard language; both meet the needs and goals of their users.

There is, however, a strong tradition of prescriptive grammar – promoted by school teachers, authorities, and the socially powerful, concerned with what they assume to be "good" or "bad" language. They seem fixated on what they hold to be correct grammar, combatting what in their view is incorrect. Objectively, there is no basis for judging

---

[3] www.merriam-webster.com/wordplay/new-words-in-the-dictionary.

some varieties of language, some ways of talking, as better than others. However, these socially motivated judgements about good and bad language can have hefty social consequences. It is necessary to realize that the sort of usage deemed "correct" and "good" by prescriptivists does count, for successful interviews for most higher-level jobs, for professional performance, for admission to graduate school, law school, or medical school. Rightly or wrongly, for everything where standard English is expected, avoidance of nonstandard or stigmatized language conveys a social advantage. William Shakespeare's [1564–1616] advice, though given in a different context, has held for centuries:

> Mend your speech a little,
> Lest it may mar your fortunes.
> (Shakespeare. King Lear, Act 1, scene 1)

In the debates about language change, one thing that all agree on is that language change happens – it cannot be prevented or avoided. All languages change all the time – except dead ones.[4] In spite of concerns, life always goes on with no obvious ill effects in the wake of language change. The language we speak today is no less able to serve our communicative needs than the language our ancestors spoke. Today's language is entirely adequate for creating "beautiful poetry, literary pieces, and expressions of love and awe and all other human feelings" (Zanuttini 2015).

So, no, language change in and of itself is neither good nor bad. It can sometimes be assumed to be beneficial, often motivated by the pull to make things easier to produce (to pronounce) or to process (to understand). And it can be thought sometimes to have detrimental consequences, sometimes creating greater burden for comprehension of language (examples can be seen in Chapter 5). However, there is no scientific basis for the frequent condemnation of linguistic change as bad nor for the rare declaration that it is good. These are social judgements about language change – they depend on the principles and prejudices of members of society, not on anything about the language involved per se. (See Campbell and Barlow 2020.)

That change in one part of language can have negative consequences for other parts is easy to see in pairs of words where a sound change can make them no longer distinct from each other, leading to confusion. An often-cited example involves the two words of English, *quean* 'disreputable woman, prostitute' (now rare in or missing from most <u>dialects</u> of English) and *queen*, where the vowel of *quean* had a lower "e" (as in *wed*),

---

[4] Or maybe even some dead languages could be said to change, too, if we compare forms used in medieval or modern Latin with Classical Latin.

distinct from the higher "e" of *queen* (formerly pronounced with the [e] sound of the vowel in *pay*). The difference in pronunciation disappeared nearly everywhere after these two vowels merged in Middle English. However, in an area of southwestern England, the two vowel sounds remained distinct and both these words, *quean* and *queen*, still survive there. *Quean* did not survive elsewhere where the two words became homophonous – it was too irreverent, too intolerable, that the word for the queen should sound exactly like the word for a prostitute.

There is a bit more to this story. In a very few places instead of the word *quean* just being abandoned to avoid the homophony of *quean* and *queen*, an initial "wh" was substituted for the "qu" of *quean* but not of *queen*, and both words survive, but with different pronunciations. The conflict caused by the merger of the vowels was avoided through this sporadic change to deflect the problem.

In another case – not polite but memorable because it involves an obscenity – English *shut*, from Old English *scyttan*, would have become *shit* by a regular sound change, the unrounding of /y/ to /ɪ/. This would have resulted in a homophony apparently too pernicious to be abided – so the vowel of *shut* was deflected to avoid the homophony (Lass 1980: 76–77). These kinds of cases show how a regular sound change (see Chapter 5), often thought to be "good" because it makes pronunciation easier, can simultaneously be "bad" where it causes loss of distinction between words of different meanings or loss of grammatical distinctions such as between present and past tenses (discussed in Chapter 5). The question of whether language change is good or bad is visited again in Chapter 5.

In the following chapters we examine the kinds of changes that languages undergo that can make them seem mysterious – the mysteries are unraveled, revealing the marvels lying behind them.

2   What's in a Word?

Words are like leaves, some wither ev'ry year,
And ev'ry year a younger race succeeds.
Horace [Quintus Horatius Flaccus, 65–8 BCE], *Ars Poetica* (or *Epistle to the Pisos*)[1]

Introduction

Though most of us may be largely unaware of changes going on in the language around us, we do tend to notice changes in words and in their meanings. These changes distress some and are sources of delight for others. People are often fascinated by the history of words. They wonder about how new words arise, why some words' meanings change, and how come some words just drop out of use and disappear. These questions are dealt with in this and the following chapter. Etymology is the study of the origin of words or phrases and of changes that have taken place in their history. A word's etymology is its origin and history. An etymon is a word from which a later word is derived. It is essentially the history that lies behind a word or other linguistic form. In this chapter, sources of new words are examined and exemplified, and the origins of English given names and surnames are looked into.

Before we leap in, it will be helpful to define and clarify a few terms that are used to talk about relatedness among languages and elements in languages. A proto-language is the once-spoken ancestral language from which related languages descend, and, in another sense, it is the language reconstructed by the comparative method (see the Glossary) that represents the ancestral language from which the compared languages descend. **Proto-Germanic** is the ancestor of English and the other Germanic languages (German, Dutch, Danish, Swedish, Icelandic, etc.), and **Proto-Indo-European** is the ancestor of the Germanic

---

[1] Vt siluae foliis pronos mutantur in annos,
prima cadunt, ita uerborum uetus interit aetas,
et iuuenum ritu florent modo nata uigentque.

languages and of several other branches of languages related more closely to one another that include Celtic, Slavic, Iranian, Anatolian, and others. (See Figure 8.1 in Chapter 8.) The story of how these relationships were discovered and determined is fascinating, taken up in Chapter 8. Note also that an **asterisk** ("*") before a word or form means that it is not attested directly in any written source but is inferred or reconstructed based on comparisons of related words or forms in related languages inherited from their shared parent language, their proto-language.[2] Cognate is a technical term for a word that has the same origin as a word in a sister language. It is a word that is inherited from a word in the parent language of the languages that share the cognate word. For example, Spanish, Portuguese, French, and Italian share a cognate meaning 'hand': Spanish *mano*, Portuguese *mão*, French *main*, Italian *mano*. They share these cognate words because they were inherited from the original Proto-Romance word *manu* 'hand'.

Let's begin by looking at a few modern examples of new and changed words (see Chapter 3 for changes in meaning). A few words newly added to English-language dictionaries include:

bling 'expensive, ostentatious jewelry or clothing'

blog 'a regularly updated website, typically done by an individual or small group'

butt-dial 'to place a call unintentionally from a mobile phone because the send button was accidentally pressed while the phone was being carried in a rear pocket'. The alternative *pocket dial* was added to the Oxford English Dictionary in 2015.

emoji 'small icons or digital images, sometimes called "ideograms" or "pictographs," used to express an idea or concept with a symbol instead of by spelled-out words'

selfie 'a photograph of oneself taken with mobile phone or handheld digital camera'

As mentioned in Chapter 1, some modern dictionaries of English have added hundreds or even thousands of new words in the last few years.

Ready examples of lost words are seen in the slang that older readers grew up with but that are now no longer in common usage with these meanings. A few examples are: *bread* 'money', *cat* 'term for any hip person', *daddy-o* 'a generally cool guy', *fuzz* 'police, police officer', and *groovy* 'enjoyable, exciting, excellent, fashionable'.

[2] For what unfamiliar symbols in examples cited in this chapter represent, see the Symbol List of phonetic and orthographic symbols at the beginning of the book.

Where Do New Words Come From?

So, where do new words come from? (We'll get back to how they get lost later.) The main sources of new words, called <u>neologisms</u>, are surveyed in what follows.

Creations from Scratch ("Creatio ex nihilo")

Creations of new words out of thin air, from nothing, are rare, but examples do exist of new words mostly created out of nothing. An example is *gas*, borrowed in English from Dutch *gas*, coined by Dutch chemist J. B. van Helmont in 1632, It was inspired by Greek *xáōs* 'chaos', where the pronunciation of the Dutch letter *g* is similar to that of the *ch* of *Bach*, corresponding to the pronunciation of the Greek letter *χ*, the first of the Greek word for 'chaos'.

Not all supposed creations from nothing are as mysterious as they might at first seem. It could be objected that in most cases, the creation doesn't totally come from absolutely nothing. In the case of *gas*, Greek *xáōs* 'chaos' is lying behind it in some way. *Zilch* 'nothing' and *bling* 'expensive, ostentatious jewelry or accessories' might seem like other likely candidates for creations from nothing. However, both these words have origin stories. *Zilch* is said to be from *Joe Zilch*, a placeholder name like *John Doe*, used for a person whose name is unknown or is intentionally not being revealed. It was used by Nunnally Johnson in a newspaper column in 1923 and as the name of an unseen character in Frank Tinney's comedy routine.[3] Of course, we might still wonder how Johnson hit upon "Zilch." For *bling*, formerly *bling bling* from rap slang, it has been suggested that it has a symbolic (expressive) or <u>onomatopoeic</u> origin, inspired or influenced either by 'blaring', bright light reflecting from jewelry, or by the sound of jewels and precious metals colliding with one another.

Literary Coinage

Another source of new words, like creation from nothing though attributed to particular writers and famous people, is literary coinage. A few cases are:

---

[3] Frank Aloysius Robert Tinney (1878–1940) was an American blackface comedian and actor. He was successful in vaudeville and on Broadway in the early twentieth century, but his career was ended by scandal.

blatant, from Edmund Spenser (between 1590 and 1596).

blurb, first used by Brander Matthews in 1906, but popularized by Gelett Burgess (American humorist) in 1907.

chortle, from Lewis Carroll (a blend of *chuckle* + *snort*).

pandemonium, 'the abode of all the demons, the capital of Hell', from John Milton's *Paradise Lost*, 1667. Milton took the pieces, however, from Greek, *pan-* 'all' and *daimōn* 'divinity, divine power, guiding spirit' (including souls of the dead).

From Proper Names

From the **names of individuals and of peoples** – including some mythical ones – English got words such as:

chauvinism, chauvinist, from Nicolas Chauvin of Rochefort, French soldier (possibly only legendary), known for excessive patriotic zeal.

guillotine, borrowed from French *guillotine*, named after the French physician Joseph-Ignace Guillotin, who suggested that the instrument be used in executions in 1789.

lynch, from William Lynch of Virginia, who set up unofficial tribunals to try suspects.

mesmerize, from Austrian physician Franz Anton Mesmer (1734–1815), whose experiments induced trance-like states in his subjects.

nicotine, from Jean Nicot, French ambassador in Lisbon, who sent samples of tobacco to the French queen Catherine de Medici in 1560. In his honor, plants of the genus are all called *nicotiana*. Nicotine, the addictive alkaloid, comes from nicotiana plants.

sandwich, named after John Montagu, the 4th Earl of Sandwich (1718–1792), who was said to spend twenty-four hours, non-stop, gambling with no other food than slices of cold meat between slices of toast.

(For more on personal names, see below.)

Some common words that originate from **names of ethnic groups** include:

cannibal, first recorded by Christopher Columbus as *caniba*, a Taino name of the feared Caribs. Columbus reported that *caniba* was how *Carib* was pronounced on Hispaniola. *Carib* is from Proto-Cariban **karípona* 'person, Indigenous person'. English borrowed *cannibal* from Spanish *canibal* 'cannibal'. Columbus believed that the Caribs in the Caribbean ate human flesh. This is generally doubted though still disputed. Thus, the words *Caribbean* and *cannibal* have the same origin, possibly lending new excitement to Caribbean cruises and vacations.

gothic, from the Goths, a Germanic tribe.

to gyp, 'to cheat, swindle', from *gypsy*, now considered improper and racist. (See the discussion of *Gypsy* in Chapter 10.)

to jew, 'to bargain to get a lower price', from *Jew*, a verb now avoided because of its negative stereotype of an ethnic or religious group.

vandal, vandalize, from the Vandals, another Germanic tribe.

to welch, welsh, 'to fail to honor a debt or obligation, to cheat by avoiding payment of debts or bets', from *Welsh*. The origin of the word with this meaning is uncertain. One often repeated possibility for its source is the belief that English debt-dodgers often fled to Wales to avoid creditors. Another less common one is the belief in a stereotype of Welsh people as dishonest.

From **place names** English got such common words as:

bikini, 'woman's two-pieced bathing suit', from *Bikini Atoll*, Marshall Islands, which was destroyed by atom bomb testing in 1946. The bikini was given this name supposedly because of its explosive impact on men.

canary, from *Canary Islands*. The islands' name is from Latin *īnsula canāria*, literally 'island of dogs', from the adjective *canārius*, derived from *canis* 'dog'.

champagne, from *Champagne*, the province in northern France for which this wine produced there is named.

denim, ultimately from French *serge de Nîmes* 'serge (a woolen fabric) from Nîmes' (a manufacturing town in southern France). **Jeans** is from *Genoa*, named for a twilled cotton cloth associated with Genoa.

geyser, from *Geysir*, a place in southwestern Iceland known for its famous geyser and thermal activity.

lesbian, from *Lesbos* island in Greece. Sappho (ca. 630–ca. 570 BCE), lyric poet, was from Lesbos. Her erotic and romantic verse embraced women as well as men, though it came to be associated with homosexual relations among women.

sodomy, from *Sodom*. Unnatural sexual relations were attributed to the inhabitants of this biblical town, reportedly destroyed by fire and brimstone for the wickedness of its people. Although Sodom is mentioned many times in the Bible, there is no agreement about what sin (or sins) of Sodom resulted in its destruction. In the Bible, it is never said to involve homo-sexual acts or even anything of a sexual nature at all. In Hebrew, *Sodom* means 'flaming, burnt', 'furrows', 'demons', derived from the verb root *sadam* (or *shadam*) 'to burn'.

turkey, from *Turkey* (now officially the *Republic of Türkiye*), short-ened from earlier *turkeycock, turkeyhen*, originally a guinea-fowl imported through Turkey. The name *turkey* was later applied erroneously to the bird of American origin. Names for turkey in numerous European languages reflect beliefs about where these birds come from, often erroneous. For example, 'India' is involved in words for turkey in Basque *indioilar*, French *dinde* (female), *dindon* (male) (from *d'* 'from' + *Inde* 'India'), Polish *indyk*, Russian *indeyka*, and Turkish *hindi*. Lithuanian *kalakutas*, Danish *kalkun*, and Finnish *kalkkuna* all ultimately reflect *Calcutta*. In Portuguese 'turkey' is *peru*, reflecting 'Peru'.

New words can also come from **brand names** (trade names). Well-known cases include:

aspirin, from Bayer's trademark for Acetylsalicylic acid.

coke, 'coca-cola, cola (drink)', from *Coca-Cola*. Words based on *Coca-Cola* are found in languages around the world, often in shortened forms, such as *coke* in English, to refer to Coca-Cola or similar drinks. Coca-Cola was invented in 1886 in Atlanta, Georgia, by John S. Pemberton, a druggist. The name reflects the names of original ingredients derived from coca leaves and cola nuts. It contained small amounts of cocaine until 1909.

dumpster, started out as a brand name, from the Dempster Brothers Inc. that joined the name *Dempster* with word *dump*, creating the Dempster Dumpster.

levis, levi jeans, named for *Levi Strauss*. Jacob W. Davis, a tailor of Reno, Nevada, invented a way to strengthen work pants using rivets, and in 1871 he went into business with Levi Strauss to mass produce them. Davis asked Strauss to help him apply for a patent, and in 1873 a patent was issued, with half of it assigned to Levi Strauss & Co.

to google, from *Google* (the search engine). According to the company *Google*, its name plays on *googol* 'a number repre-sented by *1* followed by 100 zeros' to reflect the company's mission to organize a seemingly infinite amount of information on the worldwide web. A version of *google*, however, was around earlier in *google-eyed*, a variant of *goggle-eyed* 'squinting, one-eyed, one who squints', seen in *googly eyes* (associated with *goo goo eyes*).

zipper, from a G. F. Goodrich trademark, originally for use in rubber boots.

Acronyms

Acronyms are words derived from the initial letters or syllables of each of the successive parts of a compound word or phrase. A few examples are:

BS, from 'bullshit'.

Gestapo, from German *Geheime Staatspolizei* 'secret state's police'.

humvee, hummer, from *HMMWV* 'high mobility multipurpose wheeled vehicle'. The abbreviation was pronounced *humvee*, which General Motors tried to change to *hummer* in order to market it better when it bought the rights to make the vehicle.

radar, from 'radio direction and ranging'.

scuba (scuba-diving), from 'self-contained underwater breathing apparatus'.

yuppy (yuppie), from 'young upwardly mobile professional' or 'young urban professional'.

The US Department of Justice has around 100 official acronyms.[4] You may know several of them, for example:

AG	Attorney General
ATAC	Anti-Terrorism Advisory Council (no joke!)
CIA	Central Intelligence Agency
DOJ	Department of Justice
FBI	Federal Bureau of Investigation
IRS	Internal Revenue Service

Some forms are turned into acronym-like words even though they do not originate as such. These usually involve sequences of letters from principal syllables in the word they refer to; for example: *PJs*, from 'pajamas, pyjamas'; *TB*, from 'tuberculosis'; and *TV*, from 'television'.

Compounding

Compounds are words formed by combining parts that are (or were) themselves distinct words into a single word. Some examples of relatively

---

[4] www.justice.gov/nsd-ovt/us-government-acronym-list.

new compounds in English are: *badass*; *binge-watch*; *cyberbullying*; words combining *-head* (*airhead*, *butthead*, *dickhead*, *blockhead*, *chucklehead*, *chowderhead*, *dunderhead*, *knucklehead*, *lunkhead*, *muttonhead*); *scumbucket*; *skateboard*; *studmuffin* 'a muscular or attractive male'; *superpower*; and *waterboarding*.

Other Kinds of Word-Formation

In addition to straight out compounding, new words can also be produced by adding various suffix- or prefix-like elements that derive new words. Included in this is the creation of new instances of what have been called 'neo-classical' compounds. These involve elements of Greek and Latin origin such as *auto-*, *bio-*, *trans-*, and others. Some examples illustrating these kinds of word-formations are:

-able in *bankable*, *bloggable*, *doable*, *googleable*, *microwav(e)able*. This comes from French *-able* or directly from Latin *-abilis*, depending on the word involved.

auto- in *autoerotic*, *autofocus*, *autoimmune*, *autopilot*, *autosuggestion*

bio- in *biochemical*, *biodegradable*, *biodiversity*, *bioengineering*, *biometric*, *biosphere*.

eco- in *ecofreak*, *eco-friendly*, *ecoterrorist*, *ecotourism*.

mega- in *megabyte*, *megapixel*, *megastar*.

micro- in *microbiotic*, *microbrewery*, *microenvironment*, *microprocessor*, *microsurgery*.

mini- from *miniskirt* (first attested in 1965), *mini-* spread, as in *minibar*, *minibike*, *minicam*, *minigun*, *miniseries*, *minivan*.

pre- in *pre-packaged*, *prepaid*, *presliced*, *pre-washed*.

post- *post-colonial*, *postseason*, *post-traumatic* (as in *post-traumatic stress disorder*, *PTSD*); and *post-factual*, *post-reality*, *post-truth*, mostly associated with the politics of Donald Trump in the US.

pseudo- in *pseudo-intellectual*, *pseudo-psychological*, *pseudoscience*, *pseudo-Western*.

trans- in *transcontinental*, *transgender*, *transmigration*, *transnational*, *transvestite*.

ultra- in *ultracritical*, *ultrahot*, *ultrahuman*, *ultraliberal*, *ultraleftist*, *ultramodern*, *ultraradical*, *ultrasonic*.

-ism/-ist in *racist*, *sexism*, *fattist*, *neologism*, *trumpism* 'controversial or outrageous statement attributed to US president Donald Trump or the policies advocated by him'.

We could also add *-belt*, as in *banana(-)belt, Bible(-)belt, rustbelt, snowbelt, sunbelt*, except that *belt* is not of Greek or Latin origin. It is inherited from Proto-Germanic **baltjaz* 'belt, girdle'.

Some compounds are referred to as cases of <u>amalgamation</u> (also sometimes called univerbation), in particular where the parts of the compound are no longer easy to identify because of how the parts meld together. English *nevertheless* is from *never the less* and *already* from *all ready*, from the amalgamation of separate words into single words. English has many such words. Amalgamations are underway in the frequent (mis)spellings of *alright* for *all right* (probably influenced by <u>analogy</u> with *already*) and *alot* for *a lot* 'many, much'. A few other examples of amalgamations in English are:

doff, from *do off* (as in *doff one's hat*).

don, from *do on* (as in *to don one's robe*).

however, from *how* + *ever*.

never, from Old English *ne* 'not' + *æfre* 'ever'.

wannabe, 'someone who tries to be accepted by a group, adopting its appearance and manners', from *want to be*.

Lots of amalgamations are mostly no longer recognized as such today, in spite of their origins as compounds. Some examples are:

also, from *all* + *so*.

answer, from Old English *and-* 'against' + *swaru*, from *swerian* 'to swear (an oath or promise)'.

lord, from *hlaf* 'bread, loaf' + *weard* 'keeper, guardian'.

understand, from *under* 'among, beneath' + *stand*.

woman, from *wife* 'woman' + *man*.

Blending

In blending, pieces of two or more different words are combined to create new words. Some blends are purposefully humorous or sarcastic, others are perhaps accidental, like slips of the tongue which combine parts from two or more related words. Some are created for marketing and advertising purposes. Blending is much like compounding, amalgamation in particular, but different in that blendings combine only parts of words, not whole words as compounds do, although the distinction is not always clear. Commonly cited examples that illustrate blending include: *smog* < *smoke* + *fog*; *brunch* < *breakfast* + *lunch*; *motel* < *motor* + *hotel*; *splatter* < *splash* + *spatter*; *flush* < *flash* + *blush*. Some others are:

bit (computer term), from 'binary digit'.

gaydar, a blend of *gay* and *radar*, the assumed ability to determine by intuition whether someone is homosexual.

incel, from *involuntary* + *celibate,* 'member of a group of people (mostly male, mostly online) who see themselves as involuntarily celibate, unable to find a romantic or sexual partner though desiring one'.

mansplain, from *man* + *explain,* '(for a man) to explain something, typically to a woman, in a condescending or patronizing manner'.

mocktail, from *mock* + *cocktail,* a non-alcoholic cocktail.

staycation, from *stay at home* + *vacation,* a vacation spent at home or nearby.

sexting, from *sex* + *texting,* 'sending sexually explicit photographs or messages via mobile phone'.

webinar, from *web* + *seminar,* 'an online educational presentation'.

Names of languages which borrow a lot from other languages or are highly influenced by others are the sources of such blends as ***Spanglish*** from *Spanish* + *English,* ***Finnglish*** from *Finnish* + *English*; ***Franglais*** from French *français* 'French' + *anglais* 'English' (also ***Franglish*** from *French* + *English*), ***Singlish*** from *Singapore* + *English* (for the vernacular form of English spoken in Singapore), ***Taglish*** from *Tagalog* + *English,* and ***manglish*** in feminist discourse to refer to male biases in English, from *man* + *English.*

Some elements that frequently show up in blended words become almost like suffixes. They have sometimes been called "secretions," as in:

-(a)ccino, blends based on *cappuccino*: *mochaccino/mocaccino, muggaccino, frappaccino, cyberccino* (in an internet coffeeshop), *skinniccino /skinnyccino* (small black coffee), *skimmuccino* (cappuccino made with skim milk), *decaphaccino* (cappuccino made of decaffeinated coffee), *soyaccino, kiddiccino,* and so on. *Cappuccino,* literally 'little hood', is from a figurative use of Italian *Capuccino,* 'a friar of the Minor Capuchin order' (*frate dell'ordine dei cappuccini*), thought to reflect the drink's color, seen as similar to that of the brown hoods worn by Capuchin monks.

-aholic, from part of *alcoholic*: *chocaholic, shopaholic, workaholic.*

-(a)thon, made with a portion of *marathon*: *bik(e)athon, danceathon spellathon, telethon, walkathon,* and others.

-gate, for scandals, taken from part of *Watergate.* These words relate to the Richard Nixon Watergate scandal. Watergate became so synonymous with scandal that it became common practice in the media to tack on *-gate* to name the latest scandal. Examples include: *Camillagate* (also called *tampon-gate*) (involving a telephone call between then Prince Charles, now King Charles III, and his then intimate friend and now spouse, Camilla Parker Bowles, Queen Consort); *emailgate* (about Hillary Clinton's private email server), *Monicagate* (in reference to Monica Lewinsky, made famous by US President William J. Clinton's indiscretions); *nipplegate* (also called *boob-gate*, involving Janet Jackson's breast in a wardrobe malfunction during the Super Bowl 38 halftime show); and *partygate* (a UK scandal involving gatherings of government and Conservative Party staff during the COVID-19 pandemic in 2020 and 2021, when public health restrictions prohibited such gatherings. It contributed to the downfall of Prime Minister Boris Johnson and his resignation as a Member of Parliament).

Several recent ones relate to Donald Trump:

blabbergate, from Trump's revealing highly classified information to the Russian ambassador and foreign minister.

bleachgate, from Trump's suggesting that the drinking of bleach would cure COVID-19.

pussygate, about Trump's lewd comments about women on an *Access Hollywood* tape in which he said, "when you're a star . . . you can do anything . . . grab them by the pussy."

sharpiegate, from when Trump incorrectly included Alabama in states likely to be hit by Hurricane Dorian in 2019. Although Alabama was not under threat, Trump insisted it was, showing reporters a weather map altered with a Sharpie to include Alabama in the track threatened by the hurricane.

shitholegate, from when Trump asked, "why are we having all these people from shithole countries come here?"

spygate, coined by Trump himself for his false claim that Barack Obama had planted a spy in Trump's election campaign to help Hillary Clinton win.[5]

Perhaps somewhat surprisingly, the equivalent of English 'gate' has been adopted in a number of other languages to refer to local political scandals, for example in Argentina, Germany, Greece, Hungary, and South Korea, and is used even in Mandarin Chinese.

---

[5] For a large number of additional examples of scandals with *-gate*, see https://en.wikipedia .org/wiki/List_of_-gate_scandals_and_controversies.

Clipping

New words and new versions of old words can come from "clipping," from shortening longer words, also called ellipsis, compression, and shortening. Such reduction is associated with a rapid increase in the frequency of the affected terms, often resulting in newly invented words or in ones with new and specialized meanings. English has many words that are the result of this process. A few are:

app < application
bra < brassiere
bot < robot
con < convict
dis(s) (**dissing**) < disrespect, 'to be disrespectful or insulting towards someone'
lab < laboratory
limo < limousine
memo < memorandum
nuke (nukes, to nuke) < nuclear
perp < perpetrator
pro < professional
sci-fi < science fiction

Expressive Creations

Onomatopoeia is another source of new words, created to mimic sounds in nature, as in *bam, bang, bash, boom, buzz, chirp, cuckoo, ding, hiss, hum, jingle, meow, moo, oink, peep, ping, pop, sizzle, squish, thud, whack,* and *whizz*.

Interjections (ejaculations) are another source, with words such as *ah, oh, oops, ouch, whoop-de-doo, woo-hoo, wow, yadda yadda yadda,* and *yuck*.

Some expressive words seem to have developed mostly out of nothing, new words that are both phonologically expressive and semantically affective, for example *bodacious* 'sexy, bold, impressive', *hellacious, humongous* (also *humungous*) 'very large', and *scrumptious* 'delicious, tasty'. While the origin of these words is uncertain, it is possible that *bodacious* is connected in some way to *bold* and *audacious* or perhaps *body* (as in *hot bod*), and that *humongous* perhaps reflects in some way *huge* together perhaps with associations from something like *enormous* or *monstrous*. *Hellacious* involves *hell* and an ending part that probably involves the same analogical connection with words that inspired the similar ending in *bodacious*.

Taboo

People often express amusement or repulsion, depending on their dispositions, over changes involving taboo, obscenity, and euphemism. Many of these cases involve the various kinds of semantic changes that we will see in the following chapter. We also encounter cases where a meaning may remain but a different word which had other denotations before the change is substituted for it – a kind of lexical replacement. For instance, in English, *ass* 'long-eared animal related to a horse' has essentially been replaced in America by *donkey* or *burro* because *ass* with this meaning causes discomfort since it sounds like obscene *ass* 'arse, butt, derriere'. Similarly, *cock* 'adult male chicken' is usually now replaced by *rooster* due to the associations of *cock* with 'penis' – probably *rooster*, the favored word in America to refer to the adult male chicken, has lost entirely its original association with a bird that 'roosts'. What in North America is a *bloody nose* becomes *blood nose* or *bleeding nose* in the UK and places where *bloody* is obscene, in order to avoid the taboo word *bloody*.

In euphemisms, words regarded as unpleasant very often get replaced. We see this in the many euphemistic replacements of words meaning 'toilet'. Terms for 'toilet' come to feel indelicate and so less disturbing substitutions are sought. The room where indoor toilets were installed was called a *water closet* (abbreviated *WC*) in Britain. This was soon replaced, euphemistically, by *toilet*, a loan from French *toilette* 'small cloth' (diminutive of *toile* 'cloth, towel'). *Toilet* then came to mean 'a cloth cover for a dressing table', then 'articles used in dressing', and then 'the table upon which these articles are placed', 'a dressing room with bathing facilities', and finally the 'toilet' fixture itself for bodily needs. This word is replaced in many parts of the English-speaking world by such other euphemisms as *lavatory, bathroom, restroom, washroom, commode, loo, john, head*, and so on.

Not only are words often replaced to avoid obscenities and taboo, but their pronunciation can also be modified to give more acceptable, euphemistic outcomes. For example, *pee* originated as an abbreviated, deflected form of more obscene *piss*. English has many such deflected (or distorted) euphemistic forms, for example: *dadnabbit, dang, friggin', fudge, gadzooks, gosh, jeez*, and *shucks*.

Obsolescence and Loss of Words

Some words that just dropped out of use were seen at the beginning of this chapter. Many of us are curious not just about how new words get into a language, but also about how and why some words become archaic and sometimes disappear altogether. The use of a word can fade for a number of social reasons, but a main reason is just that speakers of the language stop talking about what the word refers to. That is, change in what a society deals with can lead to vocabulary loss as well as to semantic shifts (see Chapter 3). Another reason is that some words are replaced by other words with the same meaning, often leading to loss of the older word from the language. For example, there used to be a large, active vocabulary for talking about armor, feudal society, falconry, courtly matters, and other things central to life in the Middle Ages. Most of these words have been forgotten as they ceased to be relevant to modern life.

A few examples of old words now lost or replaced by other words in Modern English follow – though sometimes some mostly abandoned words get resurrected in literature and games reflecting medieval themes.

gnathonize 'to flatter'.

jarkman 'person who could write and read Latin, and sometimes could speak it, who used this knowledge to make counterfeit licenses to which seals were set'. The seals and the falsified documents were called *jarks*. *Jarkman* was sixteenth-century slang for an educated beggar able to forge passes, licenses, etc.

kelchyn 'a fine paid by one guilty of manslaughter, generally to the kindred of the person killed'.

parnel 'slut, prostitute, priest's concubine'. From *Petronilla*, a female proper name, from the diminutive form of Latin *Petronius* and also from the name of St. Petronella, regarded as St. Peter's daughter.

stagma 'any distilled liquid, liquor'.

tyromancy 'divination or fortune-telling using cheese'.

wittol 'a husband who knows of and endures his wife's unfaithfulness, a contented cuckold'. From *woodwale*, a bird whose nest is invaded by the cuckoo, and so has the offspring of another palmed off on it as its own.

yelve 'dung-fork, garden-fork', 'to use a garden fork'.

There are many such no-longer-used words.[6]

Let us turn now to two other topics about which people often ask, the origins of place names and of personal names.

---

[6] For many more examples of now forgotten words, see https://phrontistery.info/clw4.html.

Etymology of the Names of a Few Ethnic Groups and Major Locations

The history behind some place names also tells interesting stories. We look at a few here.

Aryan comes from Latin *Ariana* 'a region in the eastern part of the ancient Persian Empire', borrowed from Greek *Areia, Aria*, from Sanskrit *ārya-* 'compatriot', later 'noble, honorable, of a good family'. *Aryan* has cognates in several other Indo-European languages: Hittite *arā-* 'friend, comrade, companion', Avestan *airya-* 'Aryan, Iranian', Old Persian *ariya-* 'Aryan, Iranian', Old Irish *aire* 'chief, noble, freeman', and Old Norse *aryoster* 'foremost, most distinguished'. The country name **Iran** has the same origin, from Persian *Iran*, from Middle Persian *Ērān* 'of the Iranians', from *ēr-* 'an Iranian', from Proto-Indo-Iranian **arya-* or **ārya-*, an autonym (self-designation), possibly meaning 'compatriot'.

Aryan was used earlier in the history of linguistics to mean Indo-European languages or peoples who speak Indo-European languages (especially of the Indo-Iranian branch), but that name was replaced by *Indo-European*. Nazi ideology had used *Aryan* as a racial supremacist term to mean white non-Jewish people of northern Europe, especially those with blue eyes and blond hair, regarded as members of the "master race." Because of this association, *Aryan* largely ceased to be used.

The name **Canada** comes from an Iroquoian language, meaning 'village, settlement', as seen, for example, in Mohawk *kana:ta* 'town'.

The name **Copenhagen** is from Danish *København*, literally 'buy-harbor', 'merchants' port', composed of Danish *køben* 'to buy' + *havn* 'harbor'. Danish *køben* 'to buy, purchase' is related to words in other Germanic languages having to do with 'buying', for example German *kaufen* 'to buy' and English *cheap*, from Old English *ceap* 'a purchase' (from *ceapian* 'to buy, sell, trade'). These words appear to be from an early Germanic borrowing of Latin *caupo* 'petty tradesman, peddler' or *cauponari* 'to haggle'. Danish *havn* is related to English *haven*, from Old English *hæfen* 'harbor, port'. Both the English and Danish words are from Proto-Germanic **hafno* 'harbor, port'. The English word *haven* later shifted its meaning metaphorically (see Chapter 3) to 'refuge'.

In the late 1300s the English word **Dutch** referred to Germans in general. It narrowed in meaning to *Hollanders* after 1600. It comes from Middle Dutch *duutsch*. That comes from Proto-Germanic **þeudo* 'national, popular', the source of Modern German *Deutsch* 'German'. The Germanic word is from Proto-Indo-European **teuta-* 'tribe'. It matches Old English *þeodisc* 'of the people, belonging to the people', used to refer to the common language of Germanic people, derived from Old English *þeod* 'people, nation, race'. The *þ* of Old English and Proto-Germanic represents the "th" sound in *thank*. English **Teutonic** meaning 'pertaining to the Germanic peoples or tribes' is borrowed from Latin *Teutonicus*, derived from *Teutoni, Teutones*, the name of a tribe from the coast of Germany near the mouth of the Elbe River, borrowed into Latin from Proto-Germanic **þeudanoz*, from the same Proto-Indo-European **teuta-* 'tribe' source.

France is borrowed into English from Old French *France*, which comes from Medieval Latin *Francia*, derived from *Francus* 'Frank'. The Franks were a Germanic tribal people on the lower River Rhine around 300 CE who conquered Romano-Celtic northern Gaul in about 500 CE. Their territory grew to what is modern France. The English name **Frank** is borrowed from Medieval Latin *francus* 'Frank', itself a Late Latin borrowing of Frankish *Frank*, the Franks' name for themselves. The sense of *frank* as 'free, at liberty' (as in 'speak frankly') is thought to have developed from this tribal name.

The Germanic rulers of France during the reign of Charlemagne (768–814 CE) were Franks, and the first Europeans encountered in the east were Franks, called *Francs* in French, *Francos* in Spanish, and *Franchi* in Italian. Roman Christians and later all western Europeans were called 'Franks', the source of the word for 'western European' that later came also to mean 'foreigner' in several languages. The name was borrowed after the first Crusade (1096–1099 CE) as Persian *farangī*, and from Persian into Arabic as *faranji*, in Ottoman Turkish as *feringhee*, and borrowed into several languages of the Indian (South Asian) subcontinent, borrowed in English in India as *ferenghee* meaning 'European, English person'. It is behind the *Ferengi*, a race of extraterrestrials in some of the *Star Trek* series, inspired by this Persian word for 'foreigner'.

Lingua franca, literally 'language of the Franks', was a pidgin language based on Romance languages, used throughout the Middle East and the Mediterranean region in the Middle Ages as a language of commerce and diplomacy. From this comes the modern sense of *lingua franca* as any language used by speakers of different languages who have no language in common to be able to communicate with each other, a bridge language among speakers of different languages.

The name **Russia** comes from *Rus*, originally the name of a group of merchants and warriors from Sweden who settled in Novgorod, near Kyiv, in the ninth century CE. The name is connected with *Ruotsi*, the Finnish name for 'Sweden, Swedish', a loanword from Old Swedish *rōþ(r)s-* 'inhabitant of *Roslagen*', called in Old Norse *Roþrslandi*, said to mean 'the land of rowing'. It was borrowed into Old Russian as *rusi* 'Russia'. This name is from Old Norse *roðr* 'steering oar', from Proto-Germanic *roþra- 'rudder', which comes from Proto-Indo-European *rot-ro-, based on the root *ere- 'to row'. Thus, the name *Russia* has Scandinavian origins, not Slavic. (See the Symbol List at the beginning of the book for the sounds that the symbols þ, ɪ, and ð represent.)

The name **Saxon**, spelled earlier also as *Sexun* and *Saxu*, refers to a tribe that lived in northern Germany who invaded Britain, settling there in the fifth and sixth centuries CE. The name is from Late Latin *Saxonem*. In Old English it was *Seaxe*. Tradition holds that its meaning was 'warrior with knives'; Old English *seax* and Old Norse *sax* meant 'knife, short sword, dagger'. In Old High German *Saxnot* was the name of a war god. These words are from Proto-Germanic *sahsq- 'knife', from the Proto-Indo-European root *sek- 'to cut'. However, not all specialists accept this proposed etymology. *Saxon* is the source of the *-sex* in the English names of Saxon kingdoms, *Essex* of 'East Saxons', *Sussex* 'South Saxons', and *Wessex* 'West Saxons'.

Where Do English Personal Names Come From?

Let's move now from names of ethnic groups and places to personal names. Many of us are curious about the origins and meanings of names, of our names, of names of relatives and famous people, and about the names we might choose for our children. Here we look into the history of some of the most common English names, first of surnames (last names), followed later by given names. The history of many of these names can also teach us about origins of words and how they can change.

Surnames

Surnames (family names, last names) started being used in Britain only after the Norman Conquest of 1066. English last names are typically of just a few types.

Surnames Reflecting Occupations

Many English surnames come from **occupations**. Some common occupational surnames follow.

> **Smith**, the most frequent surname in Britain and the US. It is an occupational name for someone who works with metal. There were many kinds of smiths – blacksmith, arrowsmith, goldsmith, shoesmith (working with horseshoes), swordsmith, tinsmiths, and others.

Stewart, from Middle English *steward* (*steuard*), meant 'official in charge of domestic affairs of a household'. In Old English it was *stigeweard* 'someone in charge of affairs of the house or estate of another person'. It comes from *stig* 'cattle pen, hall, part of a house' + *weard* 'guard'. *Stig* is the source of *sty* 'pig pen'. *Weard* 'guard' is ultimately from Proto-Indo-European *wer-* 'watch out for, perceive'.

Wright, an English and Scottish name from Middle English for a craftsman, particularly a carpenter or a joiner (cabinetmaker, finish carpenter). A number of surnames include *-wright*: *Cartwright, Shipwright, Wainwright* (on wagons), etc.

Some other common occupational surnames are: *Baker, Baxter,* a baker; *Carter,* a cart-driver; *Clarke, Clark,* for a cleric or writer – originally it usually referred to a cleric of a religious order; *Cooper,* a craftsman who makes barrels and tubs; *Fisher,* fisherman; *Fletcher,* arrow maker; *Mason*; *Miller*; *Taylor,* an occupational name from Middle English *tailor*; *Thatcher,* from someone who covers roofs with thatch; *Turner,* from someone who works a lathe; *Walker,* an English and Scottish name for what later came to be called a *fuller,* someone who beats and presses cloth to make it denser; *Webb, Webber, Webster, Weaver,* all for someone involved in weaving.

Surnames Reflecting Personal Characteristics

Some surnames that reflecting personal characteristics are:

Brown, from a personal characteristic, an English and Scottish nickname for a person with brown hair or brown complexion.

Gray, for having gray hair, originally from Scotland.

Payne, Paine, from Late Latin *paganus* 'pagan'. In Classical Latin *paganus* meant 'rustic, villager, co-combatant', from *pagus* 'country people, rural district'. It is uncertain whether the surname comes from the sense of 'villager', 'rustic', or of 'heathen'.

White, a Middle English nickname referring to people with fair hair or a pale complexion.

Young.

My own family name, ***Campbell,*** ultimately seems to involve personal attributes. The etymology that used to be promoted by the Clan Campbell goes something like this. Malcolm MacDwine (a.k.a. MacDuibhn of Gillespic) married a woman named *Beauchamp* in Normandy, said to be the niece of William the Conqueror, at that time Duke of Normandy. In Clan Campbell accounts she is listed just as

"'*Unknown Beauchamp*, Campus bellus,' heiress of Beauchamp, born 1021, Normandy, France ('uncertain')."[7] Then this Malcolm, apparently alias Archibald (or Gillespic) (ca. 1041–1091), came from Normandy to Scotland, where Latin was more prevalent and so the name was changed from French *Beauchamp* to its Latin equivalent, *Campus Bellus* 'beautiful field', later shortened to just *Campbell*. The first of my ancestors to be named "Campbell" took this surname.

However, in the more accepted etymology, *Campbell* comes from Gaelic *cambeul* 'crooked mouth' or 'curved mouth', from *cam* 'curved, crooked, deformed', and *beul* 'mouth'. Archibald (or Dugald) of Lochawe (born 1090) is believed to the first to be given the nickname *Cam Beul*. It was thought that he had a crooked mouth, or perhaps that he had the trait of talking out of one side of his mouth. The family took this as its official name, originally spelled *Cambel*.

The irony in the contrast between the "Campus Bellus" 'beautiful field' etymology and the more accurate "crooked mouth" one always struck me as hilarious.

Linguists working on the *Survey of the Gaelic Dialects of Scotland* had a more tongue-in-cheek etymology: they said *Campbell* was from Italian *campo bello*, equating the Campbells with a highland mafia, reflecting Campbell dominance in some areas and the long-held harsh attitudes sometimes held about Campbells in Scotland because of their treatment of the MacDonalds in the massacre at Glencoe in 1692. In one Scottish comedian's take on it, however, if only the Campbells had done a proper job of it, we wouldn't have to put up with all those McDonalds fast-food restaurants today.

Locational or Habitational Surnames

Several last names are of the type called locational or habitational. Some that come from the names of geographical locations include: *Fields, Ford, Hill, Lake, Rivers, Green* (a Middle English name for someone who lived by the village green), and *Wood/Woods* (Middle English name for someone who lived in or near woods). Some come from the names of towns or cities which were the places where the bearer's family lived or were identified with. Some examples of this kind of surname are: *Barton, Clayton, Eaton, Harrington, Horton, Kirby, Langdon, Maxwell, Murray, Rhodes*.

---

[7] The English surname *Beecham* comes from this *Beauchamp* name. *Beauchamp* is French, composed of *beau* 'beautiful' + *champ* 'field'.

Patronymics

Patronymic surnames come from the given name (Christian name) of a father or ancestor. Before the Norman French conquest of 1066, persons had only a single name, although a patronymic could be used to distinguish individuals, for example *John's son*. These patronymics eventually settled in as the surname in many cases. *John's son* for an individual, the son of John, became the English surname *Johnson*. Many end in *son*. The English surnames that end in -*son* are thought mostly to reflect the Scandinavian patronymic naming system, distributed throughout the territory of the <u>Danelaw</u>, seen in Map 4.1 in Chapter 4 (compare this with Map 10.3 in Chapter 10).

Many other surnames end in *s*, as in *Williams*, from *William's* (*William's child*). Many of these names may be patronymic but ultimately come from the Christian name of a male progenitor, many from biblical names or names of saints. Some of the most frequent English patronymic surnames are:

> **Anderson**, from *Andrew's son.*
>
> **Davies**, a Welsh patronymic name that evolved over time from *Dafydd's (son)*. *Dafydd* is the Welsh equivalent of *David*. **Davidson** is parallel but in English, from *David's son.*
>
> **Edwards**, from Edward's (child).
>
> **Harris**, from *Harry's (child)*. *Harry* was a common version of *Henry*.
>
> **Jones**, the second most frequent last name in Britain. It comes from *Jon*, a Welsh and Middle English name equivalent to *John*. *Jones* matches *John's (child)*.
>
> **Roberts**, from Middle English personal name *Robert*, for *Robert's (child)*.
>
> **Thompson**, from Middle English, meaning *Tom's son*. *Thomson* is the more usual Scottish version of the name. The *p* in the spelling of *Thompson* reflects a change in pronunciation that took place to make the transition from *m* to *s* easier to pronounce.[8]
>
> **Williams**, from *William's (child)*, and **Wilson**, from *Will's son*, with *Will* shortened from *William*.

Rank or Status Surnames

Some English surnames stem from terms for social status or rank. Some examples are:

---

[8] The technical name for this kind of sound change is "excrescence."

Bishop, as an English surname, is thought to have come about as a nickname for someone who was like a clergyman in appearance or behavior. The name was borrowed as *bisceop* in Old English from Late Latin *episcopus*, borrowed from Greek *episkopos* 'watcher, overseer', a title for various government officials that was taken over as a church title, composed of Greek *epi-* 'over' + *skopos* 'someone who watches over, a guardian, protector'.

Duke entered English in the early 1100s meaning 'a prince', from Old French *duc* and Latin *dux* 'leader, commander', in Late Latin 'governor of a province', derived from *ducere* 'to lead', from Proto-Indo-European **deuk-* 'to lead'.

Marshall meant 'high officer of the royal court', from Old French *mareschal* 'commanding officer of an army' and 'officer in charge of a household'. It originally referred to 'a stable officer, horse tender, groom'. It came into French from a Frankish (Germanic) loan reflecting the Proto-Germanic compound composed of **markhaz* 'horse' (seen in *mare*) + **skalkaz* 'servant'.

Given Names (Christian Names, First Names)

As mentioned, in England, originally a person had only a single name and surnames came into wide use only after the Norman Conquest of 1066. Most people had only a single given name until into the 1600s. People started adding another name in connection with their given name to make identification easier, and this was passed down as the family name. Then, having more than one given name began when Charles James Stuart, King Charles I, was baptized with his two first names. This French fashion spread to the English aristocracy, following the king's example, which then expanded to the general population, in common use by the end of the 1700s.

Given names also fall into several typical categories. The most common first names are biblical names and saints' names (several examples are presented later). Many of them come from French. Other categories are the following.

Aspirational/Inspirational Given Names

Examples of aspirational or inspirational personal names include: *Felix* ('happy'), *Grace*, *Joy*, *Hope*, *Faith*, *Charity*.

Given Names from Place Names

Examples of given names derived from the names of places include: *Austin, Brittany, Chelsea, Cody, Dallas, Dayton, Devon, Florence, Geneva, Georgia, Kent, Lorraine, Sienna.*

Given Names Taken from Times or Occasions

First names (given names) based on times or occasions include: *April, May, June, Natalie* (Christmas), *Noel* (Christmas in French), *Summer,* among others.

Given Names Taken from Objects

Some given names are based on the names of such natural objects as flowers, gems, birds, and the like. Some examples are *Jasmine, Lavender, Dawn, Daisy, Rose, Iris, Violet; Amber, Crystal, Jasper, Opal, Pearl, Ruby; Robin.*

Given Names Derived from Surnames

There are many examples of first names that are derived from family names that came to be used as given names, such as *Anderson, Avery, Brady, Cameron, Emerson, Harrison, Ross, Winston,* and many more. The origin of some first names is from the surnames of certain eminent families, as seen in the following few examples:

Howard, from the Howard family, Dukes of Norfolk
Clifford, from the Barons Clifford
Graham, from that noble Scottish family, Dukes of Montrose
Herbert, from the Herbert family, Earls of Pembroke
Russell, from the Russell family, Earls and Dukes of Bedford
Stanley, from the Stanley family, Earls of Derby

My own given name, *Lyle*, is from a surname which itself is a habitational surname. It was a Scottish surname, from Old French *l'isle* 'the island' (Modern French *l'île*), reportedly from Anglo-French *del Isle* 'from the island'. It is one of the very few names that can be traced back to the *Domesday Book* of 1086, where it is given in the Latin form of the name, *de īnsula* 'of [the] Island'. The city of *Lille* in northeastern France has the same etymology. Alternative versions of this surname are *Lyall, Lyell, Lile,* and *Lisle.* From the family name it came also to be used as a given name. *Lyle* was ranked as the 1087th most frequent name for boys in 2024, not very common, but still there are 21.6 people named "Lyle" in every 100,000 Americans, so there are a bunch of us around.

Given Names according to the Language of Their Origin

Given names in English are also classified according to the **language** of origin, as in the following cases.

> **Hebrew** (most from biblical names, several seen below). A few are **Aramaic** in origin: *Thomas, Martha,* and *Bartholomew.*
>
> **Germanic names**: *Robert, Edward, Roger, Richard, Albert, Carl, Alfred, Rosalind, Emma, Emmett, Eric,* and *Matilda.* Several Germanic names are composed with a part that meant 'wolf': *Adolf, Randolph, Rudolph.*
>
> **Anglicized versions of Celtic** names include: *Alan, Brian, Brigid (Brigit), Conor, Logan, Jennifer,* and *Sean.*
>
> **Names of Greek origin** from mythology, Classical Antiquity, or the New Testament: Alexander, Andrew, Chloe, Christopher, George, Gregory, Helen, Jason, Katherine, Margaret, Nicholas, Penelope, Peter, Stephen, Theodore, Timothy, Zoë.
>
> **Names with Latin origins**: Laura, Victoria, Mark (Latin Marcus), Justin (Latin Justinus), Paul (Latin Paulus), Cecilia, Felix, Julius, Julia, Vivian.

Not only do languages acquire new words and sometimes lose old ones, the meanings of words also can change – that is the topic of the next chapter.

3   You Get My Drift?
Meaning Change

They that dally nicely with words may quickly make them wanton.
(Shakespeare *Twelfth Night* Act 3, Scene 1)

Introduction

Languages are forever changing the meanings of some words, and as seen in the previous chapter, they also add new words and lose others. The quotation from Shakespeare just above – about words changing – exemplifies this well. The words *dally*, *nicely*, and *wanton* no longer mean what they meant to Shakespeare (pictured in Figure 3.1). For him, *dally* meant 'chat, waste time', *nicely* meant 'foolishly', and *wanton* meant 'frivolous, resistant to control'. In today's language, the citation would be something like "They that *chat foolishly* with words may quickly make them *frivolous*."

So, how do words change their meaning? Semantic change (change in meaning) deals with change in the concepts associated with a word, not with its pronunciation. In this chapter we look at the main kinds of meaning changes and at what is thought to be behind them.

Let's begin with views of why meanings change, about how such changes can be explained. One common view holds that meaning change goes through a stage where a word comes to acquire more than one meaning. A word may shift to take on additional meanings, becoming polysemous, or it may change to lose one or more of its meanings. In this view, a word can start out with an original meaning, then can acquire additional, multiple meanings, and then often the original sense is lost, leaving the word with only its newer meaning. For example, English *write* at first meant 'to cut, score'. This meaning is reflected in its German cognate *reissen* 'to tear, split'. Then, the meaning of *write* was extended to include both 'to cut, scratch' and 'to write'. The connection is through runic writing, where runes were carved or scratched on wood and stone. Compare the Old Norse cognate *rīta* 'to scratch, to write'. This stage is attested in Old English *wrītan* meaning 'to write', 'to cut'. By Modern English, *write* had come to mean only 'to write'. The sense of 'to cut' or 'to scratch' has been lost.

Figure 3.1 William Shakespeare
Source: Hulton Archive / Getty Images.

Another view is like this one, though broader in its perspective. It acknowledges that a word typically has a core meaning but also various less central, more peripheral senses when it is used in different contexts. It sees semantic change as taking place when a less central sense becomes more central or when the original core concept recedes to be more peripheral, often eventually being lost altogether.

While there may be structural linguistic or psychological factors involved in some semantic changes, it is generally understood that factors outside of language itself play a causal role in most semantic changes. Changes in society, politics, religion, and technology can cause semantic shifts. For example, *pen* originally meant 'feather, quill', a loanword from Old French *penne* 'feather, writing quill', inherited from Latin *penna* 'feather'. However, as other instruments for writing came into use, the thing referred to by the word *pen* today is not remotely connected with 'feather'. *Drive* and *fly* took on new meanings after automobiles and airplanes came into use. Examples are truly abundant of words whose meanings have changed due to sociocultural and technological change in the modern world around us.

Kinds of Meaning Change

In what follows, we look into the various kinds of meaning changes that are typically discussed in treatments of semantic change.

Widening (Broadening)

Sometimes the range of meanings of a word increases so that the word can be used in more contexts than were possible before the change. Here are a few examples.

dog, Old English had *hund* 'dog'. Old English *docga*, source of today's *dog*, was rare. In at least one Middle English source, *dog* was used to refer to a specific powerful breed of dog, and in other sources it had deprecatory, abusive senses. Later its meaning widened to include all breeds and kinds of dogs.

salary, from Latin *salārium*, a soldier's allotment of salt (based on Latin *sal* 'salt'), which then came to mean a soldier's wages in general, and then finally, as in English, wages in general, not just a soldier's pay.

town, Old English *tūn*, from which we get modern *town*, meant 'enclosure, garden, field, yard; farm, manor; homestead, dwelling house', then later 'a group of houses, village, farm', and eventually 'town'. Cognates in other Germanic languages mean 'fence, hedge, enclosure', as for example German *Zaun* 'fence'.

Narrowing (Specialization, Restriction)

Sometimes the meaning of a word gets reduced, so that after the change the word can only be used appropriately in fewer contexts than were possible before the change. The following are a few examples of narrowing changes.

deer narrowed its meaning from Old English *dēor* 'animal'. Compare the German cognate *Tier* 'animal'.

hound, 'a species of dog (long-eared hunting dog which follows its prey by scent)', comes from Old English *hund* that meant 'dog' in general. Compare German *Hund* 'dog'.

fowl, 'bird (especially edible or domestic)', has narrowed its sense from Old English *fugol* which meant 'bird' in general.

The German cognate is *Vogel* 'bird'. *Bird* comes from Old English *bird, bridd* 'young bird, nestling', which widened its meaning to include any sort of bird. The change from *bridd* to *bird* is an example of **metathesis**.

girl, which meant 'child or young person of either sex' in Middle English times, narrowed its referent in Modern English to 'a female child, young woman'.

meat originally meant 'food' in general. It later narrowed its meaning to 'meat' ('food of flesh'). This original 'food' meaning is behind the *meat* part of the compounds *sweetmeat* 'candy' and *nutmeat* 'the edible part of a nut inside the shell', and phrases such as *the meat of the matter, meat and drink*. Compare the Swedish cognate *mat* 'food'. The word *meat* occurs some 281 times in the King James version of the Bible, mostly meaning 'food', as in, for example:

"And to every beast of the earth, and to every fowl of the air . . . I have given every green herb for **meat**: and it was so." Genesis 1: 30.

" . . . and his **meat** was locusts and wild honey." Matthew 3: 4.

wife meant 'woman' in Old English times, as in the original sense of *midwife*, literally a 'with-woman'. *Wife* narrowed to mean 'woman of humble rank or of low employment, especially one selling commodities of various sorts'. This former meaning is preserved in *old wives' tales* and in *fishwife*. Finally, *wife* shifted its meaning to 'married woman, female spouse'.

Degeneration (Pejoration)

In degeneration (also called *pejoration*), the meaning of a word takes on a less positive, more negative evaluation in the minds of its users than it originally had. English *knave* 'a rogue' illustrates this well. *Knave* is from Old English *cnafa* 'a youth, child', whose meaning changed to 'servant' and then ultimately to modern *knave* with its negative meaning of 'rogue', 'dishonest, disreputable man'. The German cognate *Knabe* 'boy, lad' preserves its original non-pejorative meaning.

A few other examples of degeneration in meaning change are:

bully originally meant something like 'sweetheart, darling', a term of endearment applied to either sex. In the seventeenth century its meaning shifted to 'fine fellow', with positive senses of 'worthy, jolly, admirable' attested in the 1680s. It is seen, for example, in Shakespeare's "How now, my bully-rook?" from *The Merry Wives* *of Windsor*, meaning 'my fine fellow', a 'jolly comrade'. That sense is preserved in, for example, *bully for you!* The meaning deteriorated to 'blusterer' and then to 'harasser of the weak'.

silly, 'foolish, stupid', in Middle English times was *sely* and meant 'happy, innocent, pitiable', from Old English *sælig* 'blessed, blissful'. That meaning is still present in the German cognate *selig* 'blissful, happy'.

The frequent degeneration of terms for women reflects sexism through time, the lack of respect and equality for women in society. Many terms for women which initially were neutral degenerated so that today they have negative meanings. Some of these began as euphemisms for women or girls and then later took on negative meanings. Some cases are:

bimbo, borrowed from Italian *bimbo*, a contraction of *bambino* 'baby, little child, child's doll'. In the early 1900s in the US it started being used to refer to 'a stupid or brutish man'. By 1920 it had come to mean 'female in the sense of floozie, vamp', and in the late 1920s it had taken on associations with 'an attractive though unintelligent woman, often blond with a sensual figure, possibly wearing revealing clothing'. It was not used much after the 1930s, but then underwent a revival in the 1980s.

harlot originally meant 'tramp, beggar, vagabond'. It was borrowed around 1200 from Old French *harlot*, *herlot* 'vagabond, tramp, scoundrel'. In both Middle English and Old French it usually applied to males. For example, Shakespeare could speak of the "harlot king" in *The Winter's Tale*, Act II, Scene 1, and Chaucer (seen in Figure 3.2) used it in both positive and pejorative senses. He says in *The Canterbury Tales*:

He was a gentil **harlot** and a kynde;
A bettre felawe sholde men noght fynde.
[He was a noble rascal, and a kind (one);]
[A better comrade would be hard to find.]

Geoffrey Chaucer, *The Summoner, Prologue* (lines 649–650)

By the early fifteenth century *harlot* had acquired the sense of 'prostitute, unchaste woman', and this was reinforced in the sixteenth century by its euphemistic use to replace 'whore', 'strumpet'. *Harlot* appears forty times in the King James version of the Bible, apparently a commanding biblical concern.

madam took on the meaning of 'the female head of a house of prostitution' from its original sense of 'a title of courtesy used as a polite form of address to a woman' (from *Madame*, borrowed from Old French *ma dame* 'my lady').

mistress was borrowed from Old French *maistresse* with the meaning 'a woman who rules or has control'. In English it meant 'female governess, supervisor of novices in a convent', and came by the early fifteenth century to mean 'a woman who employs others in her service, a woman who has the care of or authority over servants or attendants'. It took on the charged meaning of 'a kept woman of a married man' also in the early fifteenth century, and went on to include eventually 'a woman in an extramarital sexual relationship, especially with a married man'.

squaw is now typically considered an offensive, derogatory, misogynist, racist slur, though its original meaning was the more neutral 'American Indian woman'. It was borrowed from Massachusett (Algonquian) *squa* 'woman'. Compare also Cree *iskwē*, and Ojibwe *ikwe* 'woman', from Proto-Algonquian **eθkwe:wa* 'woman'.

Figure 3.2 Geoffrey Chaucer
Source: GeorgiosArt / iStock / Getty Images Plus.

Elevation (Amelioration)

Meaning changes that result in a more positive sense than the word had before the change took place are cases of elevation (also called amelioration). This kind of change is seen in such examples as:

dude, 'guy, person', was elevated in meaning from what in 1883 was a word of ridicule for 'a man who affects an exaggerated fastidiousness in dress, speech, and deportment, concerned with what is aesthetically considered "good form," a dandy'.

fun, earlier meant 'cheat, trick'. It comes from the verb *to fun* that meant 'to cheat, hoax'. Something of the older sense is still seen in the likes of *to make fun of, funny business, funny stuff, funny money*, and *smells funny*.

grin, from Old English *grennian* 'to show one's teeth (in anger or pain)'. The ameliorative shift to 'to bare one's teeth in a broad smile' took place towards the end of the fifteenth century, close in meaning to today's *grin* 'to smile broadly'.

nice, 'pleasant, agreeable' – met already at the start of this chapter – is the result of elevation from its original meaning of 'foolish, stupid, senseless'.

pretty, from Old English *prættig* 'crafty, sly' – 'pretty' is more positive as a value judgement than 'crafty, sly'.

Metaphor

Some people resist metaphors because they see them as obstacles to clear communication. There are even websites that abhor metaphor. They talk about why many people don't like metaphors, though they concede that some love them. Critics think that some writers try so hard to come up with creative ways of expressing something that it just ends up as so much exaggerated twaddle. Whatever the attitude to them, metaphors abound both in daily spoken language and in writing.

Metaphor involves understanding one thing in terms of some other kind of thing thought to be similar in some way. The meaning change of *grasp* 'seize' to include 'understand' involves seeing physical 'seizing' as somehow similar to mental 'comprehension'.

Words meaning 'to kill' often attract metaphoric alternatives, as in English: to *blow away, bump off, dispatch, dispose of, do in, eliminate, erase, ice someone, knock off, liquidate, off someone, polish off, put down, put to sleep, rub out, slaughter, smoke someone, stiff someone, take care of, take out, terminate, waste, whack*, and many more.

In slang, there are many metaphoric meaning changes involving 'drunk' based on words whose original meaning is associated with being 'damaged' in some way: *bashed, blasted, blitzed, bombed, hammered, obliterated, plowed, ripped, shredded, smashed, tattered, totaled, wasted, zonked,* and many more. Another area of metaphor for 'drunk' involves being saturated with liquid: *besotted, flushed, juiced, pickled, pissed, sauced, sloshed, soaked, soused, tanked (tanked up),* among others.

A few other examples of metaphoric change are:

> **stud**, 'good-looking, sexy man' of slang origin, derived by metaphor from *stud* 'a male animal (especially a horse) used for breeding'.
>
> **mouse** by metaphor came also to be applied to a computer mouse, the small device used to move a cursor or arrow on a display screen, thought to resemble a mouse in size and shape.
>
> **thrill**, whose original meaning was 'to make a hole in, to pierce', shifted metaphorically to 'to pierce with emotion', and then later 'to fill with pleasure'.

Metonymy

Metonymy involves a change in the meaning of a word in which it comes to include new additional senses that were associated with the word's original sense but were not part of the meaning itself. However, the conceptual association between the earlier and new extended meanings may be so different from one another that they are anything but obvious. Metonymic changes typically involve things near each other in the real world, where the meaning of one of the terms shifts from its original sense to the sense of the other thing that is present in the context. Such definitions or descriptions of metonymy are frustratingly far from clear, but examples help to make it comprehensible. Some cases are:

> **bead** now means 'small piece of (decorative) material pierced for threading on a line'. However, it comes from Middle English *bede* 'prayer, prayer bead', which in Old English was *bedu, ġebed* 'prayer', related to *bid* 'to ask'. This is seen in its German cognate *Gebet* 'prayer'. The shift in meaning from 'prayer' to 'bead' came about via metonymy from 'bead' to 'prayer' – prayers were kept track of by rosary beads. It then shifted meaning to include the 'rosary bead' itself, and then eventually any 'bead', even 'beads' of water, while the sense of 'prayer' was lost.

cheek, in Old English *cēace,* the source of modern *cheek,* meant 'jaw, jawbone'. Over time it shifted its meaning to Modern English 'cheek', 'the fleshy side of the face below the eye', cheek and jaw being physically close to one another.

tea, from its sense of 'tea' the beverage, *tea* shifted to include the meaning of 'evening meal' in Great Britain and many Commonwealth countries, a meal often accompanied by tea drinking.

limey, a less direct example is *limey,* a derogatory name for English persons. It comes from the historical British naval practice of giving sailors limes to stave off scurvy.

A common sort of metonymy, sometimes thought to be connected with displacement or ellipsis (seen in Chapter 2), is the use of the name of the place (a toponym) to refer to a product characteristic of that place, as in:

champagne, from the name *Champagne,* a grape-growing region in northeast France.

cheddar (cheddar cheese), from *Cheddar* in Somerset, England.

geyser, from *Geysir,* in Iceland, a place known for its geysers and hot water springs.

sardine, from *Sardinia,* the Mediterranean island near Italy.

spa, from *Spa,* the name of a health resort in eastern Belgium that has mineral springs assumed to have curative value. The name is from Walloon *espa* 'spring, fountain'.

tangerine, from *Tangier,* Morocco.

Synecdoche

Synecdoche involves changes where a term for a part (or quality) is used to refer to the whole, or the whole is used to refer to a part, for example where *hand,* a body part, under synecdoche gives *hand* 'a hired hand, employed worker'. Some examples of words that involve meaning changes due to synecdoche follow. A few examples that may be less dramatic as cases of semantic change but are good examples of how the process of change due to synecdoche works are: *brains* for intelligence, *brass* for military officers or for shells/cartridges, *gold* in reference to an Olympic first-place medal, and *wheels* in reference to a car.

Let me beg indulgence for the first of these following examples – it is just that more shocking examples often make new concepts more memorable, if not clearer.

asshole, from *arsehole,* formerly meant just 'anus', the body part with many unpleasant associations. It changed its meaning to include also 'a contemptible or stupid person', the unpleasant body part coming to represent the whole unpleasant person.

mail was originally borrowed into English from Old French *male*, meaning 'bag, pouch' (see Modern French *malle* 'bag'), and then narrowed its meaning to 'bag for carrying letters', then to 'letters carried in that bag', and then went on to mean 'mail, post' generally. *Email* (electronic mail) is a step even further removed from the original 'bag' meaning.

And begging indulgence yet again, in some other examples a term for male or female genitals has come also to have negative meanings for a man or woman of negative character, typically obscene, as in:

dick, a nickname for *Richard*, though now much less frequent than it was in my father's time (he was Richard, though commonly called Dick). *Dick* meaning 'penis' is attested from 1891. The extension of *dick* 'penis' to mean also 'a contemptible or despicable person' started in the 1960s. The compound *dickhead* 'stupid, contemptible man' started showing up in 1969.

prick, 'penis' for 'despicable, contemptible male'. *Prick* with the meaning 'penis' illustrates an earlier metaphoric extension from *prick* 'small puncture, sharp point'. (See above for metaphor in meaning change.)

schmuck, 'penis, fool, stupid person', from Yiddish. The meaning was extended from original 'penis' to include 'fool, stupid person', applied frequently to contemptible males.

cunt, in similar fashion, became a very strong obscenity meaning 'very disagreeable or contemptible woman', from its original meaning of 'female genitals', similarly to Latin *cunnus* 'vulva', which vulgarly also meant 'a woman', probably unrelated to English *cunt*.

Displacement

Displacement (sometimes also called *ellipsis*) involves change in which one word absorbs part or all of the meaning of another word with which it is linked in a phrase, usually an Adjective + Noun, and then often the part whose meaning got absorbed gets dropped. A frequently cited example of displacement is *private*, from *private soldier*, where *private* came to mean 'ordinary/regular soldier' (contrasted with 'officer'). *Private* has taken on the meaning of the whole earlier phrase, *private soldier*. Displacement is sometimes considered a special kind of synecdoche, sometimes called phrasal synecdoche. Some other examples are:

capital < capital city
contact(s) < contact lens(es)
intercourse < sexual intercourse
proposal, to propose < marriage proposal, to propose marriage
salad < Old French *salade*, from Vulgar Latin *salata* meaning 'salted', a displacement from older *herba salata* 'salted vegetables' to just *salata*, vegetables seasoned with brine being a popular Roman dish.

Hyperbole (Exaggeration by Overstatement)

Hyperbole involves change in meaning due to exaggeration by overstatement. Some examples of this kind of semantic change are:

awesome, in the 1590s this meant 'profoundly reverential'. By 1690 it had acquired the meaning of 'inspiring dread or awe'. Today's sense of 'impressive, very good' was attested by 1961 and was very much in use by the 1980s. To say a word meaning 'inspiring dread' when the intended meaning is merely 'very good' is an exaggeration by overstatement.

spill, the Old English source of *spill* was *spillan* 'to destroy, kill, mutilate'. By late Old English times it came to mean also 'to waste'. By the early fourteenth century it was used to mean 'to shed blood', and by the mid fourteenth century it had developed the sense 'to let liquid fall or run out'.

starve, 'to suffer or perish from hunger', is from Old English *steorfan* 'to die'. Compare the German cognate *sterben* 'to die'. To say 'die' when 'suffer hunger' was intended is exaggeration by overstatement.

terribly, horribly, awfully, and other similar words today mean little more than 'very' (a generic intensifier). By overstatement they have lost their original connections with *terror*, *horror*, and *awe*.

Exaggeration by Understatement (Litotes)

Litotes is exaggeration by understatement, as in saying 'of no small importance' when 'very important' is meant. Such exaggerations by understatement are often behind permanent changes in the meanings of words. Some examples are:

bereaved, bereft, these words that today mean 'deprived by death' earlier meant just 'robbed', from Old English *bereafian* 'to rob, take away by violence, deprive', composed of *be-* 'about, around' + *reafian* 'to rob, plunder'.

kill originally meant 'to hit, strike, beat, knock'. Around 1300 *kill* came to acquire the meaning of 'to deprive of life, to put to death'. Saying a word that meant 'hit' when 'kill' was meant is an understatement.

poison involves a change in meaning due to exaggeration by understatement in French, reflected in English *poison*, borrowed from French. French inherited it from Latin *pōtiōnem* 'a drink, drinking' (derived from *pōtare* 'to drink'), which around the twelfth century gave Old French *poison*, *puison* 'a drink', especially 'a medicinal drink'. Later, around the fourteenth century, it came to mean 'a potion, a magic potion, poisonous drink', from which English borrowed *poison*.

potion is ultimately from the same Latin source, borrowed from Latin into Old French as *pocion* 'potion, draught, medicine', from which it was borrowed into English. It took on the sense of 'magical or enchanted drink' in the fifteenth century. English *potable* 'drinkable, suitable for drinking' has a straightforward history, borrowed from Old French *potable*, inherited directly from Late Latin *potabilis* 'drinkable', which is also derived from Latin *pōtare* 'to drink'.

This, then, gives the irony of how *poison*, something very bad, *potable*, something good, and *potion*, maybe somewhere between good and bad depending on context, all come from the same root, Latin *pōtare* 'to drink'.

venom came into English from Old French *venim* 'poison, malice', which is from Latin *venēnum* 'drug, medical potion' and 'charm, seduction', presumably including also 'love potion', from the Proto-Indo-European root **wen-* 'to desire, strive for'. This is apparently exaggeration by understatement, to go from a 'drug, love potion' to deadly 'poison'.

This Proto-Indo-European **wen-* 'to desire' is, incidentally, also the source of *Venus*, the Roman goddess of love and beauty, from whence we get *venerable* 'commanding respect' and *venerate* 'to treat with reverence', but also *venereal* 'description of an infection or disease that is caught or transmitted through sexual intercourse'. And that is how the goddess of love (*Venus*), poison (*venom*), respect (*venerable*, *venerate*, *veneration*), and socially transmitted diseases (*venereal*), are related, all derived from the same root.

Summary

In sum, there are numerous ways by which words can change their meanings, several kinds of semantic change. In this and the previous chapter, kinds of changes in words and in their meanings have been described and illustrated by a number of examples. Not only do these etymologies provide support for the main points of these two chapters, they also set the stage for the other kinds of language change that are often involved in the explanations of etymologies. Changes in other areas of language are the subjects of the following few chapters.

4   Language Mooching
Loanwords and Borrowing

> When a foreign word falls by accident into the fountain of a language, it
> will get driven around in there until it takes on that language's color.
> (Jacob and Wilhelm Grimm, Deutsches Wörterbuch)[1]

Introduction

This chapter, it could be said, continues the story started in Chapter 2
about where words come from, though this chapter is dedicated to words
taken over from other languages, **loanwords**. It is really common for
languages to take words from other languages and make them part of their
own vocabulary – these are called loanwords (or just loans) and the
process is called **borrowing**, and the loanwords themselves are also
often called borrowings – though there is never any intention of giving
them back. Borrowing normally implies a certain degree of bilingualism
for at least some people in both the language which borrows – usually
called the *recipient* language – and the language that is borrowed from –
called the *donor* language (sometimes the *source* language).

Here, we look at why languages borrow words from other languages.
English has rubbed shoulders with languages all around the world and in
the process has mooched new vocabulary from hither and yon. Loans in
English from various languages reveal the history of interactions with
different peoples. In Chapter 10, we see how loanwords help reveal
peoples' histories. In this chapter we look at vocabulary riches acquired
from other languages around the world.

In English, loanwords seem to be everywhere. This is evident even in
the lament against loanwords from Daniel Defoe (1660–1731, pictured in
Figure 4.1), author of *Robinson Crusoe*, ironically loaded with loans itself.
The loanwords in it are given in boldface here:

---

[1] Fällt von ungefähr ein Fremdwort in den Brunnen einer Sprache, so wird es so lange darin
umgetrieben, bis es ihre Farbe annimmt (Jacob and Wilhelm Grimm, 1854, *Deutsches
Wörterbuch*, vol. 1: XXVI).

Figure 4.1 Daniel Defoe
Source: Wikimedia Commons.

An Englishman has his mouth full of borrow'd **phrases** ... He is always borrowing other men's **languages** ... I cannot but think the **using** and **introducing foreign terms** of **art** or **foreign** words into speech while our **language labours** under no **penury** or **scarcity** of words is an **intolerable grievance**. (Defoe 1889: 222)

To wit, the source of each of these borrowed words is:

phrase, borrowed from Late Latin *phrasis* 'diction', itself borrowed from Greek *phrásis* 'speech, enunciation', derived from *phrázein* 'to tell, declare, inform'.

language, borrowed from Old French *langage* 'speech, words, oratory', from a Vulgar Latin form assumed to have been *linguaticum*, which is derived from Latin *lingua* 'tongue, speech, language'.

use, borrowed from Old French *user* 'to employ, to make use of, to frequent', inherited from Vulgar Latin *usare* 'to use', derived from Latin *úti-* 'to make use of, to consume, to take advantage of', seen in *útilis* 'useful'. English *utilize* is ultimately from this Latin root.

introduce, apparently borrowed from Latin *intrōdūcere* 'to lead in, bring in', based on *intrō-* 'inward, to the inside' + *dūcere* 'to lead'.

foreign, borrowed from Old French *forain* 'strange, foreign, external, remote', inherited from Medieval Latin *foraneus* 'on the outside, exterior', derived from Latin *foris* 'door, related to *forīs* 'out of doors'.

term, borrowed from Old French *terme* 'limit of time or place, date, duration', inherited from Latin *terminus* 'end, boundary line, line'.

art, borrowed from Old French *art* 'art, skill from learning or practice'. This comes to French from Latin *artem* (from *ars*) 'work of art, practical skill, craft, theory, science, moral quality'.

labor (*labour* in British spelling), borrowed from Old French *labor* 'toil, work, exertion, task, tribulation, suffering' (Modern French *labeur*), inherited from Latin *labor* 'effort, exertion, work, task, hardship, suffering'.

penury, borrowed from Latin *penūria* 'want, need, scarcity'.

scarcity, a shortened version of Anglo-French and Old North French *escarcete* (in Old French *escharsete*), derived from *eschars* 'scanty, scarce', source of the English loanword *scarce*.

intolerable, borrowed from Latin *intolerābilis* 'unbearable, irresistible', derived from *in-* 'not, opposite of' + *tolerābilis* 'bearable, tolerable, patient', derived from *tolerāre* 'to bear, endure, sustain'.

grievance, borrowed from Old French *grevance* 'harm, injury, misfortune, agony, sorrow', derived from *grever* 'to harm, burden, be harmful'.

About Loanwords in English

We will see more examples of borrowed words in English throughout this chapter and in others. Loanwords in English are typically identified according to the period in the history of English when they were borrowed. These periods are usually defined as:

Old English	ca. 450 to ca. 1150
Middle English	ca. 1150 to ca. 1500
Early Modern English	ca. 1500 to ca. 1750
Later Modern English	ca. 1750 to present

By far the largest number of loanwords in English is from French and/ or Latin, most of them borrowed during the Middle English period. Numerous French loanwords entered English vocabulary for both everyday things and for culture, technology, religion, law, government and administration, the military, and philosophy and intellectual matters. French developed from Latin but English also borrowed directly from Latin. For that reason, in some cases it can be difficult to tell whether English actually got a particular borrowed word from French or from Latin. Not infrequently, evidence shows that a particular word came from French and not directly from Latin, in cases where the loanword shows the results of sound changes that took place in French and in instances where the borrowed word is known from French but does not exist in Latin. For example, *clear* is from French *cler* (*clair* in Modern French spelling) and not directly from Latin *clārus*, because *clear* shows the result of the French sound change *a* to *e* (in *cler*) that Latin did not undergo.

Scandinavian (Old Norse) is in third place, behind French and Latin, for the most loans contributed to English. Though fewer in number, Scandinavian loans had a great impact on many of the most commonly encountered words of English. Most were borrowed before 1500, several of them much earlier.

As mentioned above, accounts of loanwords in English typically begin with borrowings from Latin into Proto-Germanic before speakers of Germanic tongues arrived in Britain. These early loans are inherited in the earliest English, but were not borrowed directly into English but rather into the parent language from which English descends. It is not always possible to be certain when a particular word was borrowed. Nevertheless, the following words are generally accepted as loans from Latin into Proto-Germanic and then inherited in English: *cheap, copper, cup, kettle, pin, post, pound, street,* and *wine*. There are at least 600 such loans from Latin into Germanic and inherited in Old English before the Anglo-Saxon conquest of England (Durkin 2014: 100).

The Roman conquest of Britain began in 43 CE and the Roman legions left at the beginning of the fifth century. However, Latin contributed little to the Celtic languages that would show up in later loans to English, and the Celtic languages had very little impact on Latin in England.

Germanic-speaking peoples arrived in Britain on the heels of Roman withdrawal, though exactly when and how they came and how many arrived are debated. By ca. 600 CE, most of modern England was under Anglo-Saxon control. However, the Anglo-Saxons also borrowed very little from Celtic as their territory expanded. From Celtic are *iron, leech* 'physician', *rich,* and perhaps *wire* (Durkin 2014: 69, 72). Interestingly, J. R. R. Tolkien (pictured in Figure 4.2), famous for his *Hobbit* and *Lord of*

Figure 4.2 J. R. R. Tolkien, ca. 1925
Source: Wikimedia Commons.

the Rings books, among others, contributed to the debate about whether Celtic had influenced English to preserve some sounds not retained in other Germanic languages (see Tolkien 1963).

Even later, after Old English times, English borrowed very little from the Celtic languages of Britain. Possible examples include *baby, clan, gull,* and *trousers*. More words, however, were borrowed later from Irish.

Conversion to Christianity started soon after the Anglo-Saxon arrival in England and was complete by the late seventh century, bringing numerous Latin loans into Old English with it.

Viking raids began in the late 700s, with Scandinavian invasion and conquest in the late 800s. A treaty from 886 established the Danelaw, with Scandinavian control over a large area in England east and north of a line running roughly from London to Chester. In this area Scandinavian law applied, hence the name "Danelaw," because of the many Danish invaders who settled there (see Map 4.1). Many Scandinavian loanwords came into English at this time.

The Norman Conquest of 1066 brought French domination in government, religion, and all important institutions, eventually leading to many loanwords of French origin throughout English vocabulary.

Map 4.1 The Danelaw
Map by David McCutcheon FBCart.S www.dvdmaps.co.uk.

Why Do Languages Borrow Words from Other Languages?

The two main reasons why languages take on new words from other languages are **need** and **prestige**. When people get a new item or concept from abroad, they need a new word in order to talk about it. Since the new thing has a name in the language of those from whom the new thing is acquired, very often the speakers of the recipient language just adopt the name for it from the language of the donors. The need for new words to name new things is behind the fact that words for 'automobile', 'chocolate', 'coca-cola', 'coffee', and 'tobacco', for example, are similar in many languages around the world – as these new items were acquired, speakers borrowed the names for them from other languages.

There is the story, not a particularly good one, about the guy who bragged that he knew a great number of languages because he could say 'coffee' in lots of languages – words for 'coffee' are loanwords in most languages and so typically are quite similar. *Coffee* came into English ultimately from Arabic *qahwa*, which Turkish borrowed as *kahve* – Turkish had no *w* and so substituted *v* for it. From Turkish, the word for 'coffee' reached most European languages in the early seventeenth century, including English, and is today found in languages around the world, for example Chinese *kāfēi*, Czech *káva*, French *café*, Finnish *kahvi*, German *Kaffee*, Greek *kafés*, Hindi *kofee*, Hungarian *kávé*, Indonesian *kopi*, Italian *caffè*, Japanese *kōhī*, Korean *keopi*, Māori *kawhe*, Polish *kawa*, Russian *kofe*, Swahili *kahawa*, Zulu *ikhofi*, among many others. *Mocha* comes from the place name *Mocha*, the Red Sea port of Mocha (also spelled *Mokha*, *Mukha*) in Yemen, an early place from which coffee was shipped.

And we could add *whiskey* to the list of words borrowed widely in languages around the world. Although arguably there may have been no real need for the whiskey itself, we can just assume that as speakers of these borrowing languages got the new thing, whiskey, they needed a word to go along with it, to call it by, and so borrowed the English word. Actually, first English borrowed *whiskey* from Scottish Gaelic *uisge beatha*, literally 'water of life'. *Uisge beatha* is a loan translation of Latin *aqua vītae* 'water of life'. Then from English *whiskey* it was borrowed widely: French *whisky*, German *Whiskey*, Albanian *uiski*, Arabic *alwiski*, Armenian *viski*, Balinese *wahski*, Bengali *hu'iski*, Finnish *viski*, Georgian *visk'i*, Japanese *uisukī*, Korean *wiseuki*, Portuguese *uísque*, Samoan *uisiki*, and many more.

The other main reason why words are borrowed from one language to another is prestige, because the foreign-language term is esteemed, attributed high status. English speakers were perfectly capable of talking about 'pig flesh' and 'cow flesh' using native vocabulary, but *pork*, from French *porc*, and *beef*, from French *boeuf*, were borrowed because French had high social status, more prestigious than English, during the period of Norman French dominance in England (1066–1300) and shortly thereafter. A few of the many other prestige cuisine words borrowed from French into English include: *cuisine* itself, from French *cuisine* 'kitchen'; *lettuce*, from Anglo-French *laitues*; *mutton*, from Old French *moton*, Modern French *mouton* 'sheep'; *salad*, mentioned in the previous chapter, from Old French *salade*; and *veal*, from Old French *veel* 'calf', Modern French *veau*.

As already mentioned, English has borrowed thousands of words from French. Publications and websites assert that anywhere from 30 to nearly 50 percent of the English vocabulary is of French origin. Many of these loanwords are due to their assumed higher prestige than that of their native English counterparts.

Borrowings for prestige still enter English today, but their number is low. The prestige of English now dominates in globalization, meaning that languages all over the world tend to borrow enthusiastically from English, while English now borrows much less for reasons of prestige from other languages.

A third reason for some borrowings is to be **derogatory**, to show a negative attitude, usually towards the people who speak the language from which the term is borrowed. Loans for derogatory purposes, however, are rare. One example is French *hâbler* 'to brag, boast', borrowed from Spanish *hablar* 'to speak'. Its meaning tells something of French attitudes towards Spanish speakers, at least at the time when the word was borrowed. Finnish *koni* 'nag' [old horse], with negative connotations, is borrowed from Russian *kon^y*, a neutral term for 'horse'. These words have negative connotations that are not present in their meanings in the donor languages, presumably reflecting the attitudes of speakers of the borrowing language towards speakers of the donor language.

Other examples are found in derogatory names in English for ethnic groups, such as:

> **Dago**, from Spanish *Diego* 'James', thought first to have been slang for someone born of Spanish parents, used also to mean Spanish or Portuguese sailors on American and British ships. It later expanded and shifted its reference to mean mostly 'Italian'.

> **Haji** (Hajji, Hadji), from Arabic *al ḥajjī* 'a Muslim who has made the pilgrimage to Mecca', the birthplace of Islam. The haji (also spelled *haj*) is the ritualistic pilgrimage itself, a pillar of Islam that Muslims are required to perform. The term *Haji*

was used by American soldiers in the Middle East as a derogatory term for 'Muslim'. In contrast, in several other varieties of
English *Haji* is used as a term of respect for a person who has
been on the hajj.

Kanaka, 'Hawaiian, Polynesian, Pacific Islander' ('Melanesian
fieldworker' in Australia), a negative term, from Hawaiian *kanaka*
'man, person', borrowed also into several other languages.

Kraut, for 'German', shortened from German *Sauerkraut*
'sauerkraut (pickled cabbage)'.

Nip, for 'Japanese', shortened from Japanese *Nippon* 'Japan'.

In some cases it is not clear where the negative associations come from, as
in the case of English *hausfrau* with the pejorative meaning of 'frumpy,
overly domesticated woman', borrowed from German *Hausfrau* 'house-
wife, home-maker', with only neutral connotations in German.

Loanwords of English origin in other languages can also reflect less
than positive attitudes about English-speaking people, especially
Americans, as in Japanese *wan-man* 'the type of leader who wants to
make all decisions without consulting anyone' from English *one man*,
and Japanese *bosu*, from English *boss*, where in Japanese *bosu* almost
always implies a boss involved in clandestine activities. The Russian
loanwords *biznes* 'business' and *biznesmén* 'businessman', from English
business and *businessman*, respectively, are often meant to be pejorative.

Of course, many borrowed words came not directly from their ultimate
source but through intermediary languages that borrowed the word
first – second-hand loans. For example, English *tofu* is borrowed from
Japanese *tōfu* 'soy bean curd', but Japanese borrowed it earlier from
Middle Chinese, seen in Mandarin *dòufu*, composed of *dou* 'beans' + *fu*
'rotten'. Another is *coyote*, which came into English from Spanish *coyote*,
but it was not a native word in Spanish either. Spanish borrowed it earlier
from *coyōtl*, a word of the same meaning in Nahuatl, the language of the
Aztecs. English got many terms from Spanish that Spanish had earlier
borrowed from Indigenous languages of the New World, seen below.

Loanwords in English Involving Food

We can get a sharper appreciation for the extent and impact of borrowings
in daily life from a brief look at the loanwords in English that involve the
foods English speakers eat.

The names of many things we routinely eat entered English from the
languages of many different nations and ethnic groups, enriching the diet:
tea/chai, *wonton* (from Chinese); *croissant*, *fillet mignon*, *pâté*, *soufflé* (more
recently from French); *pasta*, *pizza*, *spaghetti* (from Italian); *sake*, *sushi*,

teriyaki (from Japanese); *burrito, taco, tortilla* (from Spanish); and heaps more from various languages. A quick look at the names of common foods in your pantry or refrigerator gives a good idea of the impact of borrowed words on English vocabulary and on our everyday lives:

asparagus, from Latin *asparagus*, borrowed from Greek *asparagos/aspharagos*.

broccoli, from Italian *broccoli*, plural of *broccolo* 'a sprout, cabbage sprout', diminutive of *brocco* 'shoot, protruding tooth, small nail', from Latin *broccus* 'one having protruding teeth'.

butter, found generally in West Germanic languages but it is an early loanword from Latin *butyrum* 'butter' (surviving in Italian *burro* and French *beurre* 'butter'), borrowed in Latin from Greek *boutyron*, which meant 'cow-cheese'.

cabbage, from Old North French *caboche* 'head' (dialectal *cabbage*), from Old French *caboce* 'head', a diminutive form from Latin *caput* 'head' (ultimately from the Proto-Indo-European root **kaput-* 'head').

cake, from Old Norse *kaka* 'cake'.

candy meant 'crystallized sugar' when it entered English in the late thirteenth century from Old French *çucre candi* 'sugar candy', which was borrowed from Arabic *qandi*, which comes from Persian *qand* 'cane sugar', thought probably borrowed from Sanskrit *khanda* 'piece (of sugar)'.

cauliflower, originally *cole florye*, from Italian *cavoli fiori* 'flowered cabbage', plural of *cavolo* 'cabbage' + *fiore* 'flower'.

celery, from French *céleri*, said to be from Lombard Italian *seleri* (singular *selero*), from Late Latin *selinon*, borrowed from Greek *selinon* 'parsley' (in Medieval Greek it meant 'celery').

cheese, an old loanword in Germanic languages (Old English *cyse*) borrowed from Latin *caseus*.

cherry, from Anglo-French *cherise* (compare Modern French *cerise* 'cherry'), from Vulgar Latin *ceresia*, borrowed from late Greek *kerasian* 'cherry'.

chocolate, ultimately from Nahuatl *chokolā-tl* 'chocolate' (see below).

cookie (mostly American English), from Dutch *koekje* 'little cake', diminutive of *koek* 'cake'.

flour, from Old French *flour* 'flower' (compare French *fleur de farine* 'flower of meal/flour', that is, the 'best or finest of ground meal').

hamburger, from German *Hamburger* 'person or thing native to Hamburg'.

juice, from French *jus* 'broth, sauce, juice of plant or animal'.

ketchup, **catsup**, ultimately from Hokkien (Amoy) Chinese 'mixed pickled fish and spices' called *kôe-chiap* or *kê-chiap* 'fish sauce' (the brine of pickled fish or shellfish), see Cantonese *kōetsiap* 'pickled fish brine', from *kōe* 'seafood' + *tsiap* 'sauce'. The sauce spread to Malaysia (Malay *kĕchap*, Indonesian *kicop*), where English sailors and traders borrowed the word, perhaps via Dutch.

macaroni, from southern Italian dialect *maccaroni* (Standard Italian *maccheroni*), the plural of *maccarone*, a pasty food made of flour, cheese, and butter.

pasta, to the surprise of many, *pasta* was not common in English until after World War II, though it first entered the language in 1874, from Italian *pasta*, from Late Latin *pasta* 'dough, pastry cake, paste', borrowed ultimately from Greek *pasta* 'barley porridge'.

pie, from Medieval Latin *pie* 'a pastry with meat or fish'; earlier in English *pie* meant 'pastry'.

pizza, from Italian *pizza*. Earlier, pizza meant 'cake, tart, pie'. It is attested in English since 1935.

potato, ultimately from Taino (Cariban language of Haiti) *patata*, borrowed through Spanish *batata*, *patata* to many other languages.

rice, ultimately from Dravidian **ari/*ariki* 'rice, paddy' (compare Tamil *ari/ari-ci*), via Latin *oriza* and Greek *orúza*.

sausage, from Old North French *saussiche* (see Modern French *saucisse*), inherited from Vulgar Latin *salsica* 'sausage', derived from *salsicus* 'seasoned with salt'.

spaghetti, from Italian *spaghetti*, plural of *spaghetto* 'small thread', the diminutive of *spago* 'string, twine'.

spice, from Anglo-French *spece*, Old French *espice* (Modern French *épice*), inherited from Late Latin *species* (a plural form) 'spices, goods, wares'. In Classical Latin this meant 'kind, sort', the source of English *species*.

squash, from Narragansett (Algonquian) *askutasquash* 'the things that can be eaten raw'.

sugar, ultimately from Arabic *sukkar*, through Old French *sucre* 'sugar'.

tea, ultimately from Chinese (compare Min Chinese *tê*), probably borrowed through Malay *te* into Dutch and from Dutch to English. *Chai* is ultimately from Mandarin *ch'a* 'tea'.

tomato, from Nahuatl *toma-tl*, through intermediary Spanish *tomate* borrowed from this Nahuatl word.

yoghurt (yogurt), from Turkish *yoğurt*, though the '*g*' in English is a spelling pronunciation. The *ğ* in Turkish is silent, or is optionally pronounced as a weak /w/ when between round vowels or between a round vowel and *a* or *e*, as in the name of the Turkish president Recep Tayyip *Erdoğan*, whose last name sounds like "urdowan." Turkish *yoğurt* sounds like [yo.urt], two syllables.

And others.

Just imagine what dinner must have been like for most Europeans before Columbus, without such foods of American origin as *potatoes*, *tomatoes*, *squash*, *maize* (corn), *chili* (chili peppers), *turkeys*, and *chocolate*, not to mention *avocados*, *guavas*, *papayas*, *ananas* (pineapple), *cashews*, *pecans*, *guacamole*, *cacao/cocoa*, and *tapioca*.

How Do Languages Borrow Words from Other Languages?

So, why is it that sometimes loanwords in the recipient language do not look very much like the source words in the donor language that they are taken from? Often the word in the donor language and in the recipient language are quite similar, but sometimes borrowed words are so different that it can be hard to recognize them as loanwords. For example, seeing Hawaiian *kalikimaka* 'Christmas', most people probably would not recognize it as being borrowed from English *Christmas*. Obviously, the sounds of one language do not necessarily match the sounds in another language, and speakers of the borrowing (recipient) language typically substitute sounds in their own language that they judge to be most similar to the foreign sounds in borrowed words. Because standard Hawaiian has no *r*, *s*, or *t*, in order to borrow *Christmas*, Hawaiian speakers substituted the closest sounds that were available in Hawaiian. Hawaiian has only *a*, *e*, *i*, *o*, *u*, *h*, *k*, *l*, *m*, *n*, *p*, *w*, and ' (glottal stop), so for *r* they substituted *l*, and for *s* they chose *k*. Borrowed words are also typically forced to fit the syllable patterns of the recipient language. In this case, since Hawaiian has no consonant clusters (groups of consonants together with no intervening vowel) nor consonants at the end of words, consonant clusters were broken up by the addition of a vowel. The *chr* and *sm* and final *s* of *Christmas* were changed by adding a vowel, *kal* and *kim*, and *a* after the final *k* (that substitutes for *s*, so *ka*) – and voilà *kalikimaka* 'Christmas'.

The phrase *mele kalikimaka* 'merry Christmas', borrowed from English *merry Christmas* (*mele* with *l* substituting for the *r* of English *merry*), is a favorite of tourists. It was made famous by the song *Mele Kalikimaka* written by R. Rex Anderson in 1949. It was sung by Bing Crosby, the Beach Boys, and Jimmy Buffet, and covered by many other artists and used in a number of films – many renditions of it are available on *YouTube*.

Another example is Japanese *purasuchikku* 'plastic' borrowed from English *plastic*. Japanese *l* is limited to only a few contexts and dialects, so here *r* was substituted for English *l*. Japanese has only a very few kinds of permitted consonant clusters and word-final consonants. It does not have *s* in consonant clusters, so the consonant cluster *st* was broken up by the insertion of *u* (*su*). Moreover, in Japanese, *t* before *i* becomes *ch*, so for *ti* of *plastic*, *chi* is substituted, with *sti* ending up as *suchi* in the sound substitutions. To match *plastic* to the syllable structure of Japanese, the *pl* becomes *pur*, and final *c* ends up with a vowel, substituted by *kku*. Hence *purasuchikku*. Sound substitutions of several sorts are seen in various of the loanwords into English presented in this chapter, most not as dramatic as in these two examples.

Calques

A final sort of borrowing involves calques. A calque is a loan translation, sometimes called a semantic loan. In calquing, a word or phrase is "borrowed" from another language by literal word-for-word (or part-for-part) translation. Only the meaning is transferred from the donor language, not the pronunciation. English has many calques and there are also many examples of calques taken from English as loan translations in other languages. For example, English *black market* is a calque from German *Schwarzmarkt* (*schwarz* 'black' + *Markt* 'market'). On the other hand, Spanish *mercado negro* 'black market' (*mercado* 'market' + *negro* 'black') is a calque taken from English *black market*, after English got the calque from German. *Loanword* itself is a calque from German *Lehnwort* (*lehn*- 'loan' in compound and derived words + *Wort* 'word').

The word for 'railroad, railway' is a calque in a number of other languages based on a translation of 'iron' + 'road'/'way': French *chemin de fer* (literally 'road of iron'); German *Eisenbahn* (*Eisen* 'iron' + *Bahn* 'path, road'); Spanish *ferrocarril* (*ferro*- 'iron' in compound words + *carril* 'lane, way'); Italian *estrada ferrata* (literally 'iron-clad road'); Finnish *rautatie* (*rauta* 'iron' + *tie* 'road'); Swedish *järnväg* (*järn* 'iron' + *väg* 'road, way'); Irish *iarnród* (*iarn* 'iron' + *ród* 'roadway'); Turkish *demiryolu* (*demir* 'iron' + *yolu* 'way'), and many others.

English *skyscraper* was calqued in several languages: French *gratte-ciel* (*gratte* 'grate, scrape' + *ciel* 'sky'); Spanish *rascacielos* (*rasca* 'scratch' + *cielos* 'skies'); Portuguese *arranha-céu* (*arranha* 'scratch' + *céu* 'sky'); Russian *neboskrebo* (*nebo* 'sky' + *skrebo* 'scraper'); and German *Wolkenkratzer* (*Wolken* 'clouds' + *kratzer* 'scratcher, scraper').

English Borrowings from Other Languages

We have already seen a good number of loanwords in English from various other languages. There are hundreds of borrowings in English from French, German, Greek, and Latin. Here, we dedicate more attention to loanwords in English from less expected languages around the world. It will be helpful to be mindful that often English has borrowed a word from some language where the immediate donor language is an intermediary that itself previously borrowed the word from some third language.

Various sources report the number of words borrowed into English from a particular language, and not infrequently the percentage of the total English vocabulary that is borrowed from a particular language is given. However, the numbers reported in different sources differ greatly. Perhaps they average around 40 percent of Modern English vocabulary considered to be loanwords. These figures typically rely on databases that depend on specific dictionaries or corpora, but there are differences among databases constructed from different sources.[2] In some cases, some scholars have considered the etymology of a word to be unknown or unclear while others unhesitatingly declare the word's origin a borrowing. In short, the identification of something as a loanword is in essence a hypothesis that the word is borrowed. In many cases, the evidence in favor of borrowing is so compelling that the hypothesis becomes all but an absolute certainty. In other cases, the evidence for borrowing may vary from quite weak for some words to quite strong for others. Let's now look at some of the loanwords in English from various languages around the world.

From American Indian Languages

Algonquian

chipmunk, from Ottawa *ajidamoonh* 'red squirrel', literally 'goes down head first' (*ajid-* 'upside down, head first'). *Chipmunk* is probably influenced analogically by English *chip* and *mink*.

---

[2] See Durkin (2014) for a survey of different reports of the number of loans or percentages of loans in English and for the problems involved.

moccasin, from an Algonquian language, probably Powhatan <mockasin> (*mahkesen*).[3]

moose, from an Eastern Algonquian language, probably Massachusett *moos* (Narragansett *moos*).

opossum, from Powhatan <apasum> / <opussum> / <aposoum> (*a:passem*) 'opossum', from Proto-Algonquian *wa:p-a?θemwa*, literally 'white dog'.

papoose, from Narragansett <papoòs> or Massachusett <pappouse> 'child'.

pecan, from an Algonquian language, possibly Illinois *pakani* (compare Ojibwe *bagaan*) 'nut'.

raccoon, from Powhatan <arahkun>/<aroughcun> (*a:re:hkan*).

skunk, from a southern New England Algonquian language, probably Massachusett <squnck> (compare Abenaki *segõgw*, *segongku*, from Proto-Algonquian *šeka:kwa*, composed of *šek-* 'to urinate' + *-a:kw* 'fox').

squash (plant), seen above, from Narragansett <askútasquash> 'things that may be eaten raw', from *askut* 'green, raw, uncooked' + *asquash* 'eaten' + *-ash* 'plural suffix'.

tomahawk, from Powhatan <tamahaac>. From Proto-Algonquian *temaha·kani*, a compound of *temah-* 'to cut' + *-a·kan* 'instrument for'.

totem, from an Algonquian language, probably Ojibwe *o-doo-dem-an*, 'his totem, referring to a kin group'.

wigwam, probably from Eastern Abenaki *wìkəwam* 'house, dwelling'. Compare Ojibwe *wiigiwaam*. *Wigwam* and *wickiup* have the same Algonquian root.

woodchuck, from an Algonquian language; see Narragansett <ockqutchaun> 'woodchuck', Cree *otchek*, and Ojibwe *otchig* 'marten', later transferred to mean 'groundhog'. The English word underwent analogical change based on *wood* and *chuck*.

Nahuatl

All words borrowed from Nahuatl, the language of the Aztecs and Toltecs, were first borrowed into Spanish and then borrowed from Spanish into English. Some examples are:

---

[3] The notation <...> indicates that the material inside the brackets is presented exactly as found in the source, for example as written in some early manuscript.

avocado, from Spanish *aguacate*, from Nahuatl *āwaka-tl* 'avocado'.

chili, from Spanish *chile*, from Nahuatl *chīlli* 'chili pepper'

chipotle, from Spanish *chipotle*, from Nahuatl *chilpok-tli* meaning 'smoked chili', derived from *chīl-* 'chili' + *pok-* 'smoke' + *-tli* 'noun suffix'.

chocolate, from Spanish *chocolate*, from Nahuatl *chokolā-tl*.

cocoa and **cacao**, from Spanish *cacao*, from Nahuatl *kakawa-tl* 'cacao, chocolate bean'.

guacamole, from Spanish *guacamole*, from Nahuatl *āwakamōl-li*, a compound of *āwaka-* 'avocado' + *mōl-li* 'sauce'.

ocelot, from Spanish *ocelote*, from Nahuatl *ōsēlō-tl* 'ocelot, jaguar'.

tamale, from Spanish *tamale*, from Nahuatl *tamal-li* 'tamale'.

tequila, from Spanish *tequila*, from Nahuatl *teki-tl* 'work' + *-tlan* 'place of'.

tomato, from Spanish *tomate* (*jitomate* in Mexico), from Nahuatl *toma-tl* 'tomato'.

Quechua

Like Chinese, Quechua is actually a <u>language family</u> composed of some twenty-five related languages. Loanwords from Quechua, the language of the Incas, were first borrowed into Spanish and then from Spanish into English. Examples include:

condor, from Spanish *condor*, from Quechua *kuntur* 'condor'.

guano, from Spanish *guano* 'fertilizing excrement, especially of sea birds', from Quechua *wanu* 'dung'.

jerky, from Spanish *charqui* 'dried and salted meat', from Quechua *ch'arki* 'dried meat'.

llama, from Spanish *llama*, from Quechua *lyama* 'llama'.

pampa, from Spanish *pampa* 'pampa', from Quechua *pampa* 'pampa, large plain'.

puma, from Spanish *puma* 'mountain lion, cougar', from Quechua *puma* 'mountain lion, cougar'.

Eskimo-Aleut Languages

igloo, from Inuktitut *iglu* 'igloo'.

kayak, from Inuktitut *qayaq* 'kayak'.

malamute, 'malamute dog', from Inupiaq *malimiut*, bred by the Malamute people, an Inupiaq subgroup.

Arawakan, mostly from Taino, and from Cariban

Most loanwords from these sources were also borrowed first into Spanish and then from Spanish into English. Most of them reflect early Spanish contact with the Indigenous languages of the Caribbean.

caiman, from Spanish *caiman* 'caiman', said to be borrowed from Carib *kaymán* or *akayuman* 'crocodilian animal'.

canoe, from Taino, via Spanish *canoa*.

hammock, from Taino *hamaka* 'hammock', via Spanish *hamaca* 'hammock'.

hurricane, from Taino *hurakán* 'hurricane', via Spanish *huracán* 'hurricane'.

iguana, apparently from Taino *iwana* 'iguana', borrowed into Spanish as *iguana* 'iguana', from whence English borrowed it.

maize, from Taino *mahís*, by way of Spanish *maíz* 'maize, corn'.

potato, from the Taino *batata* 'sweet potato', via Spanish *batata* 'sweet potato'.

tobacco, from Spanish *tabaco* 'tobacco', probably from a Taino word that meant 'a roll of tobacco leaves' or 'a kind of pipe for smoking', though there are also other proposed etymologies for this word.

Tupí-Guaranían Languages

Tupí-Guaranían, with some forty-nine languages, is a branch of the very large Tupían language family of over seventy languages. There are Tupí-Guaranían languages in many South American countries, extending over 4,000 km in both length and width, one of the most widely spread language families of the world. Many of the loanwords from Tupí-Guaranían languages were borrowed first into Portuguese and then from Portuguese into English, though some came first as loans in Spanish or French and then from these languages into English. Examples include:

cashew, from Tupí *acaîu*, via Portuguese *caju* 'cashew'.

cougar, probably from Guaraní *guaçu ara* 'cougar'. It was borrowed into Portuguese from which French borrowed it as *couguar*, which was influenced by analogy from *jaguar*, where the cedilla diacritic was dropped from the <ç>. English borrowed it from French.

jaguar, from Tupinambá *îagûara*, via Portuguese *jaguar*, through French *jaguar* to English.

manioc, from Tupinambá *manioca* 'cassava root', via Portuguese *mandioca*, through French *manioc* to English.

piranha, ultimately from Tupí *pira nya*, literally 'biting fish'. The *pira* 'fish' part is clear, but the meaning of *nya* is uncertain. It was borrowed into Portuguese as *piranha* 'piranha', from which English got it.

tapioca, from Tupí *tapioca* 'juice of a pressed cassava', *tipi* 'residue, dregs' + *og*, *ok* 'to squeeze out (from cassava roots)', via Portuguese *tapioca*.

tapir, from Tupinambá *tapira*, via Portuguese *tapir*, through French *tapir* to English *tapir*.

toucan, from Tupí *tuka*, *tukana*, via Portuguese *tucano* or Spanish *tucán*, through French *toucan* to English.

Other Indigenous Languages of the Americas

abalone, from Rumsen *awlun* and Ohlone *aluan*, via Spanish *abulón*.

bayou, from early Choctaw *bayuk* 'creek, river', via French.

high muckamuck (also *mucky-muck*, *muckety-muck*), from Chinook Jargon *high muck-a-muck* 'plenty of food', from *muckamuck* 'food'.

hogan, from Navajo *hōghan* 'house, dwelling'.

manatee, via Spanish *manatí*, from a word in a Cariban language meaning 'woman's breast'. In Proto-Cariban it is **manati* 'woman's breast'. This name may be due to manatees' unique nursing behavior because their mammary glands and nipples are located behind their pectoral flippers (like in an armpit). Also, manatee calves nurse for up to two years.

sasquatch 'bigfoot', from Halkomelem *sæsq'əts* 'sasquatch'.

tepee, from Lakota *thípi* 'house'.

See Campbell (2024) for further details concerning loanwords from Indigenous languages of the Americas.

From African Languages

bwana, from Swahili *bwana* 'master'.

chimpanzee, borrowed from a Bantu language of Angola.

cola, from cola nut, from a Niger-Congo language; compare Temne *kola*, Mindinka *kolo*. The name *Coca-Cola* has this in it.

dengue, the disease is from east Africa. The name *dengue* is from West Indian Spanish *dengue*, borrowed from Swahili *dinga* 'seizure, cramp'.

gnu, from Dutch *gnoe*, borrowed from Khoikhoi *!nu* 'gnu, wildebeest', where *!n* represents a nasal click.

impala, from Zulu *im-pala* 'gazelle'.

marimba, from a Bantu language; compare Swahili *marimba*, *malimba* 'xylophone-like instrument'.

safari, from Swahili *safari* 'journey, expedition', ultimately from Arabic *safar* 'journey'.

From Australian Languages

boomerang, from Dharug (a.k.a. the Sydney language, Gadigal language) *bumariny* 'boomerang'.

kangaroo, from a native language of northeast Queensland, thought to be from Guugu Yimithir (Guugu Yimidhirr) *gangurru* 'eastern grey kangaroo'.

koala, from Dharug *gula* 'no water'.

kookaburra, from Wiraddhuri (Wiradjuri) *guuguubarra* 'kookaburra', onomatopoeic from the bird's loud, distinctive, laughing-like call.

wallaby, from Dharug *walabi* or *waliba* 'wallaby'.

wombat, from Dharug *wambad*, *wambag*.

From Hawaiian

aloha, 'hello, love', from Hawaiian *aloha* 'love, hello, goodbye'. In English outside of Hawai'i, only the meaning 'hello' tends to be known.

hula, 'Hawaiian form of dance', from Hawaiian *hula*. In older times, men used to do hula as a sign of masculinity and as a war dance. There has often been confusion between the more graceful, slow Hawaiian hula and the quicker Tahitian hula with more hip movements.

lei, 'garland of flowers or leaves or both worn around the neck', from Hawaiian *lei*.

luau, 'a Hawaiian feast or party', from Hawaiian: *lūʻau*.

ukulele, 'small guitar-like musical instrument', Hawaiian *ʻukulele* (derived from *ʻuku* 'flea, louse' + *lele* 'jump, fly'). This instrument was developed from the Portuguese instrument *cavaquinho*.

wiki, 'user-editable website', from Hawaiian *wikiwiki* 'fast, swift'. It comes from the name of the free *Wikiwiki Shuttle*, a bus service, taken by Ward Cunningham who built the first user-editable website. He called it *WikiWikiWeb*, eventually shortened to *wiki*.

From Arabic

A few of the many loanwords from Arabic are presented here. Most loanwords in English that are ultimately of Arabic origin got to English from intermediary languages that first borrowed the words and then English got them from these languages. In particular, many of the words of Arabic origin in English came via Spanish. A good number begin with *al-* (*el-*) 'the' in Arabic, that was incorporated as part of the root in the loanword when it was borrowed into Spanish or other European languages. The following are some examples of English words ultimately of Arabic origin:

adobe, from Spanish *adobe*, borrowed from Arabic *al-tūb* (*aṭ-ṭūb*) 'the brick'. Some believe this is borrowed from Coptic *tōbe* 'brick', inherited from Ancient Egyptian *ḏbt*.

alchemy, from Old French *alchimie*, inherited from Medieval Latin *alchēmia* 'medieval chemistry', the "science" attempting to transmute base metals into gold or silver, including general chemistry and metallurgy, borrowed from Arabic *al-kīmiyāʔ* 'alchemy, chemistry'. Arabic borrowed it originally from Greek *khumeiā* 'art of alloying metals'. English *chemistry* has the same origin.

alcohol, from Spanish or French *alcohol*, from Medieval Latin *alcohol* 'powdered ore of antimony', borrowed from Arabic *al-kuḥl* 'fine metallic powder used to darken eyelids', from Andalusian Arabic *kuḥul*, *quḥul*. The powder was obtained by crushing and heating it to high temperatures or distillation, and *alcohol* came to mean the spirit from distillation of wine or ethanol. English *kohl* is from this same source; it is a black powder, used as eye makeup especially in Eastern countries.

algebra, from Medieval Latin *algebra* (*algebrāica*). It is borrowed from Arabic *al-jabr* 'completing, restoring broken parts', first recorded in the title of the book *Al-mukhtaṣar fī ḥisāb al-jabr wa al-muqābala* (*The Compendium on Calculation by Completing and Balancing*), by ninth-century mathematician, astronomer, astrologer, and geographer Mohammed (Abu Ja'far) Ibn Mūsā al-Khwārizmī. It was translated to Latin in the twelfth century and it introduced Arabic numerals to Europe.

algorithm, from Old French *algorisme* 'Arabic numeral system', from Medieval Latin *algorismus,* borrowed from Arabic *al-khwārizmī* taken from the name of the mathematician Muhammad ibn Mūsā al-Khwārizmī (mentioned above with *algebra*). Medieval Latin *algorismus* is from a confused transliteration of the name *al-Khwārizmī,* literally 'native of Khwarazm' (modern Khiva in Uzbekistan). Old French changed Medieval Latin *algorismus* to *algorithme* on <u>analogy</u> with Greek *arithmos* 'number', seen borrowed in English *arithmetic.*

assassin, ultimately from Arabic *'asāsiyyīn* 'people faithful in the foundation (of the faith)', traditionally thought to be from *hashshīshīn* 'hashish-users'. It was a nickname for the Nizari Ismailis in the era of the Crusades, a fanatical Muslim sect in the mountains of Lebanon, reputed in widely circulated stories for killing opposing leaders after getting high on hashish. In Medieval Latin, Italian, and French, they were called the *assassini, assissini.* In Italian this name became generalized to mean 'assassin', borrowed into French and from there into English.

cipher (cypher), from Old French *cyfre* 'zero, nought', from Medieval Latin *cifra,* borrowed from Arabic *sifr* 'zero, empty', derived from *safara* 'to be empty'. In Europe the meaning was originally 'zero', then 'any numeral', and then later 'numerically encoded message, coded message, secret writing'.

cotton, ultimately from Arabic *quṭun, quṭn* 'cotton'. English got it from Old French *coton;* Old French got it from Old Spanish or possibly from Italian or Provençal. Spanish *algodon* 'cotton' was borrowed with the Arabic article *al-* 'the' attached, becoming part of the root of the loanword.

harem, from Arabic *harīm* (*haram*) 'women's quarters', literally 'forbidden', 'kept safe', derived from *harama* 'he guarded, forbade'. Turkish borrowed it as *harem* from Arabic, and English borrowed it from Turkish.

hashish, from Arabic *al-hashīshīya,* the singular (*hashīsh*) 'hashish, hemp, powdered hemp'. The meaning 'hashish' developed from its earlier meaning of 'dried herb, rough grass, hay, hemp' (see *assassin,* above).

magazine, from Middle French *magazin* 'warehouse, depot, store', taken from Italian *magazzino,* Medieval Latin *magazenum* 'storeroom', borrowed from Arabic *makhāzin* 'storehouses, storerooms' (plural of *makhzan*). English *magazine* also meant 'storehouse' earlier, but its more common meaning was 'storage place for ammunitions or gunpowder', and later 'receptacle for storing bullets'. The meaning of *magazine* as 'periodical journal containing miscellaneous writings' began in 1731 with the publication of *Gentleman's Magazine*, reflecting an earlier use of *magazine* for 'printed lists of military stores and information', suggesting a store of information, especially about military topics.

syrup, sherbet, sorbet were borrowed meaning 'thick, sweet liquid' from Old French *sirop* 'sugared drink', inherited from Medieval Latin *siropus, siruppus, syrupus*, borrowed from Arabic *sharāb* 'beverage, wine'. In Medieval Arabic it meant 'medicinal syrup', derived from *shariba* 'to drink'. In late medieval Europe, words involving *sirup* mostly had medicinal references.

Western European languages in the sixteenth century got another loanword involving this same Arabic root, in the shape of *sharba(t)*, which had been borrowed into Turkish as *sherbet* 'sweet lemonade', then borrowed into English as *sherbet*, and into French as *sorbet* 'sherbet, sorbet (frozen fruit juice)', and then the French version of the word was also borrowed into English as *sorbet*.

zero, from Arabic *sifr* (see *cipher* above), was borrowed into Medieval Latin as *zephirum* 'zero', which became *zefiro* in Old Italian, contracted to *zero*, then borrowed from this Old Italian form into French, as *zéro*, and on into English as *zero*.

From Japanese

bonsai, 'dwarfed potted tree, the art of tending miniature trees', from Japanese *bonsai*, from the compound of *bon* 'basin, pot' + *sai* 'to plant'.

honcho, from Japanese *hanchō* 'group leader', composed of *han* 'corps, squad' + *chō* 'head, chief'.

judo, from Japanese *jūdō*, literally 'gentle way', from *jū* 'softness, gentleness' + *dō* 'way, art'; *jū* was borrowed from Chinese *jou* 'soft, gentle' + *dō* from Chinese *tao* 'way'.

kamikaze, from Japanese *kamikaze* 'suicide flier', literally 'divine wind', a compound of *kami* 'god, providence' + *kaze* 'wind'.

karaoke, from Japanese *karaoke*, literally 'empty orchestra', from *kara* 'empty' + *oke* shortened from *okestura* 'orchestra', a loanword into Japanese from English *orchestra*.

karate, from Japanese *karate*, literally 'empty handed', *kara* 'empty' + *te* 'hand'.

tsunami, from Japanese *tsunami*, literally 'harbor wave', from *tsu* 'harbor' + *nami* 'wave'.

tycoon, from Japanese *taikun* 'great prince, great lord', later applied to 'important person, wealthy business leader', borrowed into Japanese from Chinese *tai* 'great' + *kiun* 'lord'.

From Spanish

Although Spanish is a well-known language, examples of a few of the many loanwords in English that are borrowed from Spanish are included precisely because of the striking impact of Spanish loans on English. The examples presented here do not including loans from Spanish that are mentioned in Chapter 10 and elsewhere in this book. A few examples of loanwords from Spanish in English are:

alligator, from Spanish *el lagarto* literally 'the lizard'. The final *r* doesn't belong originally, but was the result of the occasional change of final *o* sound to *r* in English words, as in other cases such as *tater* (for *potato*), *feller* (for *fellow*), and *yeller* (for *yellow*). The Spanish article *el* 'the' was incorporated into the root of the word as it was borrowed into English.

armadillo, from Spanish *armadillo* 'armadillo', from the diminutive form of *armado* 'armored'.

bodega, 'storehouse for wine, winery', 'small grocery shop', from Spanish *bodega* 'cellar', inherited from Latin *apotheca* 'storehouse', from Ancient Greek *apothēkē* 'barn, storehouse' (derived from *apo-* 'away' + *thēkē* 'receptacle'). *Boutique*, borrowed from French *boutique* 'shop', is from the same Latin and ultimately Greek sources. *Apothecary* also comes from these same sources. It entered English in the 1500s meaning 'shopkeeper', especially 'pharmacist, someone who stores, makes, and sells medicaments'.

canyon, from Spanish *cañón* 'canyon' (derived form of *caño* 'pipe, tube, gorge'), ultimately from Latin *canna* 'cane, reed'. *Cannon*, *canon*, *canal*, and *channel* all share this same Latin origin. *Cannon* comes from a derived form of Latin *canna*, borrowed into English from Old French *canon*. English *cannon* is spelled with double *n* only to distinguish it from *canon*, which ultimately has the same source, meaning 'cane, reed'. *Canon* comes from Late Latin *canōn* 'Church law, rule or doctrine from ecclesiastical authority'. In Classical Latin it meant also 'rule, measuring line', borrowed from Greek *kanōn* 'measuring rod, rule, standard of excellence'. *Canal* is from French *canal* 'canal, waterway', from Latin *canalis* 'water pipe, channel, groove', also derived from Latin *canna* 'reed, cane'. *Channel* is from Old French *chanel* 'pipe, tube, gutter, bed of a waterway', from this same Latin *canalis*.

cilantro, from Spanish *cilantro*, inherited from Late Latin *coliandrum*, Classical Latin *coriandrum* 'coriander'. English *coriander* is from the same Latin source. In some Latin American countries the plant is called *culantro* instead of *cilantro* in Spanish. Technically there is a difference between the two plants, coriander and cilantro, but the two words are typically thought to refer to the same thing.

guerrilla (often [mis]spelled as *guerilla*), means 'a member of an unofficial military group that engages in irregular warfare' and 'the actions performed by such a group'. It is borrowed from Spanish *guerrilla* 'small war', derived from *guerra* 'war'. English *war* is from the same root, since Spanish *guerra* 'war' is from the Germanic loanword *werra* 'war', the Germanic source of English *war* (seen in Chapter 2).

macho, from Spanish *macho* 'male, strong, vigorous, overly masculine', inherited from Latin *masculus* 'male, masculine', derived from *mas* 'male person, male' with a diminutive suffix. The irony of the term for a macho guy coming from a word that historically meant literally 'little man' is not to be missed.

siesta, from Spanish *siesta* 'midday nap', from Latin *sexta (hora)* 'sixth hour' (for six hours after sunrise).

vanilla, from Spanish *vainilla* 'vanilla', diminutive (small) form of *vaina* 'sheath, scabbard', inherited from Latin *vagina* 'sheath, hull of plants, pod, vagina'. So, *vanilla* and *vagina* ultimately have the same Latin source.

From Yiddish

bagel, from Yiddish *beygl*, derived from Middle High German *boug-* 'ring, bracelet', ultimately from Proto-Indo-European **bheug-* 'to bend'. Other English words from this Proto-Indo-European source include *bow*, *buxom*, and *akimbo*.

glitch, from Yiddish *glitsh* 'to slip', from German *glitschen* 'to slip, slither'.

klutz, from Yiddish *klots* 'clumsy person', literally 'block, lump'; compare German *Klotz* 'block, chunk'.

lox, from Yiddish *laks* 'salmon', from Middle High German *lahs* 'salmon' (compare Modern German *Lachs* 'salmon').

mensch, 'upright man, a decent human being', from Yiddish *mentsh* (also spelled *mensch*) 'person', from German *Mensch* 'human, person, man'.

schmooze (shmooze), from Yiddish *shmuesn* 'to converse, chat', from Hebrew *shəmū 'ōth* 'news, rumors'.

spiel (shpiel), 'sales pitch or speech intended to persuade', from Yiddish *shpil* 'play' or German *Spiel* 'play'.

English also has many loanwords from most of the languages of Europe and the larger languages of Asia, including Chinese, Dutch, Hebrew, Hindi, Irish, Italian, Persian, Russian, Sanskrit, others seen elsewhere in this book, and many others that we pass over because of limitations of space and time.

In this and preceding chapters, we have seen where new words come from, including many loanwords. We will see loanwords again in the role they play in linguistic prehistory, in Chapter 10. In the next chapter, we move on to changes in sounds. Sound changes can leave disrupted language patterns, exceptions, and irregularities that can seem mysterious until we comprehend how they change and what is behind the changes that left these kinds of marks on the language.

5   Sound Change
Costs and Benefits

In a certain respect the sound shift seems to me to be a barbarism and savagery which other, more peaceful peoples avoided, but which is connected with the tremendous progress and yearning for freedom of the Germans, which opened the Middle Ages and from which the transformation of Europe was to arise.[1]

(Jacob Grimm, *Geschichte der deutschen Sprache*)

Introduction

Why does English have such curious patterns as *goose/geese*; *wolf/wolves*; *holy* but *holiday*, and *insane* but *insanity*? How did English get so messy? Why are the vowels in *holiday* and *insanity* pronounced differently from the vowels in related *holy* and *insane*? How come English has irregular verbs like *sing/sang/sung* and *write/wrote/written*, and so many others? In Proto-Germanic and later in Old English, these verbs often followed patterns that were regular in those times, but over the centuries, various regular sound changes left them appearing irregular in today's English. In this chapter we see how many words got to have more than one form, as in *knife* : *knives*, a word root with two versions, one with *f* and the other with *v*, depending on context. Here the question of where many of these oddities, exceptions, and irregularities come from gets answered.

However, there is much more to changes in pronunciation than just these kinds of oddities. Some sound changes can be seen as beneficial; they can make pronunciation easier. In this chapter we explore various kinds of sound change and how and why sounds change as they do.

To understand how the unusual traits of languages come about, we need to understand the changes that lie behind them, that created them.

---

[1] In gewissem betracht erscheint mir das lautverschieben als eine barbarei und verwilderung, der sich andere ruhigere völker ehthielten, die aber mit dem gewaltigen das mittelalter eröffnenden vorschritt und freiheitsdrang der Deutschen zusammenhängt, von welchen Euopras umgestaltung ausgehn sollte (Jacob Grimm, 1848, *Geschichte der deutschen Sprache*, vol. 1, p. 292).

In examining sound change, we run into the major sound changes that have taken place in English, some of them very famous, such as <u>Grimm's Law</u> and the <u>Great Vowel Shift</u>. We begin by looking at several sound changes and their consequences for the history of English. Following that, we return to the question of costs and benefits, of whether sound change is good or bad, or maybe both.

It is difficult to talk about speech sounds without some terminology to describe them. Phonetics is the study of speech sounds, with explicit terms and written symbols to represent the sounds – extremely useful for talking about sounds and how they change – but unfortunately most of the terms and symbols are unknown to most people. Where possible, technical terms and symbols have been avoided here. Wherever there is need to call upon any such terms or symbols, they are explained in the text, and the terms are also defined in the Glossary and the symbols are defined and explained in the Symbol List at the beginning of this book. Many of the symbols cited are from the International Phonetic Alphabet, usually just referred to as the IPA. Phonetic symbols are usually given in square brackets (for example [s] as the "s" in *sky*).

When we talk about changes in language, the notation ">" is used to mean 'became, changed to', and "<" to signify 'came from, changed from'. A sound which comes from a sound in an earlier stage of the language (including its proto-language), is called a **reflex**. The earlier sound is said to be **reflected** by the later sound, whether it changed or remained unchanged. For example, as will soon be seen, English *f* comes from Proto-Indo-European *p (*p > *f*). Therefore, English *f* is a reflex of Proto-Indo-European *p, and Proto-Indo-European *p is reflected by English *f*.

Many sound changes were called sound "laws." Sound changes were found to be <u>regular</u>, hence law-like. Calling them "laws" comes from early scholars' decision that linguistics is a science and so it should have scientific terminology, hence "laws," analogous to the laws of physics.

Regularity of Sound Change

One of the most important basic assumptions in historical linguistics is that sound change is regular. This is a well-established principle of historical linguistics that holds that sound changes are exceptionless. That means that sounds do not change in unpredictable ways, that a sound changes systematically, regularly, throughout a language every-where where it fits the description of the change, the contexts in which the sound change takes place.

For example, *k* before *n* at the beginning of words in Old English was lost. It is still present in the spelling of such words as *knee, knife, knight, knot,* and *know,* but was lost regularly everywhere in pronunciation. It did not change in unpredictable ways. It is not the case that in words beginning in *kn,* the *k* changed arbitrarily to *g* in some words, while in others it changed to *t,* and in still others it was lost. This regularity in sound change is called "the regularity principle" or "the Neogrammarian hypothesis."

The Neogrammarians, beginning in about 1876 in Germany, became extremely influential. They were a group of younger scholars who antagonized the leaders of the field at that time by attacking older thinking and loudly proclaiming their own views, such as that sound change is regular and exceptionless. They were called *Junggrammatiker* 'young grammarians' in German, given the English translation of "Neogrammarians." In *Junggrammatiker,* the *jung-* 'young' had the sense of 'young Turk', originally intended as insulting, although the Neogrammarians adopted the term as their own name for themselves. Their slogan was: "sound laws suffer no exceptions." The importance of the regularity of sound change will be seen repeatedly in what lies ahead.

Well-Known Sound Changes That Have Affected English

In this section, we make acquaintance with several famous sound changes that in one way or another have affected English. This is a good way to get a better grasp of what sound change is and what it can do to a language.

Grimm's Law

One of the most famous sound changes of all time is Grimm's Law. It is named for Jacob Grimm (1785–1863, pictured in Figure 5.1), famous for his monumental contributions in Germanic linguistics and historical linguistics generally, but famous also, with his brother, Wilhelm, for the Brothers Grimm fairytales. Their work was situated in and motivated by German Romanticism, the dominant intellectual movement of German-speaking countries at that time that strongly fostered German nationalism. Towards the end of his life, Jacob Grimm wrote of his studies in an autobiography, "to me they have always seemed a noble and earnest task, definitely and inseparably connected with our common fatherland, and calculated to foster the love of it" (cited in Sweet 1911: 600).

Grimm's Law describes changes in a series of consonants as they developed from Proto-Indo-European into Proto-Germanic, the common ancestor of the Germanic languages, the branch of Indo-European that includes Danish, Dutch, English, German, Gothic, Icelandic,

Figure 5.1 Jacob Grimm
Source: Nastasic / DigitalVision Vectors / Getty Images.

Norwegian, Swedish, and some others. Grimm's Law established a set of regular correspondences between certain consonants in other branches of Indo-European and the corresponding sounds that they changed into in cognate words in the languages of the Germanic branch.

To understand Grimm's Law, we need a few phonetic concepts: stop, fricative, and voiced vs. voiceless. In the articulation of **stops**, the flow of air is completely blocked momentarily and then released, as in the pronunciation of *p, t, k, b, d,* and *g* in English. In **fricatives**, the airstream is not completely blocked, but is constricted so that friction (turbulence) characterizes the sound, as in English *f, s,* "*sh*" ([š], IPA [ʃ]), *v, z,* "*zh*" ([ž], IPA [ʒ]), and "th" ([θ]) and "*dh*" ([ð]), etc. **Voiced** means that the vocal cords are vibrating during the production of the sound, as in English *b, d, g, v,* "*zh*" ([ž], IPA [ʒ]), "*dh*" ([ð]), *r, l, m, n,* "*ng*" ([ŋ]), and vowels. **Voiceless** sounds are produced without the vocal cords vibrating during their production, as with English *p, t, k, f, s,* "*sh*" ([š], IPA [ʃ]), "th" ([θ]). You can feel the difference between voiced and voiceless sounds if you place your hand on your throat, on your Adam's apple, while pronouncing these sounds. You can feel the vibration with the voiced sounds but no vibration with the voiceless ones.

The changes in Grimm's Law took place long before English showed up on the scene as a separate language. Grimm's Law represents how particular consonants inherited from Proto-Indo-European have changed in Proto-Germanic, the ancestor of English and other Germanic languages. We can see the effects of Grimm's Law easily in cognate words inherited in English and shared with other Germanic languages; the same changes did not take place in the non-Germanic branches of Indo-European, and so we do not see the effects of Grimm's Law in cognates from those languages.

Grimm's Law consists of three interconnected parts which are the result of consecutive changes. These phases are:

1. Proto-Indo-European voiceless stops changed into voiceless fricatives in Proto-Germanic:

   p > f
   t > θ (the sound of "th" in English *three*, **thief**, **thumb**, etc.)
   k > h
   kw > hw

2. Proto-Indo-European voiced stops became voiceless stops:

   b > p
   d > t
   g > k
   gw > kw

3. Proto-Indo-European voiced aspirated stops became voiced stops:

   bh > b
   dh > d
   gh > g
   gwh > gw[2]

Obviously English does not have the sounds *bh*, *dh*, *gh*, and *gwh*. They are traditionally called "voiced aspirated stops." They sound like a combination of normal voiced stops and a whisper. More accurately, they are considered voiced breathy stops or voiced murmured stops. These are technical terms. "Breathy" or "murmured" means that the vocal cords vibrate as they do for plain voiced stops, *b*, *d*, *g*, and *gw*, but

---

[2] Actually, Proto-Indo-European had an additional series of stop consonants that also obeyed Grimm's Law, a series of palatal velars, *k̂*, *ĝ*, *ĝh*, pronounced on the hard palate, more toward the front of the mouth than *k*, *g*, *gh*, pronounced on the soft palate. Traditionally, this palatal series of sounds was often left out because it was believed that they could be explained as just contextual variants of their velar counterparts, *k*, *g*, *gh*, respectively. Later, however, this proved inaccurate. The palatal and velar series are distinct speech sounds in Proto-Indo-European. Here, like in many other works, we do not include the palatal series in the discussion, only because its presence is not needed to explain the main aspects of Grimm's Law and the Germanic sound changes.

are adjusted to allow slightly more air to escape when the sound is released. Voiced aspirated stops are found in Proto-Indo-European, Sanskrit, and many modern Indic languages.

These sound changes are related to one another but occurred one after another in time. This is called a <u>chain shift</u>, where in this case the earlier changes cause the later changes to take place:

bh > b, while original b > p, and original p > f
dh > d, while original d > t, and original t > θ
gh > g, while original g > k, and original k > x (h)
gwh > gw, while original gw > kw, and original kw > xw (hw).

We can often see the results of Grimm's Law in English by comparing native Germanic vocabulary with loanwords from non-Germanic languages that are cognates with the native English words, both ultimately with the same Indo-European origins. Because the languages that supply these loans to English are not Germanic, the sounds in loanwords from them have not undergone Grimm's Law.

In what follows, some cognates shared by French, Spanish, and English are presented, showing that some sound in the English word has undergone Grimm's Law but corresponding sounds in the non-Germanic French and Spanish cognates have not. The Proto-Indo-European roots from which they come are presented along with the cognates in French, Spanish, and English. In the case of the change of Proto-Indo-European *p to Proto-Germanic *f, for illustration's sake a list of other words in English involving this same Proto-Indo-European root is given, some inherited from Proto-Germanic, thus showing the effects of Grimm's Law, and others that are loanwords in English mostly from French, Latin, or Greek (non-Germanic languages), which have not been touched by Grimm's Law. This is followed by a few other Proto-Indo-European roots that also illustrate the same *p > *f change in English, together with a list of English words, both native and borrowed, that are based on each of these Proto-Indo-European roots. For the other parts of Grimm's Law, after the *p > *f change, only the information relative to the change and the French and Spanish cognates with English are presented, along with their Proto-Indo-European source.

$p > f$

Seen in such cognates as:

French *père*, 'father', Spanish *padre* 'father' : English *father* (from Proto-Indo-European *pəter* 'father').[3]

---

[3] The /ə/ phonetic symbol represents the vowel in English words such as *up, but, cup*, and the first vowel in *about, agree, attack, ugly, occur*, etc.

French *pied* 'foot', Spanish *pie* 'foot' : English *foot* (from Proto-Indo-European **ped-* 'foot').

Since French and Latin are not Germanic languages, they did not undergo the change of original Proto-Indo-European **p* > **f* in Germanic. Thus, the original *p* is seen in the loanwords in English that are borrowed from French or Latin. These are compared with native English words from the same Indo-European root, inherited from Proto-Germanic, that exhibit *f* as the result of Grimm's Law, as for example, in:

> *paternal* < Latin *paternalis* : *father*.
>
> *pedestal* < Middle French *piédestal* (the spelling of the first vowel in English *pedestal* was influenced by Latin *pede(m)* 'foot' : *foot*).

Some other Indo-European roots in which English (and other Germanic languages) have *f* but where loanwords from non-Germanic Indo-European languages have *p* are the following.

> Proto-Indo-European **peku-* 'livestock, moveable property, wealth', source of English *fee*, *fellow* of Germanic origin, and *pecuniary*, *peculiar*, and others borrowed from Latin. Let's look a bit more closely at some of these.
>
> **fee** in Old English was *feoh* 'cattle, livestock, cattle; possessions in livestock, goods, or money; wealth, riches; money as a medium of exchange or payment', from Proto-Germanic **fehu*. English *fee* is cognate with German *Vieh* 'cattle', pronounced just like English *fee*. This word underwent Grimm's Law in both consonants (*p* > *f*, and *k* > *h*).
>
> **fellow** 'companion, comrade' in Old English was *fēolaga* 'partner, one who shares with another', borrowed from Old Norse *felagi*, composed of *fe* 'money' (see English *fee*) + *lag*, from Proto-Indo-European **legh-* 'to lay, to lie down', reflecting the idea of *fellow* as 'one who puts down money with another in a joint venture'.
>
> **peculiar** meant 'belonging exclusively to one person'. The meaning 'unusual' appeared about 1600. It is borrowed from Latin *peculiāris* 'of one's own (property)'; see *peculium* 'private property', i.e. 'property in cattle', *pecus* 'cattle'.
>
> **pecuniary** is borrowed from Latin *pecuniārius* 'pertaining to money', derived from *pecūnia* 'money, property, wealth, wealth in cattle', from Latin *pecū-* 'cattle', inherited from Proto-Indo-European **peku-* 'livestock, wealth, moveable property', just as with English *fee*.

Proto-Indo-European **ped-* 'foot', source of *foot, fetter, fetch*, and of *pawn* (in chess), *pedal, pedestrian, peon, pioneer, centipede*, *expedite, pilot, pejorative, impair, impeach, pessimism,* and *impeccable* (derived from Latin *peccāre* 'to stumble').

foot, from the **pōd* variant of Proto-Indo-European **ped-* 'foot' – it illustrates Grimm's Law in both consonants (*p > f*, and *d > t*).

impeach formerly meant 'to impede, hinder, prevent', borrowed from Anglo-French *empecher* 'to hinder, stop, impede; capture, trap, ensnare' (Modern French *empêcher*), from Late Latin *impedicare* 'to fetter, catch, entangle', from *in-* 'in, into' + *pedica* 'fetter, shackle', derived from Proto-Indo-European **ped-* 'foot'.

peon, borrowed from Mexican Spanish *peón* 'farm worker', earlier 'a debtor held in servitude by his/her creditor'. In general Spanish it meant 'day laborer, pedestrian', but it originally meant 'foot soldier', from Medieval Latin *pedonem* 'foot soldier', ultimately from the Proto-Indo-European root **ped-* 'foot'. *Pawn* in chess is from the same source, from Old French *peon* 'foot soldier, a pawn in chess'.

t > θ (the sound of "th" in English thank, thought*)*

Cognates

French *trois* 'three', Spanish *tres* : English *three*, from Proto-Indo-European **trei-* 'three'.

k > h

Cognates

French *coeur* 'heart', Spanish *corazón* 'heart' : English *heart*, from Proto-Indo-European **k̂erd-* 'heart'.

French *corne* 'horn', Spanish *cuerno* 'horn' : English *horn*, Proto-Indo-European **k̂r̥-no-* 'horn'.

kw > hw

The *kw* represents the sound at the beginning of English *quick, quiet, quote*. The *hw* sound is like *h* followed by *w*, like a whispered *w*. It is the sound of "wh" in those <u>dialects</u> of English that make a distinction between such pairs of words as *which* vs. *witch, whales* vs. *Wales,* or *whine* vs. *wine*.

Cognates Many of the cognates shared by French and Spanish with English that come from words with Proto-Indo-European **kw* have changed their sounds further in modern <u>Romance languages</u> so that the *kw* is no longer heard. However, the "kw" sound is easier to see in the Latin words from which the French and Spanish cognates descend, as for example in interrogative pronouns *what, why, when, where, which*, all from the Proto-Indo-European interrogative pronoun stems *$k^w o$-, *kwi-, as in:

'what': French *quoi*, Spanish *qué* (< Latin *quid*) : English *what*.

'when': French *quand*, Spanish *cuándo* (< Latin *quandō*) : English *when*.

'which': French *qui, quel*, Spanish *cuál* (< Latin *qualem*) : English *which* (< Old English *hwilc, hwælc*).

b > p

Proto-Indo-European has very few words with *b* and it is quite possible that it did not have *b* as a native sound, found mostly in possible loanwords, such as *kannabis* 'hemp, cannabis'. Grimm's Law makes it easy to recognize English *hemp* and *cannabis* as coming from the same original word, with *k* changing to *h*, and *b* to *p* in Germanic, rendering English **hemp**.

Cognates

Spanish *labio* 'lip', French *lèvre* 'lip' : English *lip* (from Proto-Indo-European *leb-* 'lip' (?))

Proto-Indo-European ***kannabis**, the source of *hemp, canvas,* and *cannabis* (see above).

Late Proto-Indo-European ***abel-** 'apple' (?).

d > t

Cognates

French *dix* 'ten', Spanish *diez* 'ten' : English *ten*. Compare Latin *decem* 'ten'; English *ten*, from Proto-Germanic *tehun* 'ten', from Proto-Indo-European *dekm* 'ten'.

French *doigt* 'finger', *doigt de pied* 'toe' (literally 'finger of foot'), Spanish *dedo* 'finger' (*dedo de pie* 'toe' [literally 'finger of foot']) : English *toe*, inherited from Old English *tā, tahe* 'toe' < Proto-Germanic *taihwō* 'toe'. The Latin cognate is *digitus* 'finger, toe', the source of borrowed English *digit*. The meaning in English narrowed from both 'finger' and 'toe' to just 'toe'.

g > k

Cognates

> French *gens* 'person, folk, nation', Spanish *gente* 'people, folk' :
> English *kin*, inherited from Proto-Indo-European **gen-*,
> **genə-*, **gnə̥* – 'to give birth to, beget, familial and tribe group'.
> French *joug* 'yoke', Spanish *yugo* 'yoke' : English *yoke*, all
> inherited from Proto-Indo-European **yeug-*, **yug-* 'to join'.

gw > kw

Note that Proto-Indo-European **gw* changed to "v" (pronounced *w*) in
Latin before certain vowels and to *b* before other vowels, seen in the *v* and
b of Latin and French loanwords, where native English cognates, words of
Germanic origin, have *kw* (from Grimm's Law, **gw > kw*).

Cognates

> French *venir* 'come', Spanish *venir* 'come' : English *come*, from
> Old English *cuman* 'to come', inherited from Proto-Germanic
> **kwem* 'to come', from Proto-Indo-European **gwem-* 'to
> come'. In English, the *w* of the *kw* expected by Grimm's Law
> got swallowed up by the following *u* in *cuman*, **kwu > ku*.
> French *vivant* 'alive', Spanish *vivo* 'alive' : English *quick* 'quick,
> alive', from Proto-Indo-European **gwi-wo-* 'living, alive'.

bh > b

The reflexes of **bh* in French and Spanish are not straightforward. In
Latin, Proto-Indo-European **bh* changed to *f* in some contexts
(especially word-initially), but to *b* in others (especially word-
medially), and French and Spanish inherited Latin's *f* and *b*, but
these sounds later also underwent changes of their own in French
and Spanish, again depending on the context in which they appeared
in words.

Cognates

> French *foi* 'faith', Spanish *fe* 'faith' : English *bide, abide*, from
> Proto-Indo-European **bheidh-* 'trust'.
> French *fleur* 'flower', Spanish *flor* 'flower' : English *blossom*.
> French and Spanish are from Latin *flōs, flōris* 'flower', from
> Proto-Indo-European **bhel-* 'to bloom, thrive'. English *blos-
> som* is from the Proto-Germanic suffixed form **blō-s*, in Old

English *blōstm(a)* 'blossom', from an extended form of Proto-Indo-European *bhel* 'to thrive, bloom'.

dh > d

Proto-Indo-European *dh > f* in Latin in most contexts, but *dh > d* in a few contexts. French and Spanish inherited Latin's *f* and *d*, but these sounds later underwent changes of their own in these languages, again depending on the context in which these sounds appear in words. In Greek, Proto-Indo-European *dh > th* (aspirated "*t*"), then later this changed *th* to [θ], the "th" sound as in English words like **thought, thing, thanks**. Spanish *f* became *h*, and then later was dropped in pronunciation but maintained in spelling, in the context before most vowels, but not before /ue/.

Cognates

> Spanish *fuera* 'outside' < Latin *forās, forīs* 'outside, out of doors' : English *door*, inherited from Proto-Indo-European *dhwer-* 'door'.
> Spanish *hosco* 'dark, morose, maroon', Old French *fusque* 'dark, dark color' : English *dusk*, inherited from Proto-Indo-European *dhus-ko*, derived from Proto-Indo-European *dheu-* 'to rise in a cloud (dust, smoke, vapor)'; see Latin *fuscus* 'dark, dusky'.
> Spanish *hacer* 'to do, make', French *faire* (both from Latin *facere* 'to make') : English *do*. All three are from the Proto-Indo-European root *dhē-* 'to put, set'. English *do* reflects the *dhō-* version of this root, while Latin *facere* and the Romance language cognates reflect the suffixed version *dhə-k*. The semantic connection between Proto-Indo-European 'put, set' and the 'make, do' meaning in these daughter languages appears to be related to things 'laid down, done'.

gh > g

Proto-Indo-European *gh > h* in Latin and this *h* was subsequently lost in French and Spanish. This means that Germanic cognates with *g*, from Grimm's Law *gh > g*, correspond to zero (absence of a sound) in French and Spanish. The *h* is still present in Latin spelling, but it is not pronounced.

Cognates

> French *hôte* 'host' (Old French *oste*), Spanish *hueste* 'host':
> English *guest*, inherited from Proto-Germanic **gastiz*, which
> comes from Proto-Indo-European **ghos-ti-* 'stranger, guest,
> host'.
>
> French *hort* (Old French *(h)ort*) 'vegetable garden', Spanish
> *huerta* 'vegetable garden, orchard' (both from Latin *hortus*
> 'garden') : English *yard* (from Old English *geard*), from Proto-
> Indo-European **ghor-dho-*, **ghor-to-* 'an enclosure'.

gwh > b, w, gw, g

There are not many cognates with reflexes of Proto-Indo-European
*gwh in English, and **gwh* has several different reflexes depending on
the sounds following it. Proto-Indo-European **gwh* became *f* in Latin,
with *v* in some contexts, so that most loans in English from Latin or
French involving Indo-European roots with **gwh* have *f* or *v*.

Cognates

> Old French *neif* 'snow', Spanish *nieve* 'snow' : English *snow*,
> from Proto-Indo-European **s-neigwh-* 'snow'. (Compare
> Modern French *névé* 'snowfield'.) Proto-Indo-European
> **s-negiwh-* 'snow' became **snaiw-az* in Proto-Germanic,
> *snāw* in Old English, and *snow* in Modern English. Other
> English words that involve this root are *névé* 'a field of coarse,
> granular snow, partially compacted granular snow', *niveous*,
> and *Nevada*.
>
> We move on now to other well-known sound changes in the
> history of English.

The Great Vowel Shift

Between Chaucer (born 1343) and Shakespeare (born 1564), English
underwent a series of interrelated vowel changes known as the Great
Vowel Shift, in which long vowels systematically raised, and the highest
long vowels diphthongized. A <u>diphthong</u> is a combination of two vowel
sounds in a single syllable, as for example in *coin, loud, break* ([breik]).
"Diphthongization" refers to the change of a single vowel into
a diphthong. The line over a vowel, called a macron, means that it is
long, pronounced with more duration than its counterpart without the

macron. The Great Vowel Shift is another example of a <u>chain shift</u>. The following changed in the Great Vowel Shift:

ī > ai (as in Middle English [ME] /tīd/ > /taid/ 'tide') (ī is like the sound of the vowel in *beet*)

ē > ī (ME /bēte/ > /bīt/ 'beet') (ē is like the first part of the vowel in *bake* [beik])

ɛ̄ > ē (ME /mɛ̄t/ > /mēt/ > /mīt/ 'meet') (ɛ̄ is a longer version of the vowel sound in *bet, red*)

æ > ɛ̄ (ME /bæt/ > /bēt/ > /bīt/ 'beat') (æ is a longer version of the vowel sound in *bat*)

ā > æ (ME /nām/ > /næm/ > /neim/ 'name') (ā is like the first vowel of *father*)

ɔ̄ > ō (ME /bɔ̄t/ > /bōt/ 'boat') (ɔ̄ is like a longer version of the vowel sound in *bought*)

ō > ū (ME /bōt/ > /būt/ 'boot') (ō is like the first part of the vowel in *boat* [bout])

ū > au (ME /hūs/ > /haus/ 'house') (ū is like the vowel of *boot, moon*).

Umlaut

Umlaut is not only the name of the diacritic with two dots over a vowel (as in *ü, ö, ä*) but also the name of a sound change in which a back vowel (*a, o, u*) is fronted, pronounced more towards the front of the mouth, when followed in the next syllable by a front vowel, *i* or *e*, or by *y* (spelled "j" in Old English and other Germanic languages). Umlaut was important in the history of English. Understanding it helps explain the exceptional plurals in *mouse/mice* and *foot/feet*, used here to represent the class of words that have this kind of exceptional plurals.

In the beginning, Proto-Germanic just had back vowels *ū* and *ō* in these words:

*mūs- 'mouse', **mūs-iz* 'mice'* *fōt-* 'foot', **fōt-iz* 'feet'

In the first stage of three related changes, umlaut changed these back vowels to front vowels when there was an *i* or *ü* (IPA [y]) in the following syllable: *mūs-i > mǖsi* 'mice', and *fōt-i > fȫti* 'feet', giving:

mūs 'mouse', *mǖsi* 'mice'*fōt* 'foot', *fȫti* 'feet'

The vowels *ǖ* and *ȫ* are front vowels (*ü* is IPA [y]; *ö* is IPA [ø]). The *ǖ* is pronounced like *ū*, but further towards the front of the mouth, in the position of *i* (as in *feet*), like *i* pronounced with the lips rounded. Similarly, *ȫ* is like *ō* pronounced in the position of *e* in the mouth, like *e* with the lips rounded.

Later, the final *i* that had signaled the plural in these words for 'mouse' and 'foot' was lost:

mūsi > mūs 'mice' fōti > fōt 'feet'

Next, the front rounded vowels, *ū* and *ō*, became unrounded (*ū* > *ī*, and *ō* > *ē*), resulting in:

mūs 'mouse', *mīs* 'mice' *fōt* 'foot', *fēt* 'feet'

Then finally, these long vowels (*ī*, and *ē*) underwent the Great Vowel Shift (seen above), which raised long vowels (for example, *ē* > *ī*, and *ō* to *ū*), and diphthongized long high vowels (*ī* > *ai*, *ū* > *au*):

mūs > /maus/ 'mouse' mīs > /mais/ 'mice'
fōt > /fʊt/ 'foot'[4] fēt > /fit/ 'feet'

This resulted in the Modern English forms, with exceptional plurals for these words:

mouse, mice foot, feet

The spellings of these words still reflect the sounds before the Great Vowel Shift took place: where *ou* of *mouse* was how long *ū* was spelled; *oo* of *foot* spelled long *ō*; *ee* of *feet* spelled long *ē*; and *ī* as in *mice* spelled long *ī*. (See Chapter 9 for more on these spellings.)

Some other English words with weird plurals that have umlaut in their background include: *brother/brethren, goose/geese, louse/lice, tooth/teeth,* and others.

Vowel Shortening

So, what about the not very hallowed relationship between *holy* and *holiday,* or *divine* and *divinity,* and other cases like these? They involve shortening (sometimes called laxing) of vowels in certain contexts in the history of English. In the earliest form of the change, in Old English a vowel was shortened when it came immediately before a cluster of three consonants or before two consonants when they were followed by two or more additional syllables in the word. *Gospel* in Old English was *gōdspell*. Because *gōdspell* had three consonants after the *ō*, it was short-ened. Later the *d* was lost in this word, giving Modern English *gospel*. It comes literally from 'good news' (*gōd* 'good' + *spell* 'news'), ultimately a calque based on Greek *euangelion* 'good news', derived from *eu*

---

[4] The [ʊ] is the sound as in *foot, book, put.*

'good' + *angellein* 'to announce, proclaim', based on *angelos* 'messenger, envoy', also the ultimate loanword source of English *angel*.

Christmas exemplifies the shortening before two consonants when followed by two more syllables. Old English had *cristesmæsse* 'Christmas', literally 'Christ's mass' (*cristes* 'Christ's' + *mæsse* 'mass'), where all the vowels were pronounced. The *ī* was shortened to *i* because it was followed by two consonants, *st*, followed by two or more syllables, *es*, *mæs*, and *se*.

Later, in Middle English, the change was generalized so that a vowel became shortened before just two or more consonants and before a single consonant if followed by two or more syllables. This accounts for the relationship between pairs of words where the short vowel is before two consonants, but the long vowel is in related words that do not have the two consonants, such as in:

keep kept
feel felt
sheep shepherd
goose gosling
wise wisdom
wide width

And the same process is behind the shortening of vowels in related words when they were followed by a single consonant and two or more syllables, as in:

divine divinity
line linear
impede impediment
profane profanity
sane sanity
holy holiday
omen ominous
provoke provocative
pronounce pronunciation

Rhotacism

In rhotacism, a consonant changes to an *r*-like sound in some contexts. In the best-known cases, *s* changed to *r* between vowels. Probably the most famous case of rhotacism is the one that took place in Latin. Rhotacism is easy to see from Latin loanwords in English where one word has *s* while a related word involving the same root has *r* between vowels, as for example in loanwords based on the Latin root *rūs* 'country, countryside'. English *rural* is borrowed from Latin *rūralis* 'rural' that underwent rhotacism. Earlier, before rhotacism took place, it had been *rūs-alis*. However,

English *rustic*, borrowed from Latin *rūs-ticus* 'peasant, farmer', has *s*, with no rhotacism, since the *s* of *rūs-* in this word was not between vowels and so did not undergo rhotacism. Some other examples of Latin loanwords in English that show and *s* in Latin alternating with *r* due to rhotacism between vowels follow. The loanword with *s* comes first, followed by derived forms with *r* because it is between vowels:

corpus corpora, incorporate (Latin *corpus* 'body')
genus genera, generate (Latin *genus* 'genus, race, family')
justice juror, injury (Latin *iūs* 'right, legal right, law')
onus onerous, exonerate (Latin *onus* 'burden')
plus plural (Latin *plūs* 'more')

Changes involving rhotacism are relatively rare in languages, though cases are known from here and there around the world, including in English, which inherited forms that underwent rhotacism in earlier West Germanic. In West Germanic and North Germanic, *z* (from earlier *s) became *r*. The effects of this rhotacism are seen even in some very common words in English, accounting for a number of seemingly odd things. For example, Modern English *more* is from Proto-Germanic *maizōn 'greater' (Proto-Indo-European *mē-is 'more'). Here *s changed to *z* when preceded by an unstressed syllable. Then West Germanic changed all instances of Proto-Germanic non-final *z to *r. This gave *māra* 'greater' and *māre* 'more'. *Most*, from the same original root, is from Old English *mǣst* 'most', from Proto-Germanic **maista-* 'most' (Proto-Indo-European *mē-isto). *Was* and *were*, in Old English, were *wæs* and *wǣron*, respectively, where the *r* of the plural *were* is the result of the rhotacism in Proto-Germanic. Proto-Germanic *hauzjan 'hear' became Old English *hieran*, Modern English *hear*, from Proto-Indo-European **kous-* 'to hear', seen in loans in English such as *acoustic*, borrowed from French *acoustique*, which is inherited from Medieval Latin *acūsticus*, which was borrowed from Greek *akoustikos* 'pertaining to hearing or sound', see Greek *kou-ein* 'to perceive, hear'.

Voicing of Fricatives

Formerly, English had only voiceless fricative sounds *f*, "*th*" ([θ]), *s*, but when between vowels or between *l* or *r* and a following vowel, these sounds were changed. They became voiced, giving *v*, "*th*" ([ð]), *z*, respectively. This explains the relationship between pairs of words such as:

wolf   wolves
knife   knives
leaf   leaves
thief   thieves
calf   calves

bath   ba**the**
teeth   tee**the**
north   nor**the**rn

louse   lou**s**y [z] (from Old English *lūs*)
glass   gla**z**e
grass   gra**z**e
brass   bra**z**en

In all these words in earlier times, a vowel followed the *v*, "*th*" [ð], or *z*; the vowel was actually pronounced, regardless of the spelling or of today's pronunciation.

Nasal Loss before Fricatives

English lost a nasal (*n* or *m*) before a fricative sound (*f*, *s*, *θ* ["th"], etc.), simultaneously lengthening the preceding vowel. Some examples of words that underwent this change are:

Proto-Germanic (PG) **tonθ* 'tooth' to *tōθ* to Modern English *tooth* (compare the German cognate *Zahn* [tsa:n] 'tooth').

PG **fimf* 'five' to *fīf* to Modern English *five* (compare German *fünf* 'five').

PG **gans* 'goose' to *gōs* to Modern English *goose* (compare German *Gans* 'goose').

PG **munθaz* 'mouth' to Old English *mūθ* to Modern English *mouth* (compare German *Mund* 'mouth').

PG **n̥s* 'us' (from Proto-Indo-European **nes-*) to Old English *ūs* to Modern English *us* (compare German *uns* 'us').

Interestingly, in the change from Latin to Proto-Romance, nasals were also lost before fricatives, leaving the vowel long, as for example in Latin *sponsa* to Proto-Romance *spōsa* 'bride' (inherited in French as *épouse* and Spanish *esposa* 'wife') and Latin *mensa* to Proto-Romance *mesa* 'table' (as in Spanish *mesa* 'table').

Loss of Final Nasal

Why does English have both *a* and *an*, both *my* and *mine*, and *thy* and *thine*? In earlier times, these words all ended in *n*, but then their final *n* was lost unless followed by a word that started in a vowel. So, English had *an apple* but *a pear*, *mine eyes* but *my* lips, *mine uncle* but *my father*, and *to thine own self be true* but *know thy self*. Later, the *n* of these pronouns, *mine* and *thine* (but not of *an*) was lost also before words starting in vowels, so *mine eyes* > *my eyes* and *thine own* > *thy own. Mine* and more archaic *thine* remained only when the possessive pronoun functioned as a noun, as in *your guess is as good as mine, what's mine is yours,* or *your place or mine?* In the case of *an,* the *n* was retained before an initial vowel of the following word, as in *an apple,* but lost elsewhere, as in *a pear.*

English also underwent several other sound changes, but let's move on.

Sound Change: Good or Bad?

Let us return now to the question, is sound change good, bad, neither good nor bad, or both good and bad? As mentioned in Chapter 1, lots of people think it's bad. However, in spite of ardent opinions about that, by any objective measure, change in language is neither good nor bad. For communicative efficiency, sound change can be both good and bad at the same time, depending on the context. In language change, what is good for the goose can at the same time be terrible for the gander. Change that might be seen to contribute to greater effectiveness in one part of the language can have deleterious consequences for other parts of the language. There is a trade-off between what is good for pronouncing and what is good for understanding, where a particular change can simultaneously be good for one of these poles of language but bad for the other. Changes that simplify pronunciation and thus facilitate speech production can obstruct understanding and language processing. As Michel de Montaigne [1533–1592] (1686: 3: xiii) put it, "the word is half his that speaks, and half his that hears it."

Take for example the ongoing sound change that deletes final *t* and *d* in consonant clusters in essentially all varieties of English. In many words, this loss does not make understanding more difficult, for instance in *firs' thing, las' thing, slep' soundly, san' castle* ('sand castle'), *lef' school, mus' be, roun' table,* and so on. However, when the lost final *t* or *d* represents the past tense of a verb, its deletion can complicate comprehension. For example, with the possibility of final consonant cluster simplification, as this change is called, the *ask* in *they **ask** someone* or *they **ask** the question* could be present-tense *ask* or past-tense *asked.* For example, it would be present tense in *I ask someone all the time,* but it would be past tense in *they ask' [asked] somebody yesterday.* With loss of *t* or *d* in final consonant clusters, there can be confusion between whether present or past tense is intended in examples such as *they **rol(')** [roll/rolled] past, she **stop(')** [stop/stopped] shouting,* and others, causing difficulties for comprehension. This simplifying sound change makes such words easier to pronounce, but at the same time it complicates comprehension by eliminating the marker that distinguishes between present tense and past tense.[5] In this way, the sound change can be seen as good because it facilitates pronunciation but at the same time as bad because it can complicate understanding.

In the next chapter, on <u>analogy</u>, we see how languages often eliminate messy stuff, including cases created by regular sound changes.

---

[5] It is true that the context in which forms such as these are uttered can often help to disambiguate them, but definitely not always.

6   How Do Languages Clean Up Their Act?

The Might of Analogy

> Analogies, it is true, decide nothing but they can make one feel more at home.
>
> (Sigmund Freud, *New Introductory Lectures on Psychoanalysis*)

Introduction

Analogy often eliminates irregularities and exceptions, for example cleaning up the mess left in the wake of sound change. In analogical change, one thing changes to become more like something else in the language where speakers perceive the changing part as similar to the thing that it changes to. Definitions of analogical change, including this one, have never seemed very satisfying. In spite of the apparent vagueness of such definitions, however, analogical change is reasonably straightforward and easily grasped from examples, many seen in this chapter. For the <u>Neogrammarians</u>, basically anything that was not sound change or <u>borrowing</u> was considered analogy. Though this might not be reassuring, it does highlight how important analogy is in language change.

Kinds of Analogical Change

Spelling Analogies

There are a number of kinds of analogical change. The main ones are surveyed in this chapter, though let's start with a less common type – analogy involving spelling.

The *l* in the spelling of *could* was added by analogy. The past tense of *will* was *would*, and of *shall* was *should*, where the *l* of *would* and *should* was inherited as part of the root. *Could*, however, comes from *can*, whose past tense in Old English was *cūðe* (ð is the sound of "th" in *this, those*), from the infinitive *cunnan* 'to be able' – it never had an *l*. We would expect *cunðe*, but *n* before fricative sounds (*s, f,* "*th*") was lost (as seen in Chapter 5), so *cunðe > cūðe > /kud/*. The letter *l* was added to the spelling of this word, but not to its pronunciation, giving *could*, due to analogy, making it more similar to the spelling of *would* and *should*. (See Anttila 1989.)

The *s* in the spelling of *island* was never part of the pronunciation of the word, but was added on analogy to the *s* in *isle*, a word with a different origin. 'Island' in Old English was *igland*, which changed to *yland* (*iland*), inherited from Germanic. An *s* was added to the spelling, giving *island*, in the sixteenth century due to analogy with the *s* in the spelling of *isle*. *Isle*, on the other hand, has a history of its own, also involving analogy. In Middle English 'isle' was *ile* (*ille*), borrowed from Old French *ile* (*ille*), *île* in Modern French, from Latin *īnsula* 'island'. In the fifteenth century, the French started spelling it as *isle*, where the *s* wasn't there in the pronunciation but was added due to analogy with the *s* in Latin *īnsula* 'island'. This French spelling with the inserted *s* influenced some English writers to spell the English word *island*, also with an inserted *s*, one it never had in its pronunciation. The spelling with *s* eventually became standard.

Proportional Analogy

The most often talked-about kind of analogy is called "proportional analogical change," of the form, a : b = c : x, where one solves for 'x' – *a* is to *b* as *c* is to what?, *x* being whatever the answer to 'what?' is. For example: *ride* : *rode* = *dive* : *x*, where *ride* is to *rode* as *dive* is to what?, where *x* here is solved by *dove*. The original past tense of *dive* was *dived*, as it still is in much of the English-speaking world outside of North America, but *dived* was changed to *dove* under analogy with verbs like *drive* : *drove*, *write* : *wrote*, and so on, in those English dialects that have *dove*.

Bring/brought/brought changed in some nonstandard dialects to *bring/brang/brung*, on analogy with the pattern of verbs like *sing/sang/sung*.

It is important to note that the kinds of analogy talked about traditionally are not mutually exclusive. That is, there is overlapping; some changes can exemplify more than one of the traditional kinds of analogy discussed in what follows. Perhaps most kinds of analogical changes could be forced into the frame of proportional analogy, though that may not be as revealing as treating them in terms of one or another of the more fine-grained subclasses of analogy that follow.

Analogical Levelling

Many analogical changes remove alternations and irregularities, called "analogical levelling." Analogical levelling reduces multiple forms of a word, making things more uniform. For example, the earlier comparative and superlative forms of *old* had the pattern *old/elder/eldest*. This was levelled to the non-alternating pattern *old/older/oldest*. Here, *o* had been fronted by umlaut (seen in Chapter 5) due to the presence of front vowels in the second syllable, *old + -er > elder* and *old + -est > eldest*. The umlaut change left *old* with two variants forms, *old* and *eld-*. English had many words with alternations of this sort. However, analogy eliminated the effects of umlaut in many of them. It changed *elder* to *older* and *eldest* to *oldest* on analogy with words of the non-alternating pattern, for example *young/younger/youngest*. The words *elder* and *eldest* remain in the language, but only in restricted contexts with specialized meanings, no longer as the comparative and superlative versions of *old*.

Near originally was a comparative meaning 'nearer', but it became the basic form meaning 'near'. If no analogical levelling had taken place, today we would not have *near/nearer/nearest*, but instead *nigh/near/next*, from Old English *nēah* 'near'/*nēarra* 'nearer'/*nēahsta* 'nearest'. However, this pattern was levelled out. *Nearer* was created in the sixteenth century, then *nearest* was substituted for *next*. *Nigh* and *next* are still words of English, but with more limited, shifted meanings, no longer the comparative and superlative of *near*. *Nigh* in its meaning of 'near' is still heard in archaic sounding, formulaic-like phrases such as *the end is nigh, the time is nigh, well nigh impossible/nigh on impossible, nigh at hand, draws nigh/draweth nigh, nigh on 100 years, mighty nigh*, and *nigh unbeatable/nigh unbearable*.

Some English "strong" verbs have been levelled so they now follow the "weak" verb pattern. The so-called strong verbs have alternant forms, as in *sing/sang/sung* (I sing now, I sang yesterday, I have sung), *write/wrote/written*, and many others. The weak verbs have a constant single root, as in *play/played/played*. Numerous cases of former strong verbs have been levelled to weak verbs, that is, to have non-alternating stems with *-ed* or its equivalent signaling past and past participle, as in *bake/baked/baked*. A couple of cases that show the analogical levelling of strong verbs are *cleave/clove/cloven* (or *cleft*) 'to part, divide, split', which for many English speakers has become *cleave/cleaved/cleaved*, and *strive/strove/striven* has changed to *strive/strived/strived* in the speech of many.

Analogical Extension

While analogical levelling is more frequent, changes of analogical extension are also frequent, in which the alternating pattern of some forms is extended to forms that originally did not have the alternation. Various examples of analogical extension are seen in nonstandard varieties of English where past-tense forms of verbs get extended to the strong verb pattern, with alternations that formerly were not there. In my home dialect, *drag* has the alternating pattern of *drag/drug/drug*. The weak verb pattern *drag/dragged/dragged* is older; however, in some nonstandard dialects, *dragged* was replaced by *drug*, an analogical extension based on the pattern in verbs such as *dig/dug/dug*, *stick/stuck/stuck*, *hang/hung/hung*, and so on. Other cases include *squeeze/squoze/squoze* (Standard English *squeeze/squeezed/squeezed*), *arrive/arrove* (Standard *arrive/arrived*), and *sneak/snuck* (for more standard *sneak/sneaked*).

Naturally, cases of analogical extension are not limited just to nonstandard varieties; there are many examples of such changes whose results are now standard English. For example, Modern English *wear/wore*, now in the strong verb pattern, was earlier in the weak verb pattern. If Old English *werede* 'wore' had survived, today it would be *weared*. However, it changed by analogical extension of the strong verb pattern, giving *wear/wore/worn* instead, as in *bear/bore/born(e)* or *swear/swore/sworn*.

Immediate Model in Analogy

In treatments of analogical change, it is common to distinguish between immediate models and non-immediate models for the analogy. These refer to the contexts in which the relationship of similarity that is behind an analogical change is found. Most of the examples of analogy seen so far in this chapter are cases with non-immediate models, like, for example, those where the pattern of weak verbs is the model that influenced certain strong verbs to become weak verbs. The analogical influence here is from whole classes of words or grammatical patterns in the language that do not occur in speech in the near vicinity of the things that change. In the change of *old/elder/eldest* to *old/older/oldest* under influence of the non-alternating pattern exemplified by *tall/taller/tallest*, the words like *taller* or *tallest* do not occur near *elder* or *eldest* in speech. For the majority of analogical changes no immediate model exists.

An immediate model refers to a situation in which something changes due to similarity to something next to it or very near it in actual speech. Cases of analogical change based on an immediate model are often found in frequently recited lists or routines, for example in counting numbers, reciting the days of the week and months of the year, or in phrases used so frequently they become formulaic. For example, month names frequently recited together in sequence can change so that some become more similar to others. As a result, for many English speakers, because of the immediate model of *January*, *February* has changed to *Febuary*, pronounced like *febyuery*, becoming more like *January*. In my mother's dialect, the first vowel of *February* (pronounced *febyuery*) had influenced *January*, which she pronounced like *jenyueri*.

In English, *female*, stressed on the first syllable *FEmale*, earlier was *femelle*, with stress on the second syllable, *feMEL*. However, on the immediate model of *male and female*, frequently uttered together, the Middle English *femelle* changed to *female* to be more similar to nearby *male*.

Examples of analogical changes based on an immediate model are often found in numbers, typically recited together in counting. For example, in English, *four* and *five* both begin with *f*. Proto-Indo-European had **kwet-wor-* 'four' and **penkwe-* 'five'. Since **p* became **f* and **kw* become **hw* in Germanic by Grimm's Law (see Chapter 5), we expect *four* to have **hw* in Germanic (expected to be inherited as *whour* in English), not with the *f* of *four*. In this case, *four* was influenced to have *f* by the *f* of following *five*, an immediate model.

There are a number of other kinds of changes that are considered types of analogy.

Hypercorrection

Hypercorrection involves language variants that usually have different social statuses. An attempt to change a word in a less prestigious variety to make it conform with how it would be pronounced in a more prestigious variety sometimes results in overshooting the target, producing an erroneous outcome from the point of view of the variety being mimicked. In hypercorrection, speakers change things that are in fact already "correct," that already match what is in the prestige variety they are trying to mimic, getting it wrong by overcorrection. For example, in my native dialect of English (western United States) there is: *lawnd* from *lawn*; *pawnd (shop)* from *pawn*; *drownd* (present tense)/*drownded* (past tense) from *drown/drowned*; and *acrost* (or *acrossed*) from *across*. These are the results of an overzealous attempt to undo the effects of final consonant cluster simplification (seen in Chapter 5), found to one extent or another in most varieties of English, for example the loss of final *d* after *n*, as in *han'* for *hand* (common in *a han(d)ful, han(d)made*), *fin'* for *find*, *roun'* for *round*, and loss of *t* after *s*, as in *firs'* for *first* (in *firs' thing*) and *las'* for *last* (as in *las' night*). Hypercorrection added a *d* in cases such as *lawnd* under the erroneous assumption that *lawn* would be *lawnd* in Standard English, ending in a *d* that was lost after *n* in the local dialect, as with *han'* for *hand*. Re-insertion of a final *d* to *han'* would have correctly matched the standard form *hand*, but similar insertion of *d* in *lawn(d)* and *pawn(d)* did not match these words in Standard English.

A favorite bugaboo of purists is the frequently heard utterances like *for you and I, they saw you and I, between Jim and I,* or *because of Maggie and I,* where Standard English requires *me* in all cases where the pronoun is a direct object, for example *Coyote saw Roadrunner and* **me**, or follows a preposition, as in *this land is for you and* **me**, or *between you and* **me** *and the bedpost*. These cases with nonstandard "I" are examples of hypercorrection. School teachers and language pundits have long waged war on the nonstandard use of *me* (also *him, her, them, us*) as the subject of sentences, such as **me** *and Roadrunner saw Coyote,* **me** *and* **him** *saw Coyote, Roadrunner and* **me** *fought Coyote*, and so on. In attempting to correct these nonstandard instances of *me* to *I* when it is the subject of the clause, speakers got carried away and often changed *me* to *I* also in cases where *me* is required by the grammar of Standard English, hypercorrecting instances of *me* as direct or indirect objects to *I*, as in *Coyote chased you and* **I**, *Coyote threw rocks at you and* **I**, and *between you and* **I**.

What a mischievous twist! The extensive, long-term nagging against nonstandard forms of pronouns in cases such as those just mentioned resulted in the hypercorrections, and now these hypercorrections are the focus of new rants from purists.

Modern English has a good number of instances of hypercorrection where people have tried to gussy something up to make it sound more elegant but have essentially put their foot in their mouth, so to speak, by overshooting the Standard English target. An example that many have adopted is to change the plural of *process* to pronounce it like *process***eez**. In Standard English it is just plain old *processes*, a regular plural just as in the plural of most other nouns. However, apparently some people wanted to make this sound more like some of the Latin plurals that got borrowed into English, like **hypotheses** (*hypotheseez*) plural of *hypothesis*, **analyses** (*analyseez*) plural of *analysis*, and **crises** (pronounced like *criseez*) plural of *crisis*. They probably thought this pronunciation made them sound more learned, sophisticated, hence the hypercorrection. To the more critical, such an attempt at added sophistication just sounds fake.

Numerous websites today decry false Latin plurals in English, most of them instances of hypercorrection, such as:

> *octopi* as a plural of *octopus*. *Octopus* is ultimately borrowed from Greek *oktopous*, literally 'eight feet' (*okto-* 'eight' + *pous* 'foot'), the plural of which in Greek is *oktopodes*. It did not have the *-i* plural of Latin words.

> Some people attempt to create a Latin plural for *penis* in English as *peni* (sometimes *penii*), though its real plural in Latin was *pēnēs*. The Standard English plural is *penises*.

> And there is *Prii*, a playful plural of *Prius* (the automobile), perhaps said mockingly in response to the belief that many Prius drivers allegedly have snobbish attitudes? (I bought my Prius before I had learned that Priuses could come with built-in attitude.)

Folk Etymology: Linguistic Urban Legends

In folk etymologies speakers find meaningful analyses of words or phrases or pieces of grammar that were not originally there, and either the original form gets changed or new forms get introduced based on these new interpretations.

English *hamburger* may be the most often cited example of a folk etymology. It comes from German *Hamburger*, composed of *Hamburg* + *-er*, 'someone or something from the city of Hamburg'. Hamburgers are not made of 'ham' but speakers nevertheless folk-etymologized it as *hamburger*, as having something to do with 'ham', and on that basis went on to create such new words as *cheeseburger, chilliburger, fishburger, vegiburger* (*vegeburger, vegie burger*), *beefburger*, and just plain *burger*.

Some people say *it takes two to tangle*, a folk-etymologized version of the original saying *it takes two to tango*, made popular from the 1952 song "Takes Two to Tango," recorded independently by Pearl Bailey and Louis Armstrong. Here *tango* was reinterpreted by folk etymology as *tangle*, on the assumption that something about *tangle* was involved in its colloquial meaning of when 'two or more persons argue or fight'.

Some websites list *wheelbarrel* as a common "mistake" for *wheelbarrow*. *Wheelbarrow* here was folk-etymologized as associated in some way with *barrel* and accordingly changed to *wheelbarrel*. The word *wheelbarrow* involves *barrow* 'flat, rectangular frame with projecting handles for carrying a load', not a commonly known word nowadays.

Originally, *stark naked* had nothing to do with *stark*, with its meaning of 'rigid, unyielding, severe'. It was *start-naked*, based on Old English *steort* 'tail, rump'. For example, the common European bird called *redstart* has this *start* as 'tail' in its name. It has a cool scientific name, *Phoenicurus phoenicurus* – Latin *phoenīcūrus* means 'phoenix'. *Start-naked* was quite parallel in formation to modern *butt naked* and to even less polite *bare-assed*. *Start-naked* got changed to *stark naked* by folk etymology based on *stark* in its sense of 'severe, complete'.

But then, what about *butt naked*? It is actually pretty new. It came into use only after about 1970 – earlier it was *buck naked*. It is speculated that the *buck* of *buck naked* has to do with the smooth appearance of 'buckskin', similar to naked skin. The folk-etymologizing of *buck* as *butt* here seems based on *butt* as something that is visually more striking when someone is naked.

Back Formation

In back formation, a type of folk etymology, a word is assumed to be analyzable into meaningful parts that it did not originally have. Cases of back formation usually involve a root plus presumed but not real suffixes or prefixes, so that when the part thought to be a prefix or suffix is taken off, a new modified root is created. A good example that illustrates this in Modern English is *cherry*. *Cherry* entered English as a loan from Old French *cherise* (Modern French *cerise*), where the *s* originally was part of the root, but it was interpreted as representing the English plural -*s*, and so in back formation this *s* was removed, giving *cherry* as the singular and *cherries* as the plural.

Similarly, English *pea* is from Old English *pise* (singular) / *pisan* (plural), with the plural *n* seen in *oxen* and *children*. Later, the final *s* of the singular was reinterpreted as marking plural and it was backformed to *pea* singular with *peas* as its new plural. Compare *pease porridge*, preserved in the nursery rhyme "Pease porridge hot, pease porridge cold ...", which retains the *s* of the earlier singular form (and *pease-pudding* too), before the *s* was reinterpreted as the marker of plural.

A number of new English verb roots got created by back formation based on stuff in the original word that sounded like "*er*," interpreted as the -*er* suffix 'someone who does the action expressed in the verb': to *burgle* based on *burglar*; to *edit* from *editor*; to *escalate* based on *escalator*; to *letch* from *lecher*; to *orate* backformed from *orator*; to *peddle* based on *pedlar*; and to *sculpt* from *sculptor*.

Many non-American varieties of English have a verb to *orientate*, back-formed from *orientation*, competing with or replacing Standard English *to orient*. *Disorientated* is less established, but exists, derived analogically from backformed *orientated*. A few other examples include: to *automate*, backformed from *automation*; to *babysit* from *babysitter*; to *headhunt* from *headhunter*; to *hustle* from *hustler*; to *intuit* from *intuition*; to *kidnap* from *kidnapper*; to *proofread* from *proofreader*; to *reminisce* from *reminiscence*; to *self-destruct* from *self-destruction* (compare *self-destroy*); to *swindle* from *swindler*; and to *vaccinate* from *vaccination*.

Reanalysis

In reanalysis, a word or grammatical construction changes its analysis, the interpretation of its parts. It takes on a new analysis different from what it originally had, where the change affects which particular sounds belong to which particular parts of a word or construction. For example, *adder* comes from Old English *næddre*. The sequence *a næddre* was reanalyzed as *an adder*. The change came about through the reinterpretation of the article–noun sequence, where the initial *n* of *næddre* was reanalyzed not as part of the root *næddre* (*a næddre*) but rather as the *n* belonging to the article *an* before a vowel-initial root, *an adder*. Compare the German cognate *Natter* 'adder, viper'. English has several such examples:

apron, from Middle English *napron*, borrowed from Old French *naperon*, a diminutive form of *nape, nappe* 'tablecloth'. *Napkin* is related, from French *nape* 'tablecloth' + *-kin* 'diminutive suffix' from Dutch. *Napkin* preserves the original initial *n-*, but it is lost in *apron* due to the reanalysis of its initial *n* as belonging to the article *an* (*a napron* > *an apron*).

umpire entered English as *noumpere*, a loanword from Old French *nonper* 'umpire, arbiter', of *non* 'not' + *per* 'peer'. The sequence of the article *a* and a word beginning in *n* was reanalyzed as *an* + a word with an initial vowel.

uncle, Shakespeare had **nuncle** 'uncle', for example, in *King Lear*, Act I, scene iv, 170, still found in some dialects of English. It came about from reanalysis of the final *-n* of the possessive pronouns *mine* and *thine*. In earlier English the words had a final *-n* when the following word began in a vowel, as in *mine eyes*, and lacked the *-n* before words beginning in a consonant, for example, *my lips* (seen above). The original *mine uncle* was reanalyzed as *my **n**uncle*, where the *n* was assumed to be the initial consonant of *(n)uncle* and not the final *n* of the *mine, thine*.

Analogy and Sound Change

The interaction between sound change and analogy has been summarized in the slogan "sound change is regular and causes irregularity; analogy is irregular and causes regularity." A sound change applies regularly to all the words that have the particular sound in the context that is affected by the change. However, sound changes, though regular, can result in alternate forms of words, creating seeming irregularity. For example, as mentioned above, <u>umlaut</u> (seen in Chapter 5) fronted a back vowel when there was a front vowel, *i* or *e*, in a following syllable, as in *elder*, from *old* + *-er*, and *eldest*, from *old* + *-est*. The front vowel *e* of *-er* and *-est* caused the *o* of *old* to front to *e*, giving *elder* and *eldest*. The regular umlaut change introduced irregularity, leaving 'old' with two different forms, *old* and *eld-*. However, analogical change came along later and changed *elder* and *eldest* to *older* and *oldest*, respectively, on analogy with non-alternating forms such as *young/younger/youngest*. This analogical change was irregular in that it applied only here and there, to individual cases, but it undid the irregularity of having both *old* and *eld-* meaning 'old', thus eliminating the multiple forms of the comparative and superlative created by the regular sound change.

In a more complicated example, the history of the verb *to choose* in English exemplifies this interaction between analogy and sound change well. In Old English 'to choose' had several forms: *cēosan* (pronounced [čēozan]) 'to choose', *cēas* (pronounced [čæas]) 'chose [singular]', *curon* [kuron] 'chose [plural]', and *coren* [koren] 'chosen'. These come from the Proto-Indo-European root **geus-* 'to choose, to taste', which had vowel alternations in different grammatical contexts that gave also **gous-* and **gus-*. The **gus-* version is behind Latin *gustus* 'taste', the source of the loanword *gusto* in English. From this Indo-European root came Proto-Germanic **keus-an* 'to choose', with its alternants in different grammatical contexts, **kaus-* and **kuz-*. The Old English forms of 'choose' had several consonants that varied in different contexts, *č*, *k*, *s*, *z*, *r*. These varying consonants came about from two regular sound changes. In the forms *curon* [kuron] 'chose [plural]' and *coren* [koren] 'chosen', original **s* became **z* between vowels when the stress followed, and then later this *z* underwent <u>rhotacism</u>, changing to *r* (as seen in Chapter 5), yielding Old English *curon* and *coren*. <u>Palatalization</u> turned *k* into *č* ("ch", IPA [tʃ]) before front vowels, giving *cēosan* ([čēozan]) 'to choose' and *cēas* ([čæas]) 'chose [singular]'. Together, these regular sound changes left several different forms in the paradigm for 'to choose'. Later, analogy levelled out the consonant differences, leaving Modern English *choose/chose/chosen* with uniformly the same consonants. In this example, the regular sound changes, rhotacism and palatalization, created irregularity, resulting in several phonologically different forms for 'to choose' in Old English. Subsequent analogical change eliminated the alternating consonants, with only *č* ("ch") for the first consonant and only *z* (spelled "s") for the second.

The sound changes were, it is assumed, motivated by ease of pronunciation, but the result left greater complexity, with multiple forms of the verb that were more difficult to process and to learn. Analogy, often facilitating processing/understanding, reduced the complexity that the sound changes had introduced. We can say that the sound changes facilitated pronunciation but created multiple related forms, while analogy did nothing to improve the production of speech in this case, but facilitated understanding and learnability by making the consonants of the several forms of 'to choose' consistent.

The next chapter takes up grammatical change. Both sound change and analogy are behind many changes in grammar.

7   Can Languages Change Their Grammatical Spots?
Can Old Grammars Learn New Grammatical Tricks?

> The greater part of the world's troubles are due to questions of grammar.
> (Michel de Montaigne, *The Complete Essays of Montaigne*)

Introduction

This chapter is about change in grammar. A number of grammatical changes in English are unpacked and explained here because they give an appreciation for and understanding of the ways in which grammars can change. The mechanisms by which syntax can change are explicated, as is grammaticalization, and along the way some well-known grammatical changes in the history of English become familiar.

Mechanisms of Grammatical Change

There are only three basic mechanisms of syntactic change: reanalysis, extension, and borrowing (as argued by Harris and Campbell 1995). Each is explained here, with the aid of examples.

Reanalysis

Reanalysis was seen in the previous chapter as a kind of analogical change. Reanalysis is also the mechanism behind a great many grammatical changes. It involves changes in the interpretation of grammatical constructions, but it does not modify what the constructions actually look like – rather it involves a change in how speakers analyze the structure of the constructions. Reanalysis depends on the possibility for more than one structural analysis of a given grammatical construction. The following few examples illustrate it.

The be going to *Future*

English got a new future construction through reanalysis. The new *be going to* future auxiliary came about by reanalysis of (1) to have the new and different interpretation of (2).

(1)   Coyote **is going to** chase Roadrunner.
        Original interpretation: 'Coyote is going (moving over there in order) to chase Roadrunner.'

(2)   Coyote **is going to** chase Roadrunner.
        New interpretation: 'Coyote will$_{[FUTURE]}$ chase Roadrunner.'

Sentence (1) has a main verb, *be going (to)*, a verb of motion with a purposive sense. In (2), *be going (to)* has been reanalyzed as a future auxiliary.

Notice that in the reanalysis (reinterpretation) that produced (2) with the future meaning, the actual form of the sentence is unchanged: (1) and (2) are exactly the same in form, but are now different in grammatical structure, each with its own interpretation. In sentence (1) there is an ordinary main verb meaning 'is going to' ('moving somewhere to do something'). However, in sentence (2) *is going to* has now been reanalyzed as part of the grammar, a new future auxiliary *be going to*, meaning 'future' (*going to* here often pronounced as *gonna*). The sentence came to have more than one structural analysis, with both (1) and (2) possible – it underwent reanalysis, yielding (2) with its different structural analysis. As a result, the *be going to* future auxiliary became part of the grammar, a part of the English tense system.

Progressive

Another example of reanalysis is seen in the origin of the progressive in English. It is thought that it comes from an earlier construction composed of the verb *be* + *on* (preposition) + <u>gerund</u>, a noun derived from a verb by the suffix *-ing*, as in (3):

(3)   Coyote is a-hunting Roadrunner (*a-* here comes from earlier *on* 'on, at')
        [Structurally: Roadrunner is *on*-hunt-*ing* Coyote (*hunting* here is a noun)]

Later, the structure in (3) was reanalyzed as (4):

(4)   Coyote is a-hunting Roadrunner
        [Structurally: *is* ... *a-hunting* is now "progressive," a part of the grammar]

Later the *a-* (from *on* 'on') was lost, leaving *is* ... *-ing* in (5) signaling progressive:

(5)   Coyote is hunting Roadrunner

A vestige of the *a-* from the earlier preposition is still present in the progressive in some nonstandard varieties of English. It is also known from some familiar nursery rhymes and songs. For example:

Bye baby bunting,
Daddy's gone **a**-hunting,
Gone to get a rabbit skin,
To wrap baby bunting in.

Other examples are seen in the song titles "Here We Come **A**-Caroling" and Bob Dylan's "The Times They Are **A**-Changing". It is also found in the lyrics of the song "The Twelve Days of Christmas," though a bit less straightforwardly:

six geese **a**-laying (from six geese [that are] a-laying)
seven swans **a**-swimming
eight maids **a**-milking
ten lords **a**-leaping

In these lines, the progressive form of the verb *to be* isn't directly visible, the result of the optional reduction of such sentences – *six geese a-laying* is an alternative to the more complete, unreduced option *six geese **that are** a-laying*.

Extension

Extension happens after reanalysis, but unlike reanalysis, extension results in visible changes in the actual form of utterances. It does not involve other changes in meaning; rather it extends a change to apply in new situations that were not formerly possible. Extension is illustrated in the following examples.

Extension of Future Auxiliary

Extension is seen in the change that followed the newly developed *be going to* future auxiliary, seen above in (2). After the reanalysis that produced this future auxiliary interpretation had taken place, the new future auxiliary was extended so that it could appear with verbs where it previously had not been possible. Earlier the new future could occur only with verbs that could come after *go* in its sense as a verb of motion, for example, as in the original form, *Coyote is going to **eat***, meaning 'going over there to eat' (or 'going over there in order to eat'). In the extension that followed this, the new future construction could occur also with verbs where the earlier sense of *go* as a verb of motion would now make no sense, for example, *it is going to **rain** on Roadrunner and Coyote, Roadrunner is not going to **like** Coyote*, and *Roadrunner is going to **go*** – it is impossible to interpret *it is going to rain* as 'it is going over there (in order) to rain' and it makes no sense to think that *is going to go* would mean 'is going to go over there in order to go'. Or, in what seemed to me a dramatic example, overheard from a passenger in an airport concourse standing near the entrance to a restroom: *I'm going to go before I go* (that is, 'I am going [FUTURE] to go [urinate] before I go [depart]').

After *be going to* was reanalyzed from just a regular verb of motion to a future auxiliary, it was extended so it could occur before verbs that earlier could not occur with *be going to* in its earlier sense of a verb of motion, as seen in these utterances with *is going to rain, is not going to like, is going to go*, and such like.

The will *Future Auxiliary*

The other future auxiliary in English, *will*, is also the result of reanalysis followed by extension, similar in its history to the *be going to* future auxiliary. *Will* originally was an ordinary verb meaning 'want'. Vestiges of the earlier 'want' meaning of *will* are still seen in, for example, *if you will, say what you will, she willed it to be so, free will, good will on earth . . . to men of good will, have the will (to win), fire at will*, and *last will and testament. Will* changed from a main verb meaning only 'want' to meaning both 'want' and the reanalyzed *will* future auxiliary, and then later to only the reanalyzed *will* future auxiliary (except in these few vestigial contexts). Originally, this *will* 'future' could only occur with subjects capable of wanting (humans or animals), like, for example, *I will [= want] to eat, coyote will [= wants] to hunt Roadrunner*. Later, however, the reanalyzed *will* future auxiliary was extended so that it became possible to use it in situations where previously *will* could not appear, for example *it will rain tomorrow, foolhardiness will kill Coyote, Roadrunner will want to escape*, and so on – another example of invisible reanalysis followed by visible extension.

To complete the story, *want* came to replace *will* in the sense of 'want, desire'. *Want* itself was borrowed from Old Norse *vanta* with the meaning of 'be lacking, deficient' around 1200. By the early 1300s it had come also to have the meaning 'desired, lacking but needed'. *Will* is from Old English *willan* 'to wish, desire', but *will*'s sense of 'want, desire' eventually was taken over and pushed out by borrowed *want*.

The Double is *Construction*

Another thing that is new to English grammar is the double *is* construction, seen in examples such as:

(6)   The thing **is is** Coyote hates Roadrunner.

(7)   The point **is is** Coyote wants to catch Roadrunner.

(8)   The fact **is is** that Coyote wants to eat Roadrunner.

(9)   What's nice **is is** that Roadrunner always gets away from Coyote.

There are a number of ideas about how this got started, and indeed it might have had influence from more than one direction. One source appears to have been influence from sentences that started with *What*, or sometimes *Who*, followed by *is* (or sometimes some other form of the verb *to be*). These cases can have two instances of *is* together and be fully grammatical, not at all surprising, as seen in (10a), and (10b):

(10a)   What Roadrunner **is is** a faster runner.

(10b)   What the problem **is is** that Coyote is slower than Roadrunner.

However, the related utterances without *What* (or *Who*) at the beginning have only one *is*, as in examples (10c) and (10d):

(10c)   Roadrunner **is** a faster runner.

(10d)   The problem **is** that Coyote **is** slower than Roadrunner.

So (10c) and (10d) are grammatical, with a single *is*, and (10a) and (10b) are also grammatical with a *what* clause at the beginning and a sequence of *is is*. The structure in (10a) and (10b), with *is* repeated, has influenced sentences like those in (6)–(9) to become like them, with the sequence of *is is*, changing (10d) to (10e):

(10e)   The problem **is is** that Coyote is slower than Roadrunner.

This is an instance of extension of a construction to new circumstances where previously it was not possible. The reanalysis made it possible for sentences like (10d) to take a form like (10b), becoming like sentences illustrated by examples (6)–(9).

Grammatical Borrowing

In the past, it was not uncommon for scholars to believe that languages do not borrow grammar, that they do not undergo grammatical change due to language contact. However, borrowing of grammatical constructions is not at all uncommon and there are many examples in languages around the world.

   Most of the cases in English that have been claimed to involve grammatical borrowing are complicated and often less clear than we would like. English does, however, have a number of cases of borrowed grammatical prefixes and suffixes (together called affixes, parts of grammar), borrowed primarily from Latin. So, let us begin this section with them.

Ordinarily, an affix is not borrowed directly from another language, but rather enters the <u>recipient language</u> along with a number of loanwords that happen to contain the affix. The affix then can become productive enough to be combined with native stems in the borrowing language, not themselves from the source language of the borrowed affix. Borrowed affixes of this sort in English include:

-able, in some cases from French *-able*, in other cases directly from Latin *-abilis*, now found attachable to non-Romance and non-Latin stems in English words, as in *bearable, doable, google-able, laughable, lovable, microwavable, teachable, washable, unspeakable, unthinkable.*

-ism, from French *isme*, from Latin *-ismus*, borrowed from Greek *-ismos*, as in *alcoholism, Darwinism, jingoism, racism, sexism, snobbism, tokenism.*

-ist, from Old French *iste*, inherited from Latin *-ista*, borrowed from Greek *-istēs*, as in *communist, fattist, feminist, leftist, terrorist.*

anti-, from Old French *anti-* or directly from Latin *anti-*, ultimately borrowed from Greek *anti-* 'against, opposite, over', as in *antiaging, antichoice, anti-death penalty, anti-doping, anti-immigration, antinuke, anti-woke, antiwrinkle, anti-Trumpist.*

de-, from Latin *dē-* 'down, away, from among', as in *debug, debunk, defang, defog, defrock, defrost, detox.*

dis-, from Latin *dis-* 'apart, away, having negative or reversing force', as in *disinformation, dislike, disown, dishearten, distrust.*

pre-, from Old French and Medieval Latin *pre-* 'before', as in *pre-cooked, pre-game, pre-Roman, pre-owned, pre-trial.*

re-, from Old French *re-* or directly from Latin *re-* 'again, back', as in *re-open, reread, re-run, reshape, rewind.*

However, for most of the cases claimed to involve syntactic borrowing in English, competing explanations have been offered and it is not easy to present them without long-winded discussion. For that reason, let's just jump a bit sideways for a moment and look at a clear example involving languages related to English, a change in word order in French caused by language contact with German.

French and German share a word order trait because French borrowed it from German. Originally French was like other Romance languages in that it permitted sentences that have no overt subject – languages with this feature are called 'null subject' or 'pro-drop' languages. French was like Spanish, which can have sentences with no overt subject, such as *viene mañana* 'he/she/it comes tomorrow'. German, on the other hand, requires an explicit subject (it is a non-pro-drop language). French borrowed this trait through contact with German and now French also requires an overt subject, as in, for example, *il vient demain* 'he comes tomorrow', where an overt subject, such as *il* 'he', is required, now parallel to German *Er kommt morgen* 'he comes tomorrow'. Compare French *il pleut* 'it is raining' and German *es regnet* 'it is raining', where both have the required subject, with Spanish *llueve* 'it is raining', with no overt subject. Like German and French, English is also a non-pro-drop language, seen in *it is raining*, never with just *is raining* as a whole sentence.

An example of syntactic borrowing in English, albeit in Irish English, is the 'after perfect' construction [be + after + VERB-ing], as in (11):

(11)   Coyote is after hunting Roadrunner
[Meaning: 'Coyote has hunted Roadrunner']

This construction in Irish English is due to the influence of a parallel construction in Irish (a Celtic language) for expressing 'hot news', a case of grammatical borrowing from Irish into Irish English.[1]

There are many examples of borrowed syntactic constructions in other languages.

Grammaticalization

Grammaticalization is a common kind of grammatical change, but it doesn't involve any new kinds of mechanisms of change, just reanalysis followed by extension, as already seen in examples above. Informally, grammaticalization is mostly about changes in which an ordinary word becomes a grammatical marker, part of the formal grammar of a language. A couple of examples of grammaticalization have already been seen. A frequently cited one is the change seen above where English *will*, originally an ordinary word meaning 'want', was grammaticalized as a future auxiliary. *Will* came to have the grammatical function of future tense and lost its original sense of 'want'. Another frequently mentioned example of grammaticalization, also seen above, is the case of *be going to* that was grammaticalized from its verb-of-motion meaning to become part of the grammar, a future auxiliary.

Certain grammaticalization changes are found in various languages around the world, where an ordinary word follows the same pathway and ends up with the same or similar grammatical function in the different languages. The following are some of these sorts of changes.

1. Auxiliary verb < main verb, as in English *will* 'future auxiliary' < main verb 'want'.

---

[1] See Hickey (2000) for details.

2. Auxiliary verb of obligation < 'need', 'necessity', 'owe' (*should* < Old English *sceolde*, past tense of *sceal* 'owe'; *must* < Old English *moste*, past tense of *motan* 'to be able to, need to').

3. Future < 'want', 'have', 'go', 'come' (English *will* 'future auxiliary' < 'want'; *be going to* 'future auxiliary' < *be going to* 'verb of motion, with purpose'; both seen above).

4. Infinitive marker < 'to', 'for' [purposeful]. Much simplified, the English *to* infinitive comes from *to* in its 'motion toward' sense, as in (a), later reanalyzed to its 'purpose' sense, where both 'motion toward' and 'purpose' are possible, as in (b), and then later extended to 'purpose, in order to' only, as in (c), where the meaning 'motion toward' is no longer possible:

    (a) *Roadrunner went **to** Coyote's den* [to = 'direction' only]
    (b) *Roadrunner went **to** smash Coyote* [to = 'direction' or 'purpose']
    (c) *Roadrunner is using a boulder **to** smash Coyote* ['purpose' only, no 'direction']).

5. Passive < 'get', 'obtain', 'receive' (English *Coyote **got** smashed by Roadrunner*).

6. Progressive < locative + participle (English, *is hunting* < *is **a**-hunting* < *is **on** hunting* [seen above]; found also, for instance, in Cologne German *ist am Schreiben* [is on.the writing] 'is writing' and in Pennsylvania German].

Other Recent and Ongoing Grammatical Changes in English

Several recent and ongoing changes in English grammar provide examples of syntactic change. Some are of concern to purists and prescriptivists, while others seem largely to have escaped their attention and are apparently not stigmatized. The following are a few familiar ones.

English Subjunctive

The increasing loss of the subjunctive in English is an annoyance to me. I disagree with Mark Twain and Somerset Maugham. Mark Twain (1935: 303) cursed it, saying "Damn the subjunctive. It brings all our writers to shame." Somerset Maugham (1949: 323) denounced it in like manner, decrying "the subjunctive mood is in its death throes, and the best thing to do is to put it out of its misery as soon as possible." Of course, I recognize that things change and that being critical of change in language is both futile and misguided. Still, it is difficult not to feel some sadness that the subjunctive that I grew up with and cherish is all but fully lost in the speech of many people. For example, instead of saying, as in the Joni Mitchell song, *I wish I **were** in love again*, many people say *I wish I **was** in love again* or sometimes, *I wish I **would be** in love again*.

Actually, diminished use of two kinds of subjunctives in English gets talked about. The change in the so-called *were*-subjunctive is very advanced in the UK and most British Commonwealth countries, where it has receded more than in North America. This changes formal sentences such as in the title of the famous song from *Fiddler on the Roof* "If I **Were** a Rich Man" to "If I Was a Rich Man." The other is the so-called 'mandative subjunctive', also in decline though less steeply so. It is seen in examples such as:

(12)   Coyote demanded that Roadrunner **be** caught.

(13)   Coyote's demand required that Roadrunner **run** faster.

(14)   Roadrunner insisted that the sheriff **stop** Coyote.

The mandative subjunctive lives on in formal language, but is undergoing change towards loss for many speakers of Modern English, maybe unknown to or at least not used by many younger speakers.

Whom

Whom, as the direct or indirect object form of *who*, has been almost completely replaced by *who* in common spoken usage, though it is still sometimes used in writing, as in sentences such as:

(15)   **Who** did Coyote attack? (< **Whom** did Coyote attack?)

(16)   **To who** did Coyote lie? (< **To whom** did Coyote lie?)

Whom survives as an <u>archaism</u> in such idiomatic or formulaic phrases as: *for whom the bell tolls*; *to whom it may concern*; and *to whom much is given, much is required.*

Shall

Shall has mostly given way to *will* as the auxiliary verb signaling future tense, almost completely in American English, less so in the UK. In statements by prescriptivists we can sometimes read that in its 'future' sense, *shall* is required with *I* and *we*, as in *we shall overcome*, and *will* is necessary with other subjects, as for example in the titles of the songs "Will You Still Love Me Tomorrow," "He Will Break Your Heart," "She

Will," "Love Will Tear Us Apart," "Our Day Will Come," "There Will Never Be Another You," and others.

Have *Supported by* do

Questions in the past could have *have* as a main verb without some form of *do* in them, as in (17):

(17)   Have you many visitors?

Now they have changed to (18), with *do* support now required:

(18)   **D**o you have many visitors?

Change in Possessive Constructions

English has two kinds of possessives for nouns, the *-'s* suffix kind, as in *the roadrunner's success*, and the *of* phrase kind, as in *the success of the roadrunner*. Formerly, the *'s* possessive was more restricted in its occurrence, mostly only with human possessors. However, it has been extending to occur much more frequently also with non-human possessors, while the *of* phrase possessive is in decline in general, as in, for example, *the economy's collapse* at the expense of the formerly more frequent *the collapse of the economy*.

Change in Comparatives and Superlatives

Until recent times, the comparative of English adjectives of one and sometimes two syllables was generally formed by adding *-er* (*tough/ tougher, pretty/prettier*) while *more* was placed before longer adjectives (*heroic/more heroic, beautiful/more beautiful*). For superlatives *-est* was added to the one- or two-syllable adjectives (*toughest, prettiest*) and *most* preceded the longer ones (*most heroic, most beautiful*). The tendency towards use of *more* and *most* and against *-er* and *-est* even with shorter adjectives has increased markedly in recent years, so that examples such as *more clear, more odd, more ugly* are becoming common, with *most clear, most odd, most ugly* also now more common, though somewhat less frequent than in the case of the comparatives.

They *as a Singular Pronoun*

Singular *they* (*they/their/them*) has been around for centuries, as in William Shakespeare's (1623) *A Comedy of Errors* (Act 4, Scene 3, lines 1–2) where he says:

There's not a man I meet but doth salute me
As if I were **their** well-acquainted friend.

Here, *their* refers to singular *a man's*. (This sentence also, incidentally, contains a fine instance of the *were*-subjunctive.) Similarly, Jane Austen (1775–1817) used singular *they* and *their* often in her writings. For example, in *Mansfield Park*, she wrote "I would have everybody marry if **they** can do it properly", and in *Northanger Abbey*, "it is **their** duty, each to endeavour to give the other no cause for wishing that he or she had bestowed **themselves** elsewhere."

Nevertheless, until recently, teachers and prescriptivists have campaigned against singular *they*, teaching that since *a man* in sentences such as the one from Shakespeare is singular, agreement has to be with a singular pronoun, **his** *friend*. In spite of this, the use of singular *they* is on the rise, especially recently, aided by gender-neutral writing guidelines that are against so-called generic *he*, as in for example *if anyone comes, please ask **him** to wait*, where *him* is meant to include both males and females.

This sort of pronoun discomfort has been much discussed, for example, by church groups, struggling with issues of gender in language. This is seen in older vs. more recent translations of the Bible. Although the King James version has cases with singular *they*, it also has many more with generic *he*. For example, Mark 4: 25 in the King James Bible (from 1611) reads:

For **he** that hath, to **him** shall be given: and **he** that hath not, from **him** shall be taken even that which **he** hath.

The New International Version (1978), whose intent was to make the Bible easier to read and to understand, translated this verse as:

Whoever has will be given more; whoever does not have, even what **he** has will be taken from **him**.

But then, in the 1984 version, this was revised again, bringing in singular *they*:

Whoever has will be given more; whoever does not have, even what **they** have will be taken from **them**.

Indeed, in some instances, the generic *he* sounds really jarring, as for example when the chair of my department in a hiring meeting pronounced that "we are going to hire the best person for the job, regardless of **his** sex," and then repeated the sentiment again later as "we will hire the best person for the job regardless of whether **he** is a man or a woman." (He really said this; it is not made up!) Particularly jolting for its grammar, though perhaps less than for the gender of its pronoun, is what Albert Blumenthal said, addressing the New York State Assembly in 1984: "Everyone will be able to decide for **himself** whether or not to have an abortion."

The next chapter takes up how languages are related to one another, and how they are classified.

8   All in the Family
Language Classification

And the whole earth was of one language, and of one speech . . . and they said, Go to, let us build us a city and a tower, whose top may reach unto heaven . . . And the Lord came down to see the city and the tower, which the children of men builded. And the Lord said, Behold, the people is one, and they have all one language . . . Go to, let us go down, and there confound their language, that they may not understand one another's speech. So the Lord scattered them abroad from thence upon the face of all the earth . . .

(Genesis 11: 1–9)

Introduction

Although it may not be general knowledge, there are many language families in the world, about 399 in fact (listed in the appendix to this book). Most people will be unfamiliar with the names of most of them.

Languages can develop different <u>dialects</u> in different regions. Then, as further changes accumulate, speakers of the different dialects may no longer be able to understand one another. When that happens, these formerly different dialects become distinct but related languages, members of a language family. For example, in the Roman era, Latin was a single language, but over time, dialect differences developed in different regions of the empire. With the accumulation of changes in the dialects, eventually speakers from the different dialects could no longer understand one another – they were no longer mutually intelligible – and so this gave rise to the distinct languages, French, Spanish, Italian, Romanian, and others, members of the Romance family of languages, all descendants of Latin as spoken just before this diversification into related languages, the ancestor of the modern Romance languages. Linguistic classification is about these relationships among languages.

This chapter is about the world's language families, and about how languages are classified. It is also about what it takes to be able to show that languages are related to other languages, belonging to the same language family. Some of the better-known but nevertheless controversial proposals of distant linguistic kinship are also considered.

It will be useful, first, to have a good idea of some terms that are used to talk about language classification and language families.

Cognate in linguistics doesn't mean just 'related, connected', as it does in more general parlance. Rather, *cognate* is a technical term that means basically related by inheritance. Specifically, a *cognate* word is inherited from an ancestor language (a proto-language, see below) and is related to words shared by sister languages (related languages, see below) because they are inherited from a single original word in the parent language from which the related languages descend. For instance, the Romance languages, Spanish, Portuguese, French, Italian, and so on, share a cognate meaning 'hand': Spanish *mano*, Portuguese *mão*, French *main*, and Italian *mano*. These words are inherited in these languages from the original Proto-Romance word **manu(s)* 'hand', and are cognates to one another because of that shared inheritance, though they have undergone some changes in the history of the individual languages. The Germanic languages share a different cognate meaning 'hand': English *hand*, German *hand*, Swedish *hand*, Danish *hånd* (pronounced *hond*), and Icelandic *hönd*, inherited from Proto-Germanic **handuz* 'hand'. Proto-Germanic is the parent language from which these languages descend, from which they inherited their word for 'hand'.

Dialect means a variety (regional or social) of a language which is *mutually intelligible* with other dialects of the same language. Mutual intelligibility means that speakers of different dialects can understand one another's language. This is the only meaning of *dialect* accepted in linguistics today. There was an old-fashioned use of the word *dialect* to mean an exotic or little-known language, as in fanciful accounts of some romantic or heroic figure having spoken loads of "languages" and umpteen "dialects." *Dialect* has also at times been used to refer to a daughter language in a language family. There are also other confusing uses of *dialect*. For example, "dialects" of Chinese are often spoken of when in fact what is meant is the several mutually unintelligible Chinese (Sinitic) languages, Mandarin, Wu, Min, Hakka, Yue, and others. Mandarin and Cantonese (of the Yue branch) are separate languages. Similarly, several of the so-called dialects of Arabic are not mutually intelligible with each other.

Variety is a term that is similar to *dialect* but is somewhat more open-ended and inclusive. It includes any form of a language which is particular to some specific region or social group. It means any clearly identified language entity regardless of its status.

There are many definitions of **language** around, many involving notions such as system or means or method of communication, by words or signs, and so on. For language classification, *language* means any distinct linguistic entity (variety) which is mutually unintelligible with other such entities.

A **language family** is a group of languages that are related to one another because they descend from a common ancestor language that diversified over time to result in its descendant languages, called "daughter languages." A language family is the set of daughter languages, the languages that descend from a common ancestor, called a "proto-language."

The names of many language families bear the suffix -*an*, as in Indo-European, Sino-Tibetan, Algonquian, and so on. The ultimate number of language families in the world is the set of independent language families (including language isolates) that cannot reliably be shown to be related to any other language family.

A **language isolate** is a language that has no known relatives, that is, it is not related to any other language or language family. It is in effect a language family of only one member, a single language. Some of the best-known language isolates are Basque, Ainu, and Sumerian. It is often thought that there are few language isolates in the world, but in fact there are many, about 159 (see Campbell 2018).

Proto-language refers to the once-spoken ancestral language from which daughter languages descend, and, in another sense, to the language <u>reconstructed</u> by the <u>comparative method</u> that represents the once-spoken ancestral language from which the related languages descend.

An **unclassified language** is a language which has either no documentation at all or for which the available attestation is so scant that the language cannot be shown to be related to any other language. In fact, such languages are not just unclassified; they are unclassifiable, because there is not sufficient evidence upon which to base decisions of relatedness. Unclassified languages differ from language isolates. Language isolates have sufficient available information and on the basis of that information it is not possible to show that they are related to any other language.

Language families can be of different magnitudes. That is, some larger-scale families may include smaller-scale families as their branches. Unfortunately, a number of confusing terms have been used in attempts to distinguish more inclusive from less inclusive family groupings.

The term **subgroup** (also called *subfamily*, *branch*) refers to a set of languages in a language family that are more closely related to one other than they are to other languages of that family – a subgroup is a branch of a language family. As a proto-language (say, Proto-Indo-European) diversifies, it develops daughter languages (such as, in this case, Proto-Germanic, Proto-Celtic, Proto-Slavic, and others). If a daughter (for instance Proto-Germanic) itself later splits up and develops daughter languages of its own (such as English, German, Swedish, and others), then those descendants of that earlier daughter language (Proto-Germanic) constitute members of a subgroup (the Germanic subgroup), and the original daughter language (Proto-Germanic) becomes in effect an intermediate proto-language in its own right, a parent of its own immediate descendants (its daughters, English, German, and others), but still at the same time a descendant (daughter) itself, a branch of the original proto-language (Proto-Indo-European).

A number of terms have also been used for proposed but unconfirmed higher-order, more inclusive language families, hypothesized but as-yet-undemonstrated distant linguistic relationships. These terms include *stock*, *phylum*, and *macro-*, as in *Macro-Penutian*, *Macro-Siouan*, and macro-family. The entities called "stock," "phylum," and "macro-" would just be regular language families if their putative members could be demonstrated to be genealogically related to one another, and they can never be accepted language families if the proposals cannot be adequately supported. For that reason, it is better to avoid these terms and just to speak of "proposed distant relationships" or "postulated language families."

In the past, some scholars used *stock* and *phylum* to mean a confirmed higher-order language family whose members are subgroups that constitute lower-level language families themselves. For example, some might consider Indo-European a "stock" that includes "language families" on the order of Proto-Germanic, Proto-Slavic, and so on, that is, subgroups in today's usage. This, however, is problematic, because *stock* and *phylum* have so typically been applied to hypothesized but unconfirmed language families. For that reason, it is best to say that any grouping of languages whose members are definitely related to one another is simply a language family, regardless of its age or of the number of branches it may have. Proposed but unsubstantiated hypotheses of relatedness do not count as language families.

Given conflicting opinions, how is one to know what to believe? How can claims about linguistic relationships be evaluated? How do we show that languages are related and thus belong together in a language family? The question of how to determine whether languages not yet known to be related to one another may be distantly related is much debated, and is taken up below with discussion of the criteria and methods involved.

The World's Language Families

As mentioned at the start of this chapter, there are ca. 399 language families in the world. Moreover, their geographical distribution is surprising.

For example, there are some 170 independent language families (including language isolates) in the Americas. They make up 43 percent of the linguistic diversity of the world, calculated in terms of language families. How and why the Americas has come to have so many language families is an as-yet-unresolved mystery, given that the American continents were the last major land mass to be occupied by humans and yet they have a greater number of language families than any other land mass, nearly half of the world's language families. Languages belonging to these American language families are spoken from Siberia to Greenland and from the Arctic to Tierra del Fuego. They include the southernmost language of the world (Yahgan, alias Yámana, in Argentina and Chile) and some of the northernmost languages of the world (Eskimoan) (Campbell 2024).

South America alone has 100 language families, a quarter of the world's total. North America has 54, and Mexico and the parts of Central America whose languages are not genealogically connected with families in South America have 14 language families.

In comparison, there are only 31 language families in Europe and Asia. Africa has 42, Australia 30, and the Pacific 128.

Indo-European

Indo-European is by far the best-known language family. It includes such well-known languages, each with several million speakers, as English, German, French, Spanish, Portuguese, Russian, Hindi, and Bengali.

Though debate persists, most linguists favor the view that the Proto-Indo-European homeland was located in the Pontic-Caspian steppe region, north of the Black Sea, at about 4000 BCE.[1] Indo-European diversified into major branches, called subgroups or subfamilies: Albanian, Anatolian, Armenian, Balto-Slavic, Celtic, Germanic, Greek, Indo-Iranian, Italic, and Tocharian. Indo-European languages spread over most of Europe and major parts of South Asia and Southwest Asia. Well over 400 languages belong to the Indo-European family. Figure 8.1 gives all the main branches and subbranches but does not list all the individual languages that are the members of each of these branches. (See also Map 10.4 in Chapter10.)

---

[1] See Anthony and Ringe (2015).

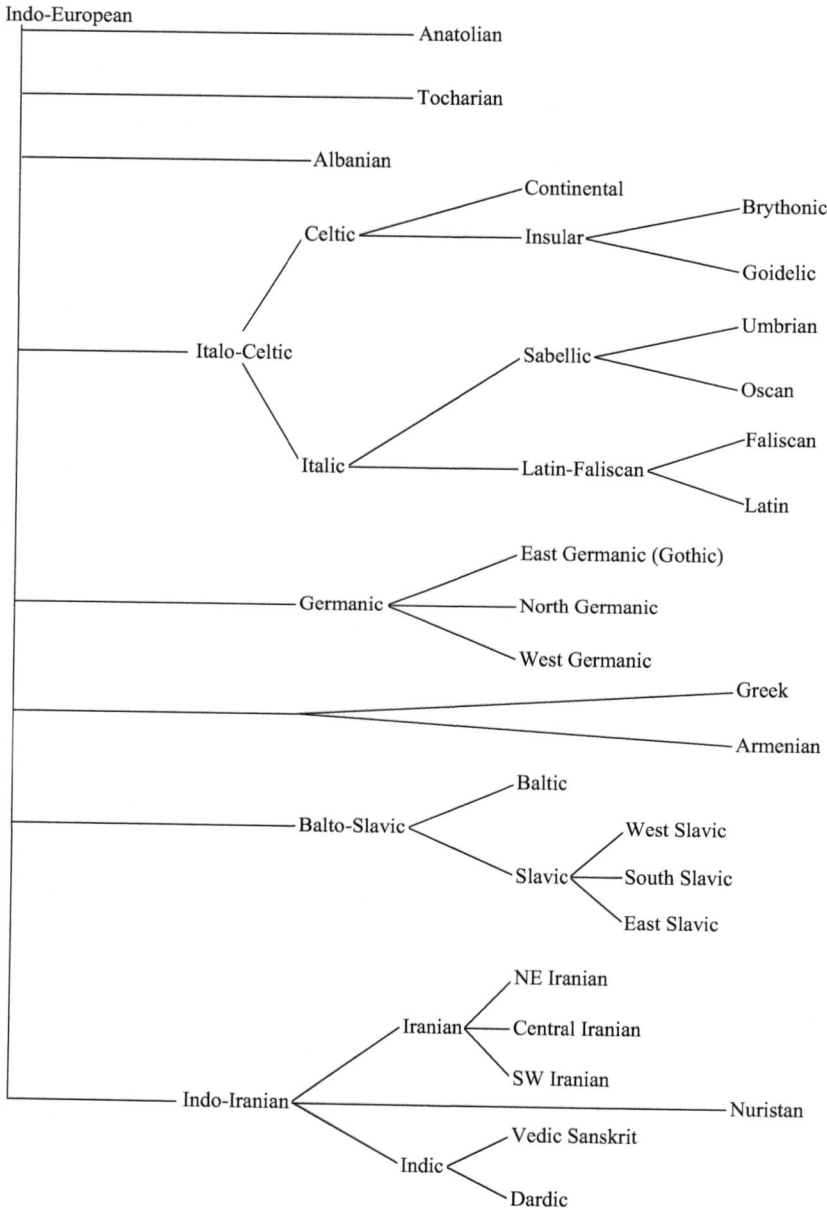

Figure 8.1 Indo-European language family tree: major branches and subbranches

The sweeping saga of how the Indo-European language family was discovered and how understanding of its internal relationships and changes developed over time, along with the emergence of the comparative method, is captivating. Recognition of the relatedness of some of the branches of Indo-European began as early as the sixteenth century, and over time, more Indo-European languages were recognized and advances in the methods of comparison continued to be made.

Several scholars observed the similarity and possible relationship between Sanskrit and various other Indo-European languages, and Sanskrit played a key role in the full recognition of Indo-European as a language family. Sir William Jones (1746–1794), with his famous declaration of the relatedness of Sanskrit with several other languages now known to belong to the Indo-European language family, is commonly credited with discovery of the Indo-European family and the comparative method. Though acknowledged as a renowned scholar even in his own lifetime, Jones was not the first to recognize that several languages, including Sanskrit, were related to each other or to utilize the comparative method. Rather, Jones reflects the thinking of his time.[2] Nevertheless, Jones' dramatic announcement and the attention it has received highlights how exciting and important the discovery of the relationship among branches of the Indo-European language family was, with the astonishing role it came to have in the history of ideas.

The story of the discovery of Hittite and the demonstration of its Indo-European affiliation is another spellbinding tale of language sleuthing. Hittite is one of several Anatolian languages that were discovered in ancient documents found in excavations of archaeological sites. Together the Anatolian languages constitute the oldest branch of the Indo-European family.[3] The inclusion of the Anatolian languages in the family resulted in widescale overhaul of the Proto-Indo-European sound system.

Uralic

Uralic is a language family of some forty members, spoken in Europe and northern Eurasia. Its largest and best-known languages are Estonian, Finnish, and Hungarian. In the traditional classification, Uralic split into two major branches, Finno-Ugric and Samoyedic. However, not all scholars now accept this division, several seeing Samoyedic as just one of several branches of the family.

---

[2] See Campbell and Poser (2008: 32–47) for details.
[3] See Campbell and Poser (2008: 74–80) for the dramatic story of how its Indo-European kinship was discovered.

Several hypotheses for the Proto-Uralic homeland have been proposed, most of them locating it just west of the Ural Mountains or in the area of the Volga River. The age of Proto-Uralic is often hypothesized at around 4,500 years ago, though some proposals suggest 6,000 years ago or even earlier.

The discovery and elaboration of the Uralic family came early and it influenced the development of the comparative method in linguistics. (See Campbell and Poser 2008 for details.)

Niger-Congo

The Niger-Congo language family is the largest in the world in terms of number of languages, with some 1,500 languages belonging to it, spoken across sub-Saharan Africa. The Bantu branch of the family has over 400 languages – some scholars count more than 600. Its biggest and best-known member, Swahili, has 16 million native speakers and some 80 million who speak it as a second language.

Niger-Congo is thought to have its homeland in west or central Africa, perhaps in the area of the confluence of the Niger and Benue rivers, in Nigeria. The date of the break-up of Proto-Niger-Congo is uncertain and varies greatly in various proposals, often cited at around 10,000 years ago.

Austronesian

Austronesian is the largest language family in terms of geographical distribution, with languages spoken from Taiwan to New Zealand and from Madagascar to Rapa Nui ("Easter Island"), over halfway around the earth. There are over 1,250 Austronesian languages. Malay and Indonesian are varieties of a single language, mutually intelligible, though often listed as separate. It is the largest and best-known language of the family. It has some 60 million speakers, and is spoken in Malaysia, Singapore, Brunei, and Indonesia (where it is called "Indonesian").

A fascinating discovery was that the Austronesian homeland was located in Taiwan, where the "Formosan languages" make up several primary branches of the family. All the other Austronesian languages, now spread widely across the Pacific, belong to the Malayo-Polynesian branch of the family. Opinions about the date of the split-up of Proto-Austronesian vary, but ca. 5,000 years ago is frequently mentioned. The date for the break-up of the Malayo-Polynesian branch is often said to be at about 4,200 years ago.

While there remain uncertainties, and opinions differ with respect to some proposed but as-yet undemonstrated language families, the list in the appendix to this chapter represents roughly the consensus among experts on what the recognized language families of the world are.

Of these some 399 language families, 91 are dormant ("extinct") – that is, no language that is a member of these 91 families has any remaining native speakers. This means that almost a quarter (23 percent) of the linguistic diversity of the world, calculated in terms of language families, is now lost. Other language families will also soon become dormant, when the last language of the language family loses its last speaker.

Complications in the Classification of the World's Languages

However, this list of the world's language families is far from definitive, for a number of reasons. Scholars are not always in agreement. Some scholars reject proposals of relatedness that others find more promising or even convincing. Sometimes opinions differ over whether a language should be considered unclassified or whether it is considered to have enough extant documentation on the basis of which it can be classified together with others or, alternatively, enough to show that it is not related to any other language and so is a language isolate.

However, the reality is that the exact number of language families in the world is unknown – unknowable – also for a number of other reasons, to which we now turn.

Dialect vs. Language

One difficulty stems from disagreements over the vexed question of separate languages vs. dialects of a single language. The boundary between relatively divergent dialects of a single language and closely related languages can be difficult to determine. Sometimes, where some specialists see a single language with dialects, others may see a family of closely related languages, not mutually intelligible. For counting the number of independent language families, it matters whether a language has diversified further into multiple languages, becoming a language family, or is but a single language with multiple dialects.

Unclassified Languages and Uncontacted Groups

Another reason why the exact number of distinct language families is uncertain is because of unclassified languages. There are literally hundreds of unclassified languages, especially among the Indigenous languages of the Americas (see Campbell 2024). Most ceased to be spoken long ago. Many of them are completely unattested; for others, the extant documentation is too scant to permit classification. Some are still spoken, but essentially undocumented. For unclassified languages, the available information is insufficient to be able to reach conclusions about possible relatives. Among these unclassified languages, it is possible that some belong to as-yet-unknown language families.

Yet another reason behind the uncertainty of the number of language families is the "uncontacted" peoples around the world, especially in Amazonia. It was estimated that there are some 100 so-called uncontacted or isolated groups around the world, most in South America, but some also in Papua New Guinea, Central Africa, and elsewhere (see Holmes 2013). The number of uncontacted groups is not known, and reports and estimates vary. For example, the website of FUNAI (Fundação Nacional do Índio [National Indigenous People Foundation] in Brazil) reports 107 isolated Indigenous groups registered in Amazonia alone.[4] The languages spoken by some of these groups are known, but in many cases it is not known whether the uncontacted group speaks an already identified language, a language currently unknown but which may belong to a known language family, or perhaps a language representing an as-yet-unidentified language family or language isolate.

Consequently, the imprecise number of approximately 399 independent language families (including 159 language isolates) is as close as we can come at present to answering the question of how many distinct language families there are in the world. It is anticipated, however, that this number will change. The total number of independent language families may be reduced if some language families come to be demonstrated through careful investigation to be related to other known language families. The languages of at least some of the uncontacted groups will become known sufficiently well for them to be compared and perhaps for their linguistic affiliation to be determined; some of these cases may turn out to be language isolates, with no demonstrable relatives, adding to the total number of language families. Probably some of the surviving unclassified languages will get described sufficiently well for them to be classified. Possibly additional heretofore unknown attestations may be discovered for some of the dormant unclassified languages sufficient to allow them to be classified. Possibly some of the undeciphered scripts will be deciphered, revealing the languages they represent (see Chapter 9). Some of these "unknowns" will become "knowns." However, adequate methods for determining relatedness among languages are crucial, and

---

[4] www.funai.gov.br/index.php/nossas-acoes/povos-indigenas-isolados-e-de-recente-contato.

hypotheses of relatedness lacking in adequate procedures or sufficient evidence will not be found persuasive.

How Are Languages Shown to Be Related to One Another? How Are Language Families Established?

To support a hypothesis that languages may be related to one another and belong to the same language family, it is necessary to determine what can constitute supportive evidence and to be able to distinguish this from what is not supportive. Here, we consider both the kinds of evidence that have successfully been deployed to demonstrate relatedness among languages and the kinds of evidence that fail to be supportive, about which caution is necessary.

Similarity vs. Adequate Evidence of Language Relationships

Discovering similarities among languages is the most frequent starting point for attempts to demonstrate family relationships among languages. However, similarities can be due to more than just inheritance from a common parent language. They may be due to:

- accident (chance, coincidence)
- borrowing (language contact)
- onomatopoeia, sound symbolism
- nursery forms
- typologically commonplace traits, language universals
- inheritance from a common ancestor – language family membership.

To make a good case for relatedness among languages, it is necessary to show that other possible explanations for the similarities are not as strong as inheritance from a common ancestor.

Unfortunately, some proponents of as-yet-unconfirmed language family relationships stop at identifying similarities among compared languages and just assume that the similarities are sufficient to show that the languages under comparison are related to one another. But assembling similarities among languages is just the beginning. Much that is offered as evidence of relatedness for proposed but as-yet-unverified hypotheses of language relationship has more plausible explanations of a different sort. These other sources of similarities among languages and the complications they can cause for hypotheses of linguistic kinship must be kept in mind when we investigate possible family relationships among languages.

First, it should be noted that seeking raw similarities can miss true cognates – real evidence of relatedness. This is seen in the following cases of cognate words among related languages which, nevertheless, do not look similar because of sound changes that the languages have undergone, even though the cognates come from a single original word in the proto-language. They exhibit non-obvious though systematic sound correspondences, which are discovered when the languages are compared carefully. A few examples are:

French *boeuf* / English *cow*, from Proto-Indo-European *g^{w}ou-* 'cow'.

French *cinq* / English *five* / Russian *p^{y}at^{y}* / Armenian *hing*, all derived by straightforward changes from original Proto-Indo-European *$penk^{w}e$-* 'five'.

French *nous* (pronounced /nu/) 'we, us' / English *us*, both ultimately from Proto-Indo-European *nos-* 'we'.

Sound Correspondences as Evidence for Classification

Nearly all scholars consider regular sound correspondences the strongest evidence for showing genealogical relatedness among languages. Sound correspondences are discovered in the application of the comparative method. A wee example from Germanic languages, English's sister languages, illustrating sound correspondences, is given in Table 8.1.

As is easy to see from these three cognate sets, there is a sound correspondence in which a *t* of the other Germanic languages corresponds to *ts* in German. Proto-Germanic had *$*t$*, which underwent the sound change *$*t$* to *ts* in German. The other sounds in these cognates also correspond regularly in cognates in these languages, though they undergo various other sound changes in the individual languages. Because this sound correspondence (*t : t : ts : t : t : t*) recurs regularly in cognates among the Germanic languages, the shared similarity cannot be explained as sheer

Table 8.1 *A few sound correspondences in Germanic languages*

Old English	Dutch	German	Swedish	Icelandic	Gothic	Proto-Germanic	Gloss
tōþ	tand	Zahn	tand	tönn	tunþus	*tanθ-s	tooth
[tōθ]	–	[tsān]	–	[tön]	–	[tunθus]	–
twā	twee	zwei	två	tveir	twai	*twai	two
–	[tvē]	[tsvai]	[tvo]	–	–	–	–
tā	teen	Zehe	tå	tá	–	*taihwō	toe
–	[te:n]	[tsee]	[to]	[taw]	–	–	–

accident. Therefore this is solid evidence to support the hypothesis that these languages are related to one another, all descendants of a common ancestor.

It is possible, of course, to compare these Germanic cognates with others from other branches of the Indo-European family to see how the Germanic sounds correspond to sounds in the other branches. As seen in Chapter 5, in Grimm's Law, given *t in Germanic, we expect d in other branches of Indo-European, and this is what we see in cognates from non-Germanic languages, for example, Latin dēnt- 'tooth', duo 'two', and digit- 'finger, toe'. These hark back to Proto-Indo-European *dent-, *dwo-, and *deik-, respectively, with Proto-Indo-European *d > *t in Proto-Germanic and then with Proto-Germanic *t > ts in German but unchanged in the other Germanic languages.

Grammatical Evidence

Many scholars think that grammatical evidence is desirable for showing that languages are genealogically related. Linguistic scholars throughout history have considered grammatical evidence valuable for establishing language families.

Many favor "shared aberrancy" (also called "submerged features," "morphological peculiarities," "arbitrary associations," "particular processes," "singular facts," "anomalous forms," and "arbitrary associations"). English good/better/best compared with German gut/besser/best is considered a good example of this kind of evidence of related-ness, since such matchings are highly unlikely to be due to borrowing or accident. In another example, in the opinion of American linguist Morris Swadesh (1951: 8), even a single "deep-seated coincidence in formation" such as that between English I–me and French je–moi can be taken as strongly suggesting common origin and not borrowing.

Note, though, that although such cases provide evidence of relatedness, this kind of irregularity or shared aberrancy is exactly what analogy (see Chapter 6) often eliminates over time, meaning that cases of shared aberrancy turn out to be rare.

Another example of shared aberrancy that gets mentioned as a good example of grammatical evidence of relatedness is the matching among irregular forms of the verb 'to be' across Indo-European languages, as seen in Table 8.2. It has been said that one need only look at the paradigm for the verb 'to be' to know whether a language belongs to the Indo-European family or not (Meillet 1967[1925]: 36).

An important and telling example of shared aberrancy helping to confirm genetic relationship among languages formerly not known to

Table 8.2 *Forms of the verb 'to be' in Indo-European languages*

	'he/she/it is'	'they are'	'I am'
Latin	est	sunt	sum
Sanskrit	ásti	sánti	asmi
Greek	esti	eisi	eimi
Gothic	ist	sind	am
Hittite	ešzi	ašanzi	ešmi (<z> = [ts])
Proto-Indo-European	*es-ti	*s-enti	*es-mi

be related comes from Friedrich Hrozný's (1915, 1917) demonstration that Hittite is an Indo-European language. This was a revolutionary discovery that rocked linguistics and led to massive modifications in the understanding of Indo-European. It involves an idiosyncratic alternation where *r* alternates with *n* in a small class of words shared by Hittite and several Indo-European languages. It is illustrated by words like Hittite *wâdar* 'water' with *r*, but *weden-as* 'water's' with *n*, not the expected *wadar-as*. This is cognate with Greek *hudōr* 'water' but *hudatos* (< *hudņtos*) 'water's'. (Note also the similarity of Hittite *wâdar* 'water' with English *water*, from Proto-Germanic *watōr* 'water'.) The unexpected alternation is seen in Latin words such as *femur* 'thigh bone' but *femin-īs* 'thigh bone's'. This irregular and unexpected alternation helped to convince the scholarly world of Hittite's affinity with Indo-European languages. I should hasten to point out that there is much more evidence confirming Hittite's Indo-European affinity than just this one case.

Basic Vocabulary

It is generally believed that potential cognates involving items from basic vocabulary are highly desirable if not necessary for supporting a hypothesis of languages being related to one another. Basic vocabulary includes very common words that have counterparts with the same meanings in almost all languages, such as terms for body parts (eye, hand, foot, nose), basic geographical and environmental terms (mountain, river, water, star, rain, hot, cold), common activities (eat, sleep, die), and low numbers (one, two, three).

However, caution is still necessary, since even words from basic vocabulary can sometimes be borrowed and thus not inherited from a common ancestor. English has a fair number of borrowings from Old

Norse, French, and Latin that involve basic vocabulary. Some examples are:

artery, from Anglo-French *arterie* 'artery', Old French *artaire* 'artery' (Modern French *artère*), inherited from Latin *arteria* 'artery', a loanword from Greek *artēriā* 'windpipe, artery'.

face, from Old French *face* 'face, appearance'.

intestine, from either from Middle French *intestin* 'intestine' or Latin *intestinum* 'gut', *intestina* (plural) 'intestines, bowels'.

leg, from Scandinavian, compare Old Norse *leggr* 'leg, leg bone, arm bone'.

mountain, from Old French *montaigne* 'mountain, mountainous region' (Modern French *montagne*).

person, from Old French *persone* 'person, human being, anyone' (Modern French *personne*) or directly from or influenced by Latin *persōna* 'person, human being, personage'.

river, from Anglo-French *rivere*, Old French *riviere* 'river bank, river, riverside'.

saliva, from Middle French *salive* 'saliva', influenced by Latin *saliva* 'spittle'.

skin, from Old Norse *skinn* 'animal hide, fur'.

sky, from Old Norse *sky* 'cloud'. Earlier it meant 'cloud' in English. The meaning of 'upper regions of the air' is known from about 1300; it replaced native *heaven* in the meaning of 'sky'.

stomach, borrowed from Old French *stomaque, estomac* 'stomach', which is inherited from Latin *stomachus* 'stomach, throat, gullet'. Earlier it was spelled *stomak*, later changed to *stomach* under influence of the spelling in Latin, though the pronunciation remained unchanged, with [k].

vein, from Old French *veine* 'vein, artery, pulse', inherited from Latin *vēna* 'blood vessel, vein, water course, vein of metal, person's natural ability or interest'.

Others would add to this list of borrowed basic vocabulary in English also *to get, to take, to give, to like, to want* (from Scandinavian), *very* (from French), *to use* and *just* (from French or Latin), and *to carry* (from Anglo-French *carier* 'transport in a vehicle', ultimately from Late Latin *carricare* 'to transport [in a cart])'. From the Leipzig-Jakarta List of Basic Vocabulary, of the 100 meanings most resistant to borrowing across languages (Haspelmath and Tadmor 2009), 12 are borrowings in English: *root, wing, to hit, leg, egg, skin, to give, to take* (from Scandinavian), and *soil, to carry, to crush, to cry* (from French).

As this shows, things that have sometimes been offered in evidence of a relationship between languages are not all indicative of true cognates.

Borrowing

In many instances, some things that have been offered in evidence of a relationship between languages turn out to be loanwords, not inherited from a common ancestor. Loanwords are a serious challenge to determining relatedness between languages. Unfortunately, loanwords mistakenly taken to be inherited cognates show up in many claims of relatedness. One example of this is from Joseph Greenberg's (1987: 108) proposed Chibchan–Paezan distant relationship, part of his <u>Amerind</u> hypothesis. As support for an assumed cognate set that Greenberg labelled as 'axe', words from only four languages were compared, but unfortunately, two of the four are loanwords. Cuitlatec (a language isolate of Mexico) *navaxo* 'knife' is borrowed from Spanish *navajo* 'knife, razor'. Tunebo (now called Uwa, a Chibchan language) *baxi-ta* 'machete' is borrowed from Spanish *machete* 'machete'. Uwa doesn't have *m* before non-nasal *a*, hence *b* substituted for *m* in this borrowed word. Many other such examples could be cited here (see Campbell and Poser 2008).

Chance (Accident)

Another thing to guard against is accidental similarity. There are hundreds of accidental similarities among unrelated languages around the world. There is even a Facebook group dedicated to such linguistic coincidences.[5] It is often suggested that 5 to 6 percent of the vocabulary of any two compared languages may be accidentally similar – of course, how similar is a judgement call.

Examples of accidentally similar words are easy to find, even among related languages. For example, English *much* and Spanish *mucho* 'much', though very similar in these two Indo-European languages, come from very different sources. Spanish *mucho* is from Latin *multus*, inherited from Proto-Indo-European **ml̥-to-*, the suffixed form of **mel-* 'strong, great'. Spanish *mucho* underwent the Spanish sound changes of *l* to *y* before *t*, and then *yt* to *ych* to *ch* (*multus* > *multo-* > *muyto* > *muycho* > *mucho*). *Much* in English comes from Old English *micel, mycel* 'great, much', which came from Proto-Germanic *mik-ila, which is from Proto-Indo-European **meg-* 'great'. Compare Latin *māgnus* 'big, great', from this same

---

[5] This website is at www.facebook.com/groups/linguisticcoincidences/?fref=nf.

Proto-Indo-European root. Another often mentioned similarity is English *day* with Spanish *día* 'day'. They are not cognates since they do not obey Grimm's Law (seen in Chapter 5) as true cognates do. English *day* is from Old English *dæg*, from Proto-Germanic **dagaz* 'day'. Spanish *día* comes from Latin *diēs* 'day', from Proto-Indo-European **dyē-*, a variant of **deiw-* 'to shine'.

Accidental similarities are not hard to find, seen in such random examples as: Proto-Jê **niw* 'new' / English *new*; Māori *kuri* 'dog' / English *cur*; Lake Miwok (Utian, California) *hóllu* 'hollow' / English *hollow*; Gbaya (Niger-Congo, central Africa) *be* 'to be' / English *be*; Yana (language isolate, California) *t'inii-* 'small' / English *teeny, tiny*; Persian *bad* 'bad' / English *bad*, among massive numbers of others. Lack of systematic sound correspondences helps sort out such accidental similarities.

Semantic Constraints

Most historical linguists believe that when attempting to find language family relationships for potential cognates in different languages it is important for the words to be identical or very nearly the same in meaning. It is risky to present similar-sounding words that have markedly different meanings as potential evidence of relatedness among languages under the assumption that meaning shifts have taken place. Of course meaning can change (as seen in Chapter 3), but in hypotheses of linguistic kinship, the greater the meaning latitude permitted in compared forms, the easier it is to find forms which sound similar that have no historical connection. Many unpersuasive examples of compared words which have quite different meanings have been presented as evidence in various hypotheses of a distant family relationship.

For example, in the Nostratic hypothesis, mentioned below, there are a number of cases of proposed cognates that are based on words in the different languages that have very different meanings. The following are some examples, where the meanings separated by slashes are those of distinct words in different languages that are assumed to be cognate with the other words in the set: 'lip'/'mushroom'/'soft outgrowth'; 'grow up'/'become'/'tree'/'be'; 'crust'/'rough'/'scab'; among others.

Examples presented as cognates in the Amerind hypothesis have proposed cognates with the following very divergent meanings: 'excrement'/'night'/'grass'; 'body'/'belly'/'heart'/'skin'/'meat'/ 'be greasy'/'fat'/'deer'; 'child'/'copulate'/'son'/'girl'/'boy'/'tender'/'bear'/'small'; and 'field'/'devil'/'bad'/'underneath'/'bottom'.

Onomatopoeia

Onomatopoeic words imitate sounds in the real world associated with a word's meaning, things like *bow-wow* for the noise of dogs barking and *cock-a-doodle-doo* for roosters crowing. The connection to the sounds in nature can be so strong that it inhibits some onomatopoeic words from undergoing otherwise regular sound changes. For example, English *peep*, from earlier *pīpen*, should have become /paip/ by regular sound change in the <u>Great Vowel Shift</u> (seen in Chapter 5). Indeed, *pipe* did undergo this change. However, *peep* was prevented from doing so by the influence of onomatopoeia, keeping the word sounding more like the sound baby birds make that it refers to. Examples involving onomatopoeia must not be relied on in proposals of <u>distant genetic relationship</u>, since they may be similar across languages because they independently imitate the same sound in nature and not because they are inherited from a common ancestor.

One way to reduce the sound-imitative factor is not to rely for evidence of relatedness on words that are known cross-linguistically often to involve imitative forms, for example, words meaning 'blow', 'breathe', 'suck', 'laugh', 'cough', 'sneeze', 'break'/'cut'/'chop'/'split', 'cricket', 'crow' (and many bird names in general), 'frog'/'toad', 'lungs', 'baby'/'infant', 'beat'/'hit'/'pound', 'call'/'shout', 'choke', 'cry', 'drip'/'drop', 'hiccough', 'kiss', 'shoot', 'snore', 'spit', 'suck', and 'whistle'.

Unfortunately, onomatopoeic words are often found in proposals of distant genetic relationships. One illustrative example is the words from various languages meaning 'to blow' for which the forms *pui, pʰu, puhi, pu, pi, fwo* have been given as evidence for the Amerind hypothesis presented by Greenberg (1987: 196).

Nursery Forms

It is generally recognized that nursery words, the *mama–nana–papa–dada–caca* sort, should be avoided in considerations of potential linguistic relationships, since they typically share a high degree of cross-linguistic similarity which is not due to common ancestry.

Short Forms and Unmatched Segments

How long proposed cognates are and the number of matched sounds within them are important, since the greater the number of matching sounds in a proposed cognate set, the less likely it is that accident accounts for the similarity. It is easy to find accidental similarities across languages for short forms (composed of only a consonant and a vowel [CV], a vowel and a consonant [VC], or just a consonant [C] or a vowel [V]). Similarly, it is also easy to find accidental similarity if only a small part of a word is compared to words in other languages when the various other sounds in the compared forms are not similar. Comparisons involving short forms are not convincing.

The Sound–Meaning Isomorphism Criterion

A generally accepted principle permits only comparisons that involve both sound and meaning together. Similarity in sound alone (for example, the presence of tone contrasts in compared languages) or similarity in meaning alone (for example, grammatical gender in the languages compared) are not reliable. These things often develop independently of genealogical relationship. Such similarities can be due to <u>diffusion</u>, accident, or typological tendencies.

Only Linguistic Evidence

Another principle permits only linguistic information, no non-linguistic considerations, as evidence of family relationship. Shared cultural traits, mythology, folklore, and genes must be eliminated from arguments for linguistic relatedness. The wisdom of this principle becomes clear when the many strange proposals of linguistic relatedness based on non-linguistic evidence are taken into account. For example, some earlier African classifications proposed that Ari (Omotic) belongs to either Nilo-Saharan or Sudanic 'because the Ari people are Negroes', that Moru and Madi belong to Sudanic because they are located in central Africa, or that Fula is Hamitic because its speakers herd cattle, are Muslims, and are tall and Caucasoid. Clearly, language affinities can be independent of cultural, biological, or geographic considerations such as these.

Erroneous Analysis of the Structure of Compared Words

Unfortunately, misanalyzed words can make comparisons seem more similar than they are, in two ways. A clear example of how missing word divisions can skew comparisons is seen in Greenberg's (1987: 229) example of Rama (a Chibchan language) *mukuik* 'hand', which he considered evidence for his Amerind hypothesis. Actually, *mukuik* is from Rama *mu-* 'your' + *kwi:k* 'hand'. The root *kwi:k* 'hand' is not similar to Greenberg's postulated Amerind *ma-ki* 'hand', once it is understood that *mu-* is the prefix meaning 'your' and not part of the root meaning 'hand'.

Another example is Greenberg's (1987: 152) comparison of Tzotzil (Mayan, of Mexico) *tiʔil* 'hole' with Lake Miwok (Utian, California) *talok^h* 'hole', Atakapa (language isolate, Louisiana) *tol* 'anus', Totonac (Totonacan, Mexico) *tan* 'buttocks', and Takelma (language isolate, Oregon) *telkan* 'buttocks'. Greenberg considered these as evidence supporting his postulated <u>Penutian</u> branch of his proposed Amerind. The Tzotzil word is actually *tiʔ-il*, composed of *tiʔ* 'mouth' + -*il* 'indefinite possessive suffix', together meaning 'edge, border, outskirts, lips, mouth', but not 'hole'. The appropriate comparison with the root *tiʔ* 'mouth' bears little resemblance to the other forms or meanings in this comparison set. Critics were wont to point out that examples such as this one show that the method used couldn't tell its anuses from a hole in the ground.

Erroneously added divisions in words to segment off assumed different meaningful pieces is the other way in which misanalysis can skew comparisons. For example, for Yurumanguí (a language isolate of Colombia), Greenberg (1987: 214, 246), in his Amerind hypothesis, segmented the word *joima* 'saliva' as *jo* 'mouth' + *ima* 'water'. However, there is no evidence in Yurumanguí that *joima* has any internal analysis. Greenberg assumed that *joima* 'saliva' was connected with *čuma* 'to drink,' which he segmented as *č-uma* with no evidence that *č-* is a prefix of Yurumanguí. There is no basis for any of the four pieces he posited, *jo* 'mouth,' *ima* 'water,' *č-* 'prefix,' and *uma* 'drink,' though these unmotivated segmentations seem to suggest greater similarity with some of the forms in other languages to which Greenberg compared the Yurumanguí word. (See Poser 1992.)

Spurious Forms and Scribal Errors

Many proposed cognates turn out to be just erroneous, due to mistakes in handling data. Errors of these kinds can make compared elements seem similar when in fact they are not. For example, in the proposed evidence for their Mayan–Mixe-Zoquean hypothesis, Brown and Witkowski (1979) compared Mixe-Zoquean words meaning 'shell' with K'iche' (Mayan) *sak'*, said to mean 'lobster'. However, the K'iche' word actually means 'grasshopper' – a mistranslation of the Spanish gloss *langosta* found in a K'iche'–Spanish dictionary. In Guatemala *langosta* means 'grasshopper', though it means 'lobster' in other varieties of Spanish. While a 'shell'–'lobster' comparison is pretty implausible, a comparison of 'shell' with 'grasshopper' is extremely unlikely to involve words inherited due to common ancestry that later underwent such semantic shifts.

In another case, Gurov (1989) suggested that Kusunda (a language isolate in Nepal) was related to the Yeniseian languages (of Siberia). One of his only nineteen lexical parallels, all unclear, was Kusunda *tou* 'snake', where he misread the gloss 'snake' as 'smoke' and compared it to Proto-Yeniseian **du(h)* 'smoke' (cited by van Driem 2001: 260).

In his evidence for his proposed Amerind, none of Greenberg's (1987) Quapaw (Siouan) words is actually from Quapaw. They are from Biloxi or Ofo. Apparently, Greenberg mistakenly jumped a line in his notebooks as he entered the supposed but erroneous Quapaw forms.

A favorite example of mine of scribal problems involves Beothuk, a language isolate of Newfoundland, known only from three short vocabulary lists; a number of later copies made of these three originals are also extant. However, as John Hewson (1982: 181) pointed out, "the vocabularies are full of errors of every kind." They were taken down in chaotic English spellings, and "none of the native informants knew sufficient English to communicate in any satisfactory manner, so that the only means of interpreting the meaning of Beothuk words was through mime, drawing and pointing." Hewson (1982: 181–182) explained some of these errors. In one case, about what Albert Gatschet gave as *stiocena* 'thumb', Hewson wrote:

This item had started life as *Ifweena* "thigh" in the Leigh vocabulary . . . When Leigh came to copy his vocabulary for John Peyton . . . he wrote the English *thumb* and then instead of copying the Beothuk word *pooeth*, inadvertently wrote instead the Beothuk word *ifweena* which happens to be the next word down the page in the original Leigh vocabulary . . . Consequently, in the so-called Peyton copy of Leigh, the entry appears as: *Itweena* "thumb." Another copy of this item was made by James P. Howley and sent to Sir William Dawson . . . who in turn copied it out by hand and sent a copy to the Reverend Dr. Silas Rand . . . Mr. Rand in turn copied it out and sent a copy to Gatschet. By the time this item had gone through all these varying copyings, the original capital *i* had become an *s*, the following ambiguous *f* [the only example of an *f* in the corpus] had become a *t*, the *w* had become an *i* and an *o*, the double *e* had become *ce* and only the *na* had survived intact.

Clearly comparison of *stiocena* 'thumb' with words of other languages in a search for possible relationships would give no valuable result, given that the word recorded as *ifweena* 'thigh' is what it really was about. Unfortunately, "data" of this sort were utilized in several attempts to classify Beothuk with other languages, especially with Algonquian.

Distant Genealogical Relationships

Judging from reports in the media, we might imagine that proposals of distant genealogical relationships among languages is one of the most burning topics in contemporary linguistics. Postulated but unconfirmed remote language families such as <u>Amerind</u>, <u>Nostratic</u>, and <u>Proto-World</u> have been featured enthusiastically in newspapers, television documentaries, semi-scientific journals and magazines, and various other media outlets. And yet these same proposals have been roundly rejected by mainstream historical linguists. Why should this be? The answer is because the evidence presented in favor of these claims was not sufficient to show that an explanation other than inheritance from a common ancestor couldn't provide a better account of the similarities detected.[6]

The following lists some of the better-known hypotheses that would group together languages which are not yet known to be related. The list gives an idea of what is involved.

Altaic, a proposed grouping of Turkic, Tungusic, and Mongolian, to which some proposals also add Japonic, Koreanic, and others.

Amerind, Joseph Greenberg's (1987) unsuccessful proposal which would lump together all the 170 or so language families of the Americas except Eskimo-Aleut and NaDené.

Indo-Uralic, Indo-European + Uralic.

Nilo-Saharan, Greenberg's (1963) grouping which contains most African languages not otherwise classified as belonging to one of his other three large African groupings.

Nostratic, in various versions. The best-known one groups Indo-European, Uralic, Altaic, Kartvelian, Dravidian, and Afroasiatic, though some add also Chuckchi-Kamchatkan, Eskimo-Aleut, Sumerian, and Nivkh.

Penutian, in various versions which group a large number of American Indian language families and isolates.

Proto-World (Global Etymologies), whose supporters believe all the world's languages are demonstrably related.

Transeurasian, a name that those favoring an expansive version of the Altaic hypothesis have adopted in order to avoid confusion about the status of Altaic. Transeurasian was intended to include supposed core Altaic (Turkic, Mongolic, and Tungusic), plus also Japonic and Koreanic. Some suspect that it is primarily a change in name only in order to avoid the negativity surrounding the Altaic hypothesis.

Yeniseian-NaDené, Yeniseian + NaDené.[7]

---

[6] For detailed discussion of how major language families have been established and the methods needed, see Campbell and Poser (2008).

[7] For a critical assessment of the more prominent of these hypotheses, see Campbell and Poser (2008) and Campbell (2024).

What Is the Prognosis for Discovering New Family Relationships among Languages?

Most proposals of remote linguistic relationships have not been successful, usually either because the methods employed have been inadequate or because the evidence presented is insufficient to show that it could not be explained better in other ways, or both. Nevertheless, there are a number of success stories where previously unknown or disputed relationships later came to be established, relying on adequate methods and evidence. Some examples are:

Algic, demonstrated to the satisfaction of all, showing Yurok and Wiyot of California and the Algonquian languages belong to the same language family.

Austroasiatic, with Munda and Mon-Khmer.

Austronesian, with the Formosan branches of the family firmly established, related to the Malayo-Polynesian languages.

Harákmbut-Katukinan, Harákmbut + Katukinan.

Hittite and the other Anatolian languages, demonstrated to be Indo-European.

Lule-Vilelan, with Lule + Vilela.

Macro-Jê, now confirmed. Several things formerly thought to be possibly independent language families are now joined in a large, more inclusive language family.

Pano-Takanan, Panoan + Takanan.

Sino-Tibetan, together with clarifications of the relatedness of several languages to the family.

Tikuna-Yurí, Tikuna + Yurí.

Tlapanec-Subiaba's membership in Otomanguean, now demonstrated.

Uto-Aztecan, once contested, now demonstrated to the satisfaction of all.

These success stories lend support to the belief and hope that additional cases of language family relationships will probably be demonstrated in the future. Although language relatedness and language classification must be based on application of proper methods, there is good reason to be optimistic about possible future discoveries in the classification of the world's languages.

9   Writing and the Magic of Writing Systems

And perhaps the Druids were in the right, who . . . did not make use of letters . . . because they thought the use of them impaired the memory.
(James Burnet [Lord Monboddo], *Of the Origin and Progress of Language*)

Introduction

In this chapter, the origin and development of writing systems are examined, with the development of English writing conventions in focus. We look at how old written records can be utilized to understand more about the history of a language, illustrated with examples mostly from the history of English writing. And we look at mystical beliefs about letters and writing.

An important notation used in this chapter is < ... >. It indicates that the material in the brackets is presented exactly as found in the source, for example as written in some early manuscript.

There is definitely no lack of history and folklore in which writing, written symbols, and writing systems are considered mystical and magical. Writing evolved to record economic transactions, taxes and tribute, administrative proceedings, and so on, but writing also served religion and mystical beliefs. It was widely believed in ancient, and even modern, times that written symbols and words possess ritualistic powers of their own. This is easy to see in the many magical symbols and texts of spells, curses, and incantations from hither and yon written on tombs, sarcophagi, ritual objects, and personal possessions, for protection or as warnings. The assumption that words can have magical power is seen in such words as *abracadabra, alakazam,* and *hocus pocus.* The origin of none of these three words is clear.

The often-encountered connection between writing and ritual or religion is clear in the Ancient Egyptian god Thoth, seen as the inventor of writing, wisdom, and secret knowledge. Over the centuries, a number of **grimoires** were produced, textbooks of magic and sorcery, the manuals for many occult and secret societies. The word *grimoire* is borrowed from

French *grimoire*, which perhaps surprisingly is an altered form of *grammaire* 'grammar'. This comes from Classical Latin *grammatica*, which means 'grammar' but also meant the methodical study of literature and rhetoric more broadly. By the Middle Ages, *grammatica* came to mean primarily the study of Latin and came also to mean learning in general, the kind peculiar to the learned class. The mostly illiterate masses believed that this included also magic and astrology, and so French *grammaire* came to be a name sometime used to refer to these occult themes. It is in this sense that it came into earlier English as the now archaic *gramarye* 'occult learning, magic, or sorcery', also 'necromancy' or 'enchantment', as well as in the modified form *grimoire* 'conjuring book, textbook of magic'.

Especially closely linked with written symbols is **Kabbalah,** a mystic branch of Judaism which has as one of its chief beliefs that there is a mystic power in Hebrew letters. *Kabbalah* is from Hebrew, meaning 'reception, received lore, tradition', 'tradition of mystical interpretation of the Old Testament', and from that 'any secret or esoteric "science"'.

Runic Writing

It would be far beyond practical to attempt to survey all cases where letters or characters in writing systems have been associated with magic and ritual. Instead, let's just focus for a moment on runic writing as a forceful representative. Runes were carved on pieces of wood, stones, bones, weapons, tools, jewelry, amulets, memorial stones, and churches. Some runic inscriptions were read from right to left, others from left to right. Nearly all Germanic peoples used runes, but most inscriptions were discovered in Scandinavia.

If we google "runes," a vast number of sites would have us believe that for medieval people, the runes were magic, and they would leave no doubt about the superstitious beliefs many hold today, too, about runes, thought to be a writing system for wizardry and witchcraft. However, the belief in the extent of rune magic is exaggerated, mostly a notion from the twentieth century. Most of the runic inscriptions that have been found convey more mundane messages for practical, everyday purposes, although they did also have associations with Norse religion, poetry, and magic. Runic magic relates more to medieval and modern times than to the Viking age. Calling on the magic of "Viking runes" probably would not have been recognized by the Vikings. (More on the magic of runes below.)

The runes are in fact phonetic characters in a family of writing systems from early northwest Europe called Futhark (see Figure 9.1). The name **Futhark** is an <u>acronym</u> based on the first five letters of the alphabet.

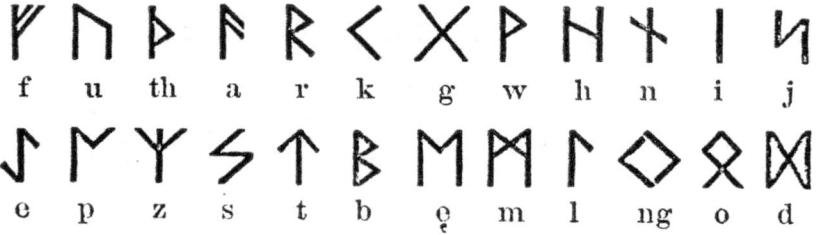

Figure 9.1 Runic alphabet
Source: Nastasic / DigitalVision Vectors / Getty Images.

Elder (Older) Futhark was used from about 100 to 800 CE. **Younger Futhark** is from 800 to 1100 CE. It is more simplified; it is also the source of most of the runic characters seen in games, on T-shirts, and in tattoos today. There is also **Anglo-Frisian Futhorc**, from which the **Anglo-Saxon Futhorc** comes. Medieval runes were in use from about 1100 to 1500 CE.

The word *rune* didn't refer only to the writing, but included in its meaning also poem and song. According to the sagas, runic inscriptions could help predict the future, protect against misfortune, be used for healing and for curses and spells. The poem *Hávamál* tells how Odin hung himself from the world tree Yggdrasil in order to learn wisdom. He hung on the tree, pierced by a spear, for nine nights and days, and just as he was about to die, he found the runes, grabbed them, and lived. The *Hávamál* and other poems associate these runes with the songs of magical spells that Odin could recall on demand.

The English word *rune* has a solid but convoluted history, which tells us more about the meaning and use of runes in the past. Old English had *rūn* 'runic letter, secret, mystery, (secret) council'. This word can be reconstructed to Proto-Germanic **rūnō*, which is also the source of Old Norse *rūn* 'runic character, secret sign'. This is from Proto-Indo-European **rū-no* 'mystery, secret', thought to be derived from **reuh-* 'to intone, mumble'. It is also the source of Gaelic *run* 'secret, mystery, deceit, desire'. Had Old English *rūn* survived, it would have come down to us as *rown*, but it was abandoned in the mid 1400s, when runes were no longer used. Modern English *rune* is a resurrection, reintroduced by scholars in the late 1600s from Scandinavian sources. Finnish *runo* 'poem, poetic meter, song, verse, lyric' is borrowed from Germanic. All of this helps to confirm that the original sense of *rune* included at least 'poetic song' as well as 'secret marks, writing'.

Other Writing Systems

Let's turn now to the history of some other writing systems.

Alphabetic Writing from Phoenician to English

The modern English alphabet has a whole string of earlier alphabets and scripts in its genealogical bloodline. In fact, most Old World alphabets have the same common ancestor. The Proto-Sinaitic script (mid 19th century BCE to mid 16th century BCE), illustrated in Figure 9.2, was the ancestor of the Phoenician alphabet. The Phoenician alphabet (10th century BCE to 2nd century BCE) is considered the ancestor of most modern alphabets. It is shown in Figure 9.3.

The Phoenician alphabet begot the Greek alphabet, from whence the Etruscan alphabet, which lies behind the Latin (Roman) alphabet, from whence the alphabets of most western European languages, including English. The very name *alphabet* reveals this origin. *Alphabet* comes from a combination of the names of the first two letters of the Greek alphabet, *alpha* (uppercase *A*, lowercase *α*) and *beta* (uppercase *B*, lowercase *β*). These letter names, however, are not originally Greek; rather, they are borrowed from Phoenician. Characters in the Phoenician script represent consonants but not vowels; such systems are called "abjad" writing. The Greek name *alpha* is borrowed from the name of the first letter of the Phoenician alphabet, *'aleph*, ⟨. It represented a glottal stop – not a sound of Greek nor of written English. It is like the sound in the pause between

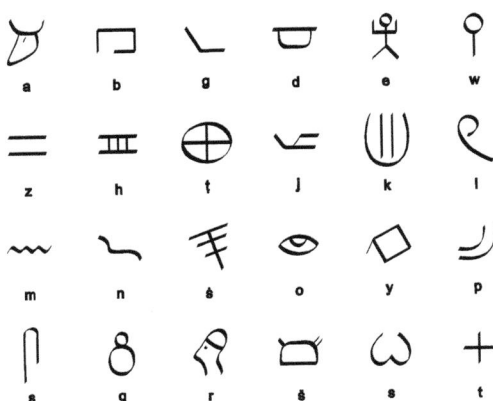

Figure 9.2 Proto-Sinaitic script
Source: iSidhe / iStock / Getty Images Plus.

Figure 9.3 Phoenician alphabet
Source: Adobest / iStock / Getty Images Plus.

the two parts of *oh-oh!* It represented the first sound in the Phoenician word *'aleph* 'ox', for which this letter was named. The sign depicts the head of an ox – the <A> of modern alphabets now seems turned upward, with the top originally depicting the ox's snout and the two lines at the bottom representing its horns. However, Greek had no glottal stop and so Greeks took this symbol to represent *A* instead, the first vowel of *alpha*, the first letter of the Greek alphabet. The second part of *alphabet* is from the second letter of the Phoenician alphabet, ◁ *bēt*, which means 'house'. It represents the first sound of *beta*, the borrowed name of the Greek letter, *B*. The symbol for Phoenician *bēt* represents a house, more clearly seen in its form in the Proto-Sinaitic script, and in the corresponding signs for 'house' in Egyptian hieroglyphics, ⊏⊐. The name *alphabet* comes from the combination of the names for these first two letters in Greek, *alpha* and *beta*, borrowed from Phoenician.

History of Alphabetic Symbols Used to Write English

Anglo-Saxon scribes used the Latin (Roman) alphabet, a descendant of sorts of the Phoenician, Greek, and Etruscan alphabets, to write Old English, but they added some letters not present in the Latin alphabet:

<æ>, called 'ash' after the runic letter *æsc*, the vowel of *bat, mash*

<þ>, the runic letter 'thorn', for the "th" sound as in *think, bath*

<p>, the runic letter 'wynn', for *w* as in *wide, beware*

<ð> 'edh', a modification based on the Latin letter *d*, used to represent the "th" sound of *this, other*. In Old English it represented the pronunciation of "th" between vowels or between *r* and a vowel, as in *eorðe* 'earth', although scribes often used it interchangeably with *þ*, to represent both kinds of "th" pronunciations in the Old English, as in *thin* (with [θ]) and in *this* (with [ð]).

After the Norman Conquest of 1066, Norman French scribes spelled English according to French orthographic conventions. The non-Latin letters that had been used to write Old English were dropped. Digraphs – two letters to represent a single sound – came into use, for example <ch> for the "ch" sound /č/ (in *church*) and <th> for the "th" sound /θ/ (of *thank*). The combinations <ph>, <th>, and <ch> were known in Latin and French spellings of words of Greek origin, and <h> came to be used in other digraphs to represent English sounds not present in Latin or French. One of these was <gh> for, [x] as in *right* or *thought*, where earlier the sound represented by <gh> was pronounced as the last sound in *Bach* ([x]). Another was <sh> for "sh" ([š], IPA [ʃ]), as in *shoot*). Yet another was <wh> for "hw," as in *which, where*, in varieties of English that contrast the pronunciation of *which* with that of *witch*, and of *whine* with that of *wine*.

The letters <i> and <j> were not originally distinct; <j> was just a longer curved version of <i> used for writing the last *i* in Latin words that ended in double *i*, as in <filij> for *filii* 'sons'. For English scribes <y> was the version of <j> used for the second *i* in these cases and for the last *i* of words in general (as in *merry, mighty*), and also sometimes for *i* in other places in words, as in older spellings such as <wyfe> or <wife> and <tyme> or <time>. In short, <j> was just a long "i", and <y> was just another way of writing <j> or <i>. This accounts for such differences in spelling as *holy* but *holiest* and *holiday* (from *holy day*), *carry* but *carried*, *pretty* but *prettier*, *mighty* but *mightiest*, and so on. Originally there was no dot over *i* and *j*, and the dot is still lacking from capital (uppercase) *I* and *J*. The dot owes its origin to a small sloping line that came to be placed above the very slim letter *i* to distinguish it from letters composed of more

Figure 9.4 INRI
Source: Wikimedia Commons.

strokes such as *m*, *n*, and *u*, often difficult to distinguish in the handwriting of scribes. The dot was also placed over *j*, since it was just considered a variant of *i*. The word *jot* comes in here in its meaning of 'stroke, smallest letter'. It comes from the Greek letter *iota*, like English *i*.

The lack of distinction between <I> and <J> is illustrated well in the '*INRI*' caption on Roman Catholic representations of crucifixes and paintings of the crucifixion of Christ (see Figure 9.4). It is an abbreviation of the title Pontius Pilate was reported to have had written on the cross of Jesus, *Iesvs Nazarenvs Rex Ivdaeorvm*, or in more conventional modernized spelling, *Jesus Nazarenus Rex Judaeorum* 'Jesus of Nazareth, King of the Jews'.

Association of <j> with the "j" sound "dzh" ([ĵ], IPA [dʒ]) as in *jam*, *judge*, *banjo* is due to developments in French. Latin *j* (pronounced like "y" in *yes*, *young*, *royal*), came to be pronounced in French as "dzh" at the beginning of words due to a sound change – "y" > "j" (as in *jam*, *judge*, and so on, today). This new "j" sound was still spelled in English as <j>, which no longer represented the "y" sound, as it did in the earlier spelling convention used to write English. Early French loanwords in English reflect an earlier pronunciation with the <j> as the "dzh" sound ([ĵ], IPA [dʒ]), as in *jolly*, *journey*, *juice*, and so on. Later, this "j" sound ("dzh") in French changed further to a "zh" sound ([ž], IPA [ʒ]), as the middle sound in English *pleasure*, *azure*, *Asia*, although the convention of writing <j> to represent the "j" sound ("dzh") had already become established for English orthography before this later French sound change (of the "dzh" sound to a "zh" sound) took place. Thus, these

French words, the source of the English loans with <j> pronounced as "dzh", are in Modern French *joli* 'pretty', *journée* 'day's earnings, day's travel', and *jus* 'juice', all pronounced now with the "zh" sound ([ž/], IPA [ʒ]) at the beginning.

The letters *u*, *v*, and *w* have a similar history. In Latin spelling, which persisted in earlier French orthography, *u* and *v* were interchangeable, used for either the vowel sound "u" ([u]), as in *abuse*, *moon*, *soup*, or for the consonant sound "v" ([v]), as in *very*, *vile*, *brave*), seen above in *Iesvs Nazarenvs Rex Ivdaeorvm* 'Jesus of Nazareth, King of the Jews' (in modern spelling, *Jesus Nazarenus Rex Judaeorum*). In Classical Latin, the <v>, when it represented a consonant, had the sound of "w" (as in *witch*, *weasel*, *war*) – as in the quote *veni*, *vidi*, *vici* [weni, widi, wiki] 'I came, I saw, I conquered' attributed to Julius Caesar around 47 BCE in describing a decisive victory in a battle. In the early Christian era, Latin changed this "w" pronunciation to a "v" sound ([v]), as in *vine*, *valley*, *veal*, though the two letters, <u> and <v>, continued to be used essentially interchangeably for both the "u" and the "v" sounds. The *u* shape of the letter in time came to be associated with vowels and the *v* shape with consonants, and eventually they came to be considered as distinct letters.

The letter <w> was not used in Latin. The Norman French scribes needed a way to distinguish the "v" and "u" sounds from the "w" sound in English. For earlier Anglo-Saxon writers, the symbol <ρ>, called *wyn* or *wen*, was used for *w*, but all symbols for writing English not found in the Latin alphabet were dropped by the Norman French scribes. They started writing <u> twice, together, to represent the "w" sound, a digraph with double *u*, as seen in the name of the letter, 'double-u', although the orthographic distinction between <u> and <v> had not yet been settled and so "double u" could be written either as *uu* or as *vv*, later conjoined into a single letter, *w*.

English orthographic practices had a few other unexpected quirks. For instance, some words that today are spelled with *o* should have been spelled with *u* according to expectations from the actual pronunciation. For example, in words with a *v* after a "u" sound, a spelling of <uv> would have been expected. However, the scribes wrote <ov>, for example in *move* (with the sound of "u" of *boot*) or in *love*, which in varieties of English in northern England is still pronounced with the "u" of *book*, and not with the "uh" of *luck* as in North American and other varieties of English. The orthographic convention used by the scribes was to close the <u> in writing, making it into an <o>, in order to distinguish "uv" in writing from sequences of letters difficult to identify in squiggled handwriting, such as *um*, *un*, *uv*, and *uw*. So, <love> 'love', from Old English *lufu*, was never pronounced with any sound we would ordinarily associate with the spelling of <o> or the pronunciation of [o].

Philology: Getting Language History from Older Written Sources

There are a variety of techniques for getting information about the history of a language from older written records. Today this is often called <u>philology</u>. The utility of these techniques for this purpose in any given case naturally depends on various things – on the kind of writing, the structure of the language, the quantity of written records, accessibility, the interpretive ability of the scholar, for example. Essentially, anything that can be put to use for unraveling further the history of the language involved is fair game. Often, the information we can obtain for understanding the history of the language and its structure at the time when the texts were written is a matter of luck, a question of what may happen to show up in the sources available. Some valuable sources of information for interpreting the sounds behind the written symbols include rhymes, meter, variations in spellings, clues from related languages and dialects, and, in rare cases, descriptions of pronunciation given by writers from earlier times. It will be fun to look at a few examples utilizing these kinds of sources of information.

Rhymes and Poetry

In Middle English texts, the word *night* was spelled variously as <niht>, <nyʒt>, <nyght>, <nicht>, among others. Even though the sound represented variously by <gh>, <ʒ>, <ch>, and <h> is lost from Modern English *night* /nait/, evidence from multiple sorts leads to the conclusion that the sound represented in these spellings of *night* and other similar words was the sound of <ch> in the German name *Bach*. In technical terms this sound is a voiceless velar fricative [x], like a "k" sound but without the airstream being completely blocked, open enough to create friction during the production of the sound. Some of the evidence for the conclusion that these spellings represented [x] in Middle English comes from Middle English poetic texts, where words spelled with <gh>, <ʒ>, <ch>, and <h>, as in spellings of *night*, rhyme only with other words spelled in this way and never with words which contain the same vowel but lack <gh>, <ʒ>, <ch>, or <h>. For example, Chaucer rhymes *knight* with *wight* 'strong' but never with *white*. (See Lass 1992: 30.)

Clues from Related Languages

Sometimes we can get clues to the interpretation of what was written from related languages. In the case of Middle English spellings with <gh>, <ʒ>, <ch>, <h>, Modern English has no matching sound; however, we can be more confident in the hypothesis that this represented the <ch> sound of *Bach* (the velar fricative [x]) because English's closest relatives have [x] in cognate words, as in Dutch *nacht* ([naxt]) and German *Nacht* ([naxt]) 'night'.

Variant Spellings

Alternative spellings of the same thing can provide an indirect source of information about changing pronunciations in the past. They sometime give clues concerning what was changing and when the change took place, called "occasional spellings." English spelling conventions were starting to regularize in the 1600s, as printers began to use uniform spellings, but spelling was not fixed. Occasional spellings rather than the more expected ones from the period show ongoing changes in pronunciation. For example, variants such as *ceme/came*, *credyll/cradel* 'cradle', and *teke/take* show that the former "a" sound (as in *father*) had changed or was changing to something closer to the modern "e(i)" sound (as in *eight*) in these words. Examples such as *symed/semed* 'seemed', *stypylle/stepel* 'steeple', reflect the change of long "e" to long "i", part of the Great Vowel Shift (seen in Chapter 5). Spellings of *marcy/mercy* 'mercy', *sarten/certein* 'certain', *parson/persoun* 'person', and so on, show that "er" changed to "ar" in the pronunciation of the writers of these forms. This change was fairly general in the speech of certain classes of people, but it was ultimately lost as people changed their pronunciation back to the more common or prestigious versions of words with these sounds. However, it left English with such doublets as *clerk/clark*, *person/parson*, *vermin/varmint*, and *university/varsity*.

Interpretation Based on Foreign Material

A clear example comes from Gothic, a Germanic language and so a sister of English, known only from earlier written records. The principal source of information on Gothic is Bishop Wulfila's (311–382) translation of the Bible from Greek to Gothic, part of which has survived. The orthography was based on the Greek spelling conventions in use at the time when Wulfila (portrayed in Figure 9.5 and also known as *Ulfila, Ulfilas, Wulfilas*) wrote.

   The Gothic spellings with <ai> are interpreted as representing [ɛ:] (like "e" in *bed, ten, set*, only pronounced longer), and those with <au> as [ɔ:] (like the *o*-like sound in words such as *caught, bought, paw, walk*, though lengthened, in English dialects that have not merged this sound with [a]). This is based on the value of <ai> and <au> in Greek spelling at the time. This interpretation is confirmed by the Gothic spellings of Greek names and words that appear in the text and are known to have

Figure 9.5 Bishop Wulfila, translator of the Gothic Bible
Source: Wikimedia Commons.

had [ε(:)] and [ɔ(:)] in Greek, the source language. Some examples are *Ailisabaiþ* 'Elizabeth', *Nazaraiþ* 'Nazareth', and *praúfetus* 'prophet', *Gaúmaúrra* 'Gomorrah', and *Naúbaímbaír* 'November'. This evidence from the spelling of foreign names and words in Gothic confirms the phonetic interpretation of Gothic <ai> and <au>.

Kinds of Writing Systems

Some writing systems are called **hieroglyphic** (from Greek *hieros* 'sacred' + *glúphein* 'to carve'). They are usually mixed systems with signs representing logograms (whole words) together with some phonetic signs and others. Ancient Egyptian hieroglyphic writing is a prime example. Other hieroglyphic scripts are early Sumerian and ancient

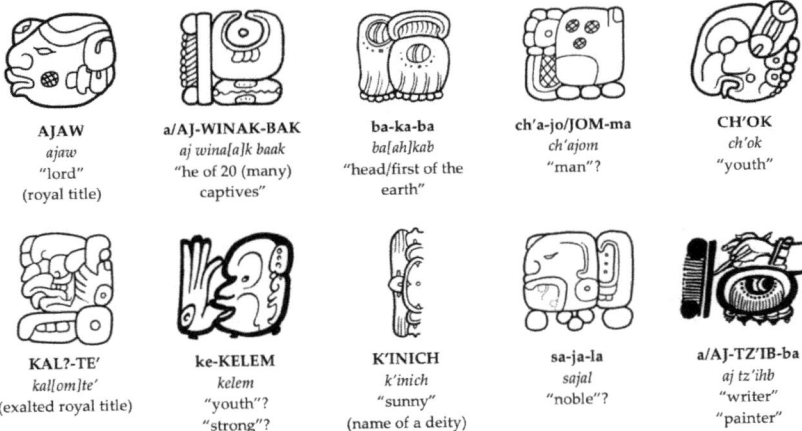

AJAW
ajaw
"lord"
(royal title)

a/AJ-WINAK-BAK
aj wina[a]k baak
"he of 20 (many)
captives"

ba-ka-ba
ba[ah]kab
"head/first of the
earth"

ch'a-jo/JOM-ma
ch'ajom
"man"?

CH'OK
ch'ok
"youth"

KAL?-TE'
kal[om]te'
(exalted royal title)

ke-KELEM
kelem
"youth"?
"strong"?

K'INICH
k'inich
"sunny"
(name of a deity)

sa-ja-la
sajal
"noble"?

a/AJ-TZ'IB-ba
aj tz'ihb
"writer"
"painter"

Figure 9.6 Maya hieroglyphic writing
Source: https://archive.org/details/maya-hieroglyphs-202312/Harri%2
0Kettunen%2C%20Christophe%20Helmke%20-%20Introduction%2
0to%20Maya%20Hieroglyphs-Wayeb%20%282020%29.pdf.

Maya writing, among others. (See Figure 9.6 for an example of Maya hieroglyphic writing.)

A number of early scripts were written in **cuneiform** ('wedge-shaped', from Latin *cuneus* 'wedge'). Cuneiform writing was done by making impressions in clay tablets with a reed stylus that left wedge-shaped marks. Some ancient languages written in cuneiform are Akkadian, Elamite, Hittite, Hurrian, Luwian, Urartian, later Sumerian, and others. Figure 9.7 shows an example of Assyrian cuneiform writing.

Some scripts are **syllabaries**. Their characters represent syllables, or more often only a consonant and vowel (the beginning of a syllable). Some languages written in syllabaries are Mycenaean Greek (Linear B; see Figure 9.8), Japanese, Cherokee, and Cree.

Rebus signs are like logograms that have been recruited into phonetic service. This is sometimes seen as the first step towards signs coming to represent sounds directly in a writing system. Rebus signs deploy signs for words (logograms) that are easier to depict graphically to represent other words or parts of words that are difficult to depict but that sound like ones that are easier to draw – rebuses are like visual puns. These signs exploit homophonous or nearly homophonous words. For example, in English

Figure 9.7 Specimen of Assyrian cuneiform writing, from a slab from Nimroud, in the British Museum
Source: duncan1890 / DigitalVision Vectors / Getty Images.

Figure 9.8 Linear B syllabary
Source: Wikimedia Commons.

the phrase 'to be or not to be' can be represented with rebuses, in a series of pictures with '2' (for *to*), 'bee' (for *be*), 'oar' (for *or*), 'knot' (for *not*), and '2' and 'bee' again (for *to be*).

Many scripts are **alphabetic**, where each symbol (letter) usually represents a single sound, whether a consonant or vowel, as in the English alphabet.

Some better-known writing systems include the following:

Akkadian cuneiform (2500 BCE to 100 CE)

Anatolian hieroglyphics (called 'Hittite' hieroglyphics, though representing the Luwian language, ca. 1400 to 700 BCE)

Aztec writing (ca. 1400 to 1600 CE, logographic with rebus signs)

Brahmi script (syllabary, 400 BCE to 300 CE), ancestor of many South Asian and other scripts, for example those used for Burmese, Thai, and Tibetan, as well as Devanagari, used to write Sanskrit and its descendants (*Praktits*), including Hindi, Marathi, Bengali, Gujarati, Nepali, and others

Cherokee syllabary (from 1821 CE to present), illustrated in Figure 9.9

Chinese (1500 BCE to present, logographic) – Chinese kanji was influential in the writing that developed for several other East Asian languages

	A	E	I	O	U	V
	D a	R e	T i	Ꭳ o	Oʼ u	i v
G/K	Ꭶ ga Ꭺ ka	Ᏻ ge	Ᏹ gi	A go	J gu	E gv
H	Ꭽ ha	Ꭾ he	Ꭿ hi	Ꮀ ho	Ꮁ hu	Ꮂ hv
L	W la	Ꮈ le	Ꮅ li	G lo	M lu	Ꮑ lv
M	Ꮉ ma	Ꮋ me	H mi	Ꮊ mo	Ꮄ mu	
N	Ꮕ na Ꮏ hna Ᏽ nah	Ꮑ ne	h ni	Z no	Ꮄ nu	O⸱ **nu**
QU/ KW	Ꮖ qua	Ꮗ que	Ꮘ qui	Ꮙ quo	Ꮚ quu	Ꮛ quv
S	Ꮝ s Ꮠ sa	4 se	Ꮖ si	Ꮢ so	Ꮣ su	R sv
D/T	Ꮣ da Ꮤ ta	Ꮥ de Ꮦ te	Ꮧ di Ꮨ ti	V do	Ꮪ du	Ꮫ dv
DL/ TL	Ꮬ dia	Ꮭ tia	L tie	C tli	Ꮮ tlo	Ꮯ tlu	P tlv
TS/J	G tsa	Ꮴ tse	Ꮵ tsi	K tso	Ꮷ tsu	C tsv
W	G wa	Ꮺ we	Ꮻ wi	Ꮼ wo	9 wu	6 wv
Y	Ꮿ ya	ẞ ye	Ᏸ yi	Ᏺ yo	G yu	B yv

Figure 9.9 Cherokee syllabary
Source: Wikimedia Commons.

Coptic (100 BCE to present), adopted from Greek with five letters added from Egyptian hieroglyphics

Cree 'syllabics' (syllabary, 1840 CE to present)

Cyrillic alphabet (800 CE to present), invented by the brothers, Saint Cyril and Saint Methodius, based on the Greek alphabet. It is used to write Russian, Ukrainian, Serbian, Bulgarian, Macedonian, and the non-Slavic languages Chechen, Kazakh, Uzbek, Kyrgyz, Tajik, Chuvash, and Mongolian

Egyptian hieroglyphics (3100 BCE to 400 CE), mixed hieroglyphic, with both logographic and syllabic signs

Elamite (ca. 3300 to 500 BCE). Proto-Elamite script (3100–2900 BCE) developed from early cuneiform. Later Elamite cuneiform was adapted from Akkadian cuneiform, after c. 2500 BCE

Etruscan alphabet (700 BCE to 100 CE), adapted from the Greek alphabet

Hittite cuneiform (1650 to 1200 BCE)

Japanese writing (400 BCE to present), first based on Chinese kanji logographic characters, to which hiragana and katakana syllabaries were added, based on Chinese characters to represent Consonant + Vowel signs

Korean Hangul (1443 CE to present), syllabary, partially alphabetic, created by King Sejong the Great in 1443

Latin (Roman) (7th century BCE to present), modified version of Etruscan alphabet, source of most European alphabets, though some are closer to the Greek alphabet in origin

Linear A (Cretan, Minoan, 1800 to 1400 BCE), remains undeciphered

Linear B (Mycenaean Greek) (1500 to 1200 BCE), syllabary

Maya hieroglyphic writing (ca. 400 BCE to 1600 CE), mixed with logographic and syllabic signs

Mixteca (Mixteca-Puebla) writing (1200 to 1600 CE), mostly logographic, with rebus signs

Ogham (200 to 500 CE), alphabetic, for writing Old Irish

Phoenician alphabet (1050 to 300 BCE)

Proto-Sinaitic (Proto-Canaanite) script, abjad (consonantal) writing (from 1700 BCE, perhaps as early as 1900 BCE, which evolved into the Phoenician script and several regional scripts)

Runic writing (called 'Futhark', 150 to 1600 CE), in two forms: earlier Continental Germanic Futhark and later Anglo-Frisian Futhorc

Sumerian (3300 to 100 BCE), hieroglyphic, evolved into cuneiform

Tibetan (600–700 CE to present), its ultimate ancestor was the Brahmi script

Zapotecan script (ca. 500 BCE to 1000 CE), hieroglyphic

Note that the Indus 'script' or Indus Valley "writing" (ca. 2600–1900 BCE), which is often listed as an undeciphered writing system, is disputed and may not be writing at all (see Farmer et al. 2004 for details). Similarly, whether the Rongorongo of Rapa Nui (Easter Island) is actual writing is also disputed.

Origins of Writing

It was sometimes thought that the earliest writing systems evolved out of tally systems for economic purposes, to keep track of inventories and transactions. For example, the 'sheep' sign ⊕ in Sumerian writing is associated with keeping track of transactions involving sheep. However, scholars of writing systems today believe that tally systems are distinct from true writing. It has also been proposed that some writing systems develop out of iconographic representations – conventionally recognized symbols, often with religious connections. However, there is doubt that the representations of linguistic features in true writing developed from earlier pictorial elements either. The beginning of writing systems seems generally to be independent of numeral systems and art. In modern English, we use the Roman alphabet alongside Arabic numerals, two separate systems with independent origins. Some letters of the English alphabet can be traced back to signs that were more pictorial in origin. For example, as mentioned, the letter 'A' ultimately comes from a Phoenician letter that depicts an ox's head, called *'aleph* which means 'ox', where the first sound in *'aleph* 'ox' is the sound that this letter represents. However, there is no evidence that portraits of oxen predated the use of this sign to represent the associated sound.

Interesting explanations have been offered for commonalities observed among many ancient writing systems. Some involve direction of reading and writing. Top-to-bottom reading or writing order apparently developed in reflection of the vertical orientation of the dominant figures in the pictorial scenes that the writing accompanied. Since a depiction of a person or animal or scene in nature is usually scanned from the head or top downward, the direction of the writing followed the same direction. In several early scripts the writing is in columns, read from top to bottom rather than in rows, for example Sumerian, Chinese, and most Mesoamerican systems.

Left-to-right order developed in scripts involving painting or recording in clay, where the writing was on materials that could smudge easily. Since most scribes are right-handed, writing from left to right in the direction away from the symbols just written avoided smearing those symbols. The word 'to write' in a number of languages comes from 'to paint', as in Proto-Mayan *ts'ihb* 'to paint', later 'to write'. In contrast, as seen earlier, English *write* comes from Proto-Germanic *wrītan* 'to cut, scratch, tear', as runes on wood or stone. Old English *wrītan* meant 'to score, outline, draw the figure of', and then later also 'to write'.

The reading and writing order from left to right is very common, but there are scripts that are written right-to-left, for example those used for writing Arabic, Hebrew, and Persian. In some situations, writing was both left-to-right and right-to-left, called **boustrophedon**, from Greek *boustrophēdon* 'ox-turning' (composed of *bous* 'ox' + *strophē* 'turn'). This name evokes the image of an ox drawing a plow across a field and turning at the end of each furrow to return in the opposite direction. In boustrophedon every other line of writing reverses the direction. The writing order of some archaic Greek stone inscriptions and of a few scripts such as Safaitic and Sabaean was boustrophedon.

In writing systems, signs and characters tend to face left. Since most writing is from left to right, the signs face the direction from which the reader reads or the scribe writes. That is, in scripts where signs or characters have any pictorial association, figures face the direction from which one reads. Sign orientation mostly follows from reading order, where a consistent orientation of signs makes it easier for the reader to process them. In boustrophedon, characters change their orientation in alternate lines to face the direction in which the line is read.

The next chapter is about how linguistic information helps us to understand prehistory.

10   Thereby Hangs a Tale
Linguistic Prehistory

> I fully believe that the harmony of languages is the best means of determining the origin of nations, and virtually the only one that is left to us where historical accounts fail.
>
> (In a letter from Gottfried Wilhem von Leibniz to Hiob Ludolf [1687]. Quoted in Aarsleff 1982: 95)

Introduction

Linguistic prehistory relates and integrates information about language history with information from archaeology, ethnohistory, human genetics, and ethnographic analogy to obtain a clearer, more complete picture of a people's past. Linguistic prehistory has been associated with other names: linguistic archaeology, linguistic paleontology, and applied historical linguistics. It has a long and sometimes checkered history. All the tools for investigating language change and the history of languages can provide information useful in linguistic prehistory. This chapter is dedicated to linguistic prehistory, seen here in its application in a few informative cases. It is important also to be aware of its limitations.

History Told by Loanwords

Loanwords often provide a great deal of historical and cultural information about the sorts of interactions and relationships that existed between the speakers of languages in contact. Loanwords, by definition, involve contacts among speakers of different languages.

Spanish Impact on the American West

We start with a straightforward example from the role of Spanish in the history of America's Old West. Spanish is the source of a large portion of the English vocabulary that is emblematic of the cultural identity of the Old West, with its cowboys, horses, cattle, ranching, and stereotypical kind of law and order. This story is told in loanwords from Spanish such as the following:

Terms for horses and the like:

bronco < *bronco* 'rough, rude'.

buckaroo < *vaquero* 'cowhand' (derived from *vaca* 'cow').

burro < *burro* 'burro', 'donkey'.

cayuse 'a feral horse, horse of low quality, an Indian pony' < *caballo-(s)* 'horse(s)', perhaps first borrowed from Spanish into Chinook Jargon and from there into English.

mustang < *mestenco* 'lacking an owner'.

palomino 'horse with pale cream-colored or golden coat and cream-colored to white mane and tail' < *palomino* 'dove-like' (see Mexican Spanish *palomo* 'pale cream-colored horse'; compare *paloma* 'dove').

pinto 'pinto', 'a horse with white patches and a darker background on its coat' < *pinto* 'painted'.

Cattle herding and ranching terms:

chaps (pronounced "shaps") < *chaparreras* 'open leather garment worn by riders over trousers to protect them from thorny bushes'.

corral < *corral* 'corral'.

lariat < *la reata* 'the strap, rein, or rope', from *reatar* 'to tie again' (see *atar* 'to tie [up]').

lasso < *lazo* 'knot, bow, lasso'.

ranch < *rancho* 'hut or house in the country'.

rodeo < *rodeo* 'a round-up' (from *rodear* 'to go round').

stampede < Mexican Spanish *estampida* 'crash, uproar'.

Geography and Western environment:

adobe 'sun-dried bricks, a structure made of adobe bricks' < *adobe* 'adobe'.

arroyo 'a water-carved gully in a dry region' < *arroyo* 'brook, small stream'.

canyon < *cañón* 'ravine, gorge, canyon'.

mesa 'flat-topped hill with steep sides' < *mesa* 'table', 'plateau'.

manzanita 'an evergreen bush of western North America (*Arctostaphylos manzanita*)' < *manzanita* 'little apple' (see *manzana* 'apple').

pinyon (piñon) < *piñón* 'pine nut, kind of pine'.

Western law and order:

calaboose 'jail, prison'< *calabozo* 'prison cell, dungeon'.

desperado 'a reckless or desperate man, especially a criminal' < Older Spanish *desperado* 'without hope, desperate' (compare Modern Spanish *desesperado* 'without hope').

hoosegow 'jail' < *juzgado* 'courthouse, judged, court, tribunal', derived from *juzgar* 'to judge' (*d* between vowels is not pronounced in many colloquial varieties of Spanish).

renegade < *renegado* 'disowned, renegade, turncoat'.

vigilante 'a member of a self-appointed group of citizens who undertake law enforcement without legal authority' < *vigilante* 'one who is vigilant' (derived from *vigilar* 'to watch, keep an eye on').

The large number of loanwords from Spanish with these meanings reveals the massive impact of Spanish on the culture and economy of the old American West, characterized by its horses, cattle, and ranching.

German Wine Making

Another straightforward case that illustrates loanwords contributing historical information comes from wine-making terms in German. Most of them are borrowed from Latin: German *Wein* 'wine' < Latin *vīnum*, *Most* 'new wine, must' < *mustum* 'unfermented wine', *Kelter* 'wine-press' < *calcātūra* 'trample, stamping with the feet', and so on. The inference drawn from these loans is that German-speaking people acquired knowledge of viticulture and wine production from the Romans (Polenz 1977: 23).

Romani History Told Primarily by Loanwords

A very telling example of linguistic prehistory, based mostly on loanwords, is that of the migrations of the Rom (Romani-speaking people, formerly called "Gypsies"). As seen in Chapter 2, the name *Gypsy* comes from *Egyptian*, reflecting the erroneous earlier belief that the

Rom came from Egypt. The word *gypsy* has many negative connotations. For example, the word *to gyp* (*gip*) 'to cheat, swindle' (now considered offensive) is derived from *gypsy*. For that reason, *Rom* (or *Roma*) for the people and *Romani* for the language are used today, and *gypsy* is avoided.

A lot is known of the origins, migrations, and history of the Rom, nearly all of it from linguistic evidence, especially from loanwords. Comparison with related languages established long ago that Romani belongs to the Indo-Aryan languages (also called Indic), a branch of Indo-European of northern and central India. While in north central India, Romani borrowed several words from Sanskrit, words meaning 'believe' and 'thirst', for instance. Their first move was to northwest India, before the second century BCE, where words from Dardic languages, another branch of Indo-Aryan, were borrowed, for example words for 'man-male', 'whip', 'to arise', 'six'. These loanwords document that migration. Because of what is known from the history of sound changes and of the break-up of Indic languages, it is clear that Romani speakers could have left India no later than ca. 1000 CE.

The second move was to Persia (modern Iran) before 650 CE, where Romani borrowed many words from Persian, 'bag', 'blind', 'breath', 'bridge', 'chicken', 'church', 'donkey', 'fortress, town', 'friend', 'goat', 'handful', 'handle', 'honey', 'linen', 'mule', 'pear', 'saddle', 'silk', 'sin', 'sock', 'spur', 'star', 'wax', 'wool', 'worm', for example, and from Kurdish, 'axe', 'forest', 'garlic', 'honey', 'landlord/host', 'nut', 'steel', 'raise', and others.

From here the Rom split, with one branch going southwest into the eastern Mediterranean region, the other moving east and north. Since there are no Arabic loans in European Romani, it is inferred that they left Iran before the Muslim conquest of 650 CE – there are Arabic loans in all the languages in regions reached by Islam, so the Romani speakers must have left Iran before the arrival of Islam.

The third move is less clear. Some scholars believe that Romani speakers moved to the Caucasus region, on the Black Sea, during the Armenian Trebizond Empire, before ca. 1040 CE, where Romani borrowed from languages of the region, from Armenian ('bewitch', 'button', 'co-parent-in-law', 'deep', 'dough', 'flax', 'forehead', 'hair', 'heart', 'honor', 'horse', 'leather', 'melon', 'oven', 'tin', 'piece'); from Georgian ('plum', 'eyelash', 'tallow', etc.); and from Ossetic ('boot', 'sock', 'wagon'). One branch of Romani speakers remained in Armenia. However, other scholars point out that contact with these languages may have been possible in eastern and central Anatolia (modern Turkey [Türkiye]) and so, they hypothesize, there is no need to postulate a separate movement into the Caucasus region.

The invasion of the Seljuk Turks in ca. 1040 is thought to have brought about the fourth Rom move, to the Byzantine Empire in Anatolia, during which time Romani came under Greek influence, taking on some grammatical patterns and borrowing many Greek words, 'anvil', 'bell', 'bone', 'buckle', 'cherry', 'crow', 'dew', 'embrace', 'flower', 'grandmother', 'hour', 'kettle', 'key', 'lead', 'market', 'nail', 'nine', 'road', 'seven', 'Sunday', 'tent', 'town', 'tablecloth', and others.

Since Romani shows no Turkish loans, it appears that the European Romani speakers must have left Anatolia before the Turkish invasions, pushed perhaps by both the Black Death, which reached western Anatolia in 1347, and the invasion of the Ottoman Turks, who arrived 1265–1328. Byzantium was sacked and Constantinople (today's Istanbul) fell in 1453.

In their fifth move, actually a series of waves, Romani speakers arrived in southeastern Europe, in the Balkans by ca. 1350, where they came under the influence of Serbo-Croatian and other South Slavic languages, borrowing many words, for example from Serbo-Croatian (perhaps also from Bulgarian and Macedonian) 'bean', 'bed', 'body', 'boot', 'cloak', 'dear', 'green', 'gun', 'hut', 'ice', 'inn', 'king', 'mountain', 'old woman', 'onion', 'paper', 'rat', 'room', 'sand' / 'dust', 'sin', 'sheet', 'stable', 'street', 'thick', 'world', 'time', 'vein', 'wild'. After this, the European Romani speakers do not share a common history.

In the sixth move, or wave, documented in historical sources, Romani spread throughout Europe during the fourteenth century. Documentary history establishes the Rom as present in Ragusa (Dubrovnik) in 1362, in Hildesheim, Germany, in 1407, in Brussels, Belgium, in 1420, and in Bologna, Italy, in 1422.[1]

This surprising case shows how, from linguistic evidence alone, primarily from loanwords, a remarkable amount of the history of the Rom and their migrations has been recovered. (See Map 10.1.)

Ironically, with their origins in the Indo-Aryan (Indic) branch of Indo-European, the Rom are the truest "Aryans" in Europe, despite Nazi views to the contrary. In the Holocaust (1939–1945), Nazi genocide killed at least 250,000 European Rom. Some informed accounts estimate that the total number may have been as high as 500,000. Sadly for linguistic prehistory and for a number of ethnic groups, Nazis had called upon misguided views of the classification of Indo-European languages and their speakers, where "Aryan" came to be associated with their concept of

---

[1] For details of the history of Romani and the Rom migrations, see Igla (1997), and Matras (2002). See Pereltsvaig and Lewis (2015: 164–167) for a somewhat different view of some of the stages in these migrations.

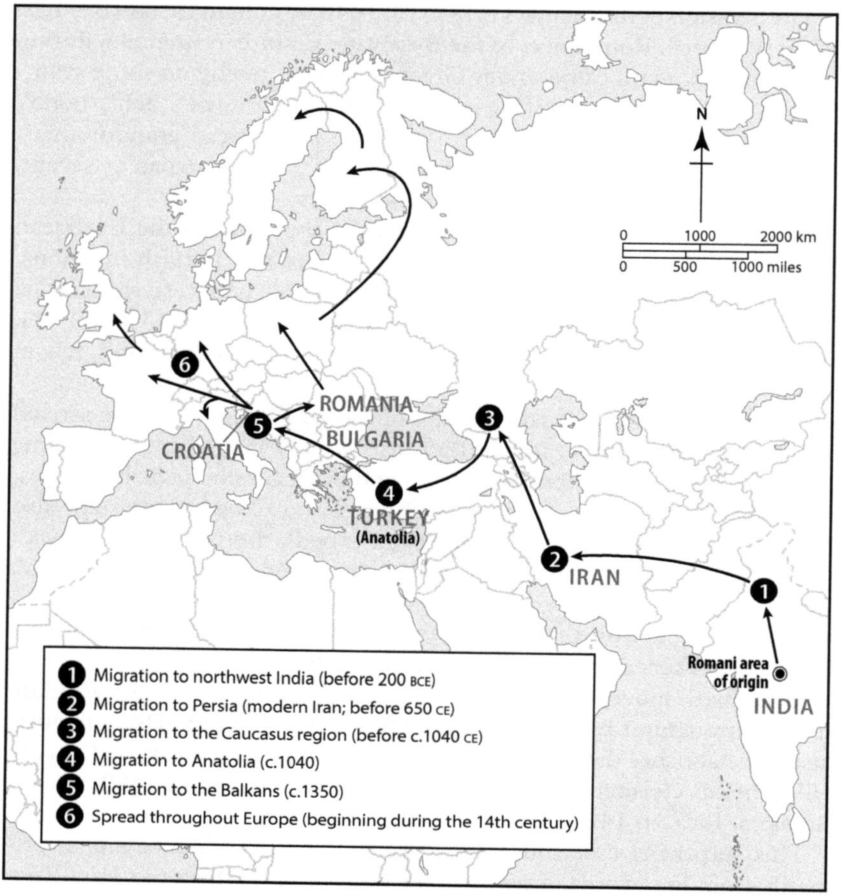
N
0 1000 2000 km
0 500 1000 miles
ROMANIA
BULGARIA
CROATIA
TURKEY
(Anatolia)
IRAN
Romani area of origin
INDIA
1 Migration to northwest India (before 200 BCE)
2 Migration to Persia (modern Iran; before 650 CE)
3 Migration to the Caucasus region (before c.1040 CE)
4 Migration to Anatolia (c.1040)
5 Migration to the Balkans (c.1350)
6 Spread throughout Europe (beginning during the 14th century)

Map 10.1 Romani migrations
Map by David McCutcheon FBCart.S www.dvdmaps.co.uk.

Herrenrasse 'master race' or *Herrenfolk* 'master people', where the purest stock of Aryans were assumed to be the Nordic (Germanic) peoples.

Place Names (Toponyms)

Another source of information that can contribute to interpreting a people's past is place names. The linguistic origins of place names across the map of England provide a dramatic example of how such names can provide information that reveals the history of speakers of the languages involved.

The geographical distribution and meaning of place names in England reflect the history of these places. For example, toponyms which end in *-caster*, *-cester*, and *-chester* reflect Latin *castra* 'camp', originally 'military post'. This was borrowed into Old English as *ceaster*, seen today in *Lancaster*, *Gloucester*, *Chester*, *Colchester*, *Dorchester*, *Leicester*, *Winchester*, and so on, telling of the Roman military presence in these places. These names provide information on the distribution and history of the Roman occupation in England that lasted nearly 400 years, from invasions that began in 43 CE until after Roman magistrates were expelled from Britain in around 410 CE. (See Map 10.2.)

Germanic invaders arrived soon after. The Venerable Bede (672–735), in his *Ecclesiastical History of the English People* (731 CE), gave what he took to be the exact year, 449 CE, for the arrival of the Anglo-Saxons in England, from three tribes which he named as the Angles (from Anglen, a small area of northern Germany), the Saxons (of Lower Saxony in northern Germany), and the Jutes (from Jutland, in Denmark). They came to be called "Anglo-Saxons," eventually shortened and changed to "English." In truth, not all the invaders came from the same place and at the same time. The people were more mixed than was once thought, and the assumed rapid replacement of Britons by Anglo-Saxons actually went on over centuries, and is not complete even today.

The Celtic speakers and their language had vanishingly little impact on the language of these new arrivals, with only a very few Celtic loanwords in early English, two examples being *bin* and *hog*.

As seen in Chapter 4, the area with heavy settlement from Scandinavia during Old English times is called the "Danelaw," north and east of a line running roughly from Chester to London (see Map 4.1). This area contains a great many place names of Scandinavian origin (see Map 10.3). These names reveal where Scandinavian invasion and settlement took place, and what its distribution in England was.

Many names of Scandinavian origin are easy to recognize from linguistic elements of Scandinavian origin that they contain. For example, *-by* is from Old Norse *by* 'village, town, settlement', seen in the English town names of *Busby*, *Crosby*, *Derby*, *Grimsby*, *Kirby*, *Rugby*, *Selby*, *Wetherby*, and so on. The *-thwaite* and *-waite* of other place names is from Old Norse *þveit* 'clearing', seen in *Braithwaite*, *Curthwaite*, *Linthwaite*, *Micklethwaite*, *Seathwaite*, *Thornthwaite*, *Waite Farm*, *Waite Ho*, and *Ivin Waite*. The town name *Twatt* in the Shetland Islands is also from Old Norse *þveit*. It has not escaped would-be amusing but crude commentary, passed over here in silence. Another is *-ay* or *-ey* from Old Nores *ey* (*øy*) 'island', as in *Orkney*, *Ramsay*, *Selsey*, *Guernsey*, *Jersey*, and so on. Yet another is *-kirk* from Old Norse *kirk* 'church', in *Colkirk*, *Falkirk*, *Kirkby*,

Map 10.2 Roman *castra* place names
Map by David McCutcheon FBCart.S www.dvdmaps.co.uk.

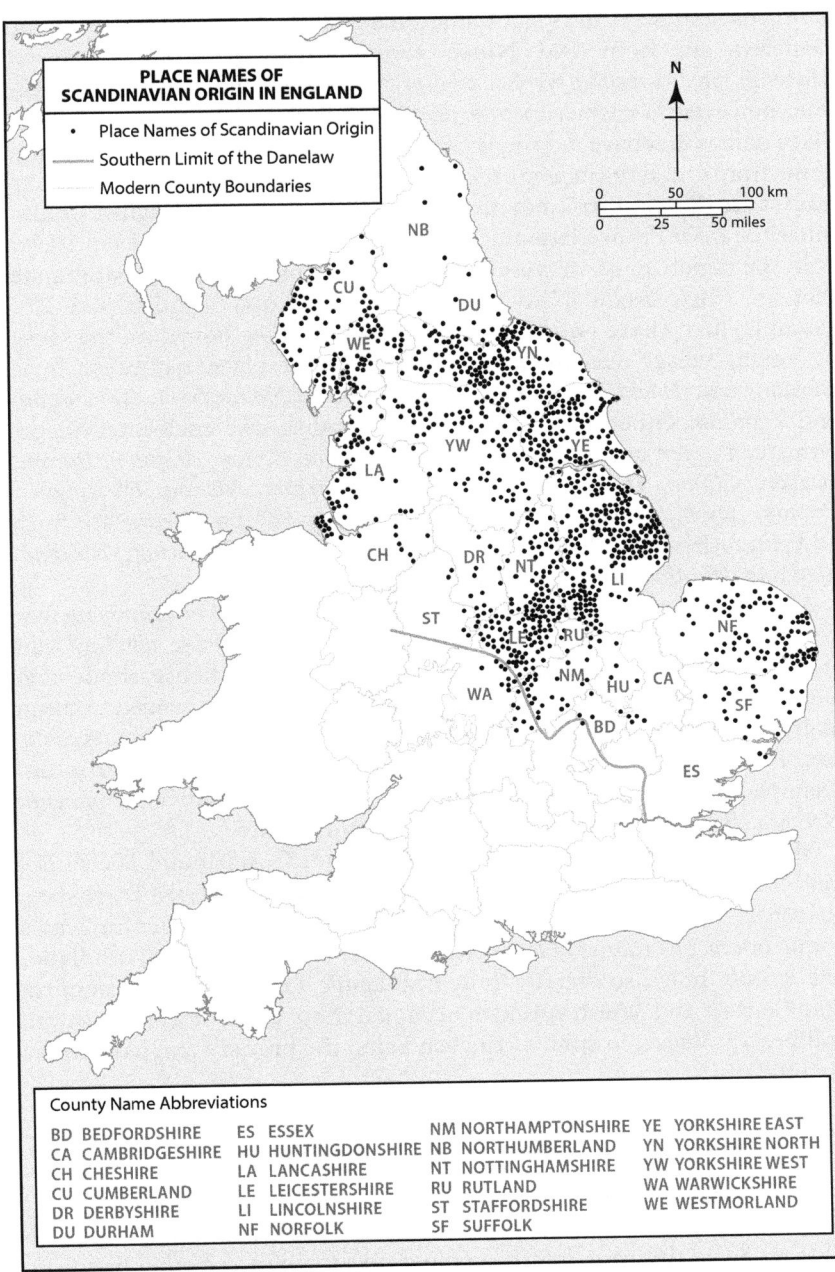

Map 10.3 Scandinavian place names in England
Map by David McCutcheon FBCart.S www.dvdmaps.co.uk.

Kirkstead, and *Kirkwall*. Place names that end in *-thorp* or *-thorpe* in the Danelaw are from Old Norse *þorp* 'village', seen in *Gunthorpe*, *Mabelthorpe*, *Mapelthorpe*, *Scunthorpe*, *Winthorp*, and *Thorpeness*. This one, however, is trickier to interpret because there are also some other place names that have *thorp* in them, outside the area of the Danelaw, that come from Old English *þrop* or *þorp* 'village, hamlet, farm, estate, group of houses in the country', not from Scandinavian but of English origin, inherited from Proto-Germanic **thurpa* village, hamlet'. (See Map 10.3.)

In the region south or west of the Danelaw, place names predominate that are Anglo-Saxon (Old English) in origin, not Scandinavian. For example, many have *-ham*, from Old English *-hām* 'home', in the sense of 'town, village', as in *hamlet*. It is seen in place names such as *Birmingham*, *Buckingham*, *Chatham*, *Durham*, *Nottingham*, *Tottenham*, and *Waltham*. Others have *-ton* from Old English *-tūn* 'enclosure, village, farmstead', seen in the likes of *Arlington*, *Bolton*, *Boston*, *Brighton*, *Burton*, *Buxton*, *Clifton*, *Darlington*, *Hamilton*, *Kensington*, *Merton*, *Paddington*, *Preston*, *Southampton*, and so on. Place names ending in *-ing* are from Old English *-ingas* 'people of', seen in *Epping*, *Pickering*, *Reading*, *Spalding*, *Worthing*, among others.

Another pair of similar place-name elements that could be confusing that are revealing in their distribution are *-wick* from Old Norse *vik* 'bay' and *-wich* 'settlement' from Old English *wic* 'dwelling place, house, abode' that later came to mean 'village, hamlet, town', and still later changed to mean 'dairy farm', as in *Gatwick* that meant 'goat-farm'. Scandinavian *-wick* is seen in *Berwick*, *Brunswick*, *Keswick*, *Lerwick*, *Prestwick*, *Wick*, and so on. Examples of place names containing *-wich* of English origin are *Bromwich*, *Horwich*, *Ipswich*, *Norwich*, *Prestwich*, *Sandwich*, *Woolwich*.

Meanwhile, place names with **pen** are from Cornish and Welsh *pen* 'hill, headland, top', seen in *Penarth*, *Penderyn*, *Pendle*, *Penbroke*, *Penrith*, *Pentlepoir*, and famously in *Penzance*, familiar from Gilbert and Sullivan's comic opera *The Pirates of Penzance*, from Cornish *penn* 'head, headland, hill' + *sans* 'holy', so literally 'holy headland'. These toponyms confirm that Cornish and Welsh speakers occupied these areas of west Cornwall and nearby Wales, in spite of English being the primary language of the area today.

Indo-European Linguistic Prehistory

A very instructive case is that of Indo-European-speaking peoples and how their prehistory is reflected in evidence from the languages (see also Chapter 8). In this case, it is the comparative method and other linguistic tools that provide most of the evidence.

By the mid 1800s, scholars were able to say how the known Indo-European languages were related to each other and how they had diversified, and they were able to make informed hypotheses about both the material and non-material culture of the speakers of Proto-Indo-European and about their <u>homeland</u>. This was based solely on the evidence obtained from the languages and on their geographical distribution.[2] Information from archaeology and human genetics was not available at that time, and the archaeological data that was available seemed to clash with the most probable linguistic interpretations. For example, it was hypothesized that the Indo-European homeland – the place where Proto-Indo-European was spoken before it diversified into the branches of the family and spread out – was in the steppes to the north of the Black Sea (see Map 10.4). However, it was objected that no likely archaeological culture was known from that area at that time. Possible supportive archaeological evidence did not appear for another hundred years. (See Mallory and Adams 1997 for details.)

Reconstruction of Proto-Indo-European vocabulary by the comparative method has provided a clear view of important aspects of Proto-Indo-European culture, valuable information on, for example, the social structure, kinship, subsistence, economy, law, religion, environment, technology, original homeland, and more. Much of this information is of the kind not easily retrievable via archaeology from material culture. In what follows, the <u>glosses</u> (meanings) of the reconstructed Proto-Indo-European vocabulary items are presented to show what they reveal about the culture of the speakers of Proto-Indo-European.[3]

The speakers of Proto-Indo-European clearly had **agriculture**, as revealed by reconstructed words meaning 'grain', 'wheat', 'ear of grain, chaff', 'field', 'garden, enclosure', 'to plough', 'plough', 'harrow', 'hoe', 'sow', 'harvest', 'sickle', 'quern', among others. They also had **domestic animals** and knowledge of **animal husbandry**, as seen in their words for 'horse', 'pig', 'piglet', 'sheep', 'ram, fleece', 'ewe', 'lamb, kid', 'goat', 'he-goat, stag, ram', 'bovine', 'bull, ox', 'cow' (two terms), 'milk', 'to milk', 'buttermilk', 'butter', 'livestock' ('moveable wealth'), 'herdsman', 'graze', and so on. They also had 'salt', 'honey', 'mead', and 'broth'.

Reconstructed terms involving **wagons** and **transport** include 'wagon', 'wheel' (three terms), 'axle', 'shaft' (of a cart or wagon), 'yoke', and 'reins', as well as 'boat' and 'to row'.

[2] See famous early works by Kuhn (1845), Pictet (1859–1863), and Schrader (1883 [1890]).
[3] See Campbell (2020: 382–393) for the actual reconstructed words. The Proto-Indo-European words listed here were assembled by Michael Weiss, published in Campbell (2020). See also Mallory and Adams (1997).

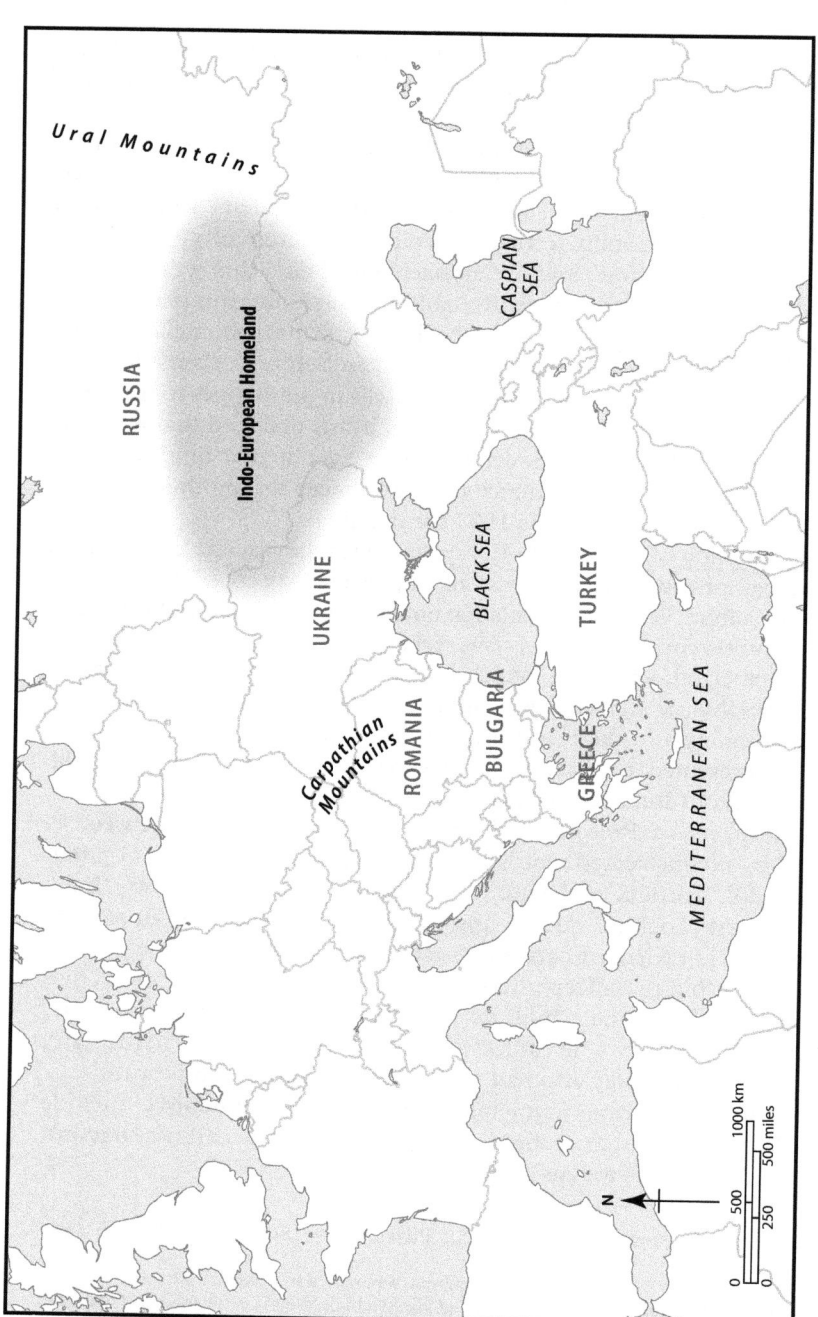

Map 10.4 Proto-Indo-European homeland
Map by David McCutcheon FBCart.S www.dvdmaps.co.uk.

Much is known of their **religion** and **beliefs** from the rather large reconstructed vocabulary that includes terms for 'holy' (four terms), 'god' (derived from *dyeu- 'sky, day, god/sungod', derived from *dei- 'shine'), 'sky-father', 'pray' (three terms), 'invoke, call', 'priest, seer/ poet', 'to worship', 'consecrate', 'libation', 'magical glory', 'sorcery', 'phantom', and 'dragon'.

Warfare and **fortification** are represented by the reconstructed words for 'to conquer', 'hillfort', 'fort', 'sword', 'spear', 'spear-point', and 'booty'. In the realm of **legal terms** we find that they had 'law, deed, thing laid down or done', 'religious law, ritual, norm', 'penalty' (derived from 'to pay, atone, compensate'), and 'make whole' (legal expression 'to pay for damages').

Their **social structure** and **social interaction** are represented by terms meaning 'king', 'free born', 'master', 'housemaster', 'group' (a settlement composed of a number of extended families, later extended to mean the complex of buildings they occupied, and, still later to mean the socio-political unit), 'family', 'member of one's group' (self-designation of the Indo-Iranians), and 'stranger, guest/host, someone with whom one has reciprocal duties of hospitality' (an outsider could be both guest and potential foe).

The reconstructed vocabulary of Proto-Indo-European provides a remarkably detailed view of the culture of a prehistoric people, the speakers of this language. Importantly, much of the cultural information recovered from the inventory of reconstructed vocabulary includes non-material culture, the sort not usually recoverable from archaeology.

Olmec Identity

A case that I am fond of, because I was involved in its development, is about the ethnolinguistic identity of the Olmecs and the impact that the Olmecs had on the culture and languages of the other peoples of Mesoamerica. Mesoamerica is a culture area that extends from the Pánuco River in northern Mexico to Costa Rica. It is characterized by shared traits among the cultures of the area. The Olmecs are responsible for the first highly successful civilization of Mesoamerica. It started developing on the southern Veracruz coast of Mexico, in about 1700–1500 BCE, with its florescence from 1200 to 400 BCE. Because the Olmec civilization was the earliest in Mesoamerica, it had a huge impact on the other languages and cultures of the region.

The Olmecs were identified as speakers of a Mixe-Zoquean language (see Campbell and Kaufman 1976), based mostly on the geographical distribution of Olmec archaeological sites that coincides with the distribution of Mixe-Zoquean languages and on some 150 early loan-words from Mixe-Zoquean encountered in languages throughout Mesoamerica. Mixe-Zoquean is a language family of some twenty languages, spoken across the Isthmus of Tehuantepec, the primary region of the Olmec archaeological sites. Many of these loanwords have significant cultural content, including the names for many items that are diagnostic for cultural items of the Mesoamerican culture area. It was concluded that Mixe-Zoquean speakers had to have had a culture with a lot of clout, important enough to contribute much to other cultures during Olmec times, when the Mesoamerican culture area was being formed. Examples of Mixe-Zoquean borrowings into the various other languages of Mesoamerica include the following, represented here only by the glosses of the loanwords.

> **Maize complex**: 'to grind corn', 'nixtamal (leached corn for grinding)', 'tortilla', 'corn dough', and others.
>
> **Other cultivated plants**: 'cacao', 'gourd', 'small squash', 'pumpkin', 'tomato', 'bean', 'sweet potato', as well as 'guava', 'papaya', 'sweet manioc', and others.
>
> **Ritual and calendric terms**: 'incense' (crucial to all Mesoamerican ritual), 'to count, divine' (borrowed as 'twenty-year period', 'twenty', 'calendar', 'calendar priest', and 'day names in various calendars of the region'), 'sacrifice'/'axe', 'woven mat' (which functioned as 'throne' for rulers), 'paper', etc.
>
> **Others**: 'child'/'infant' (a central motif in Olmec art), 'fog'/'cloud', 'iguana' (a day name), 'opossum', 'pot', 'rabbit' (a day name), 'ripe', 'salt', 'tortilla griddle', and 'turkey', among others.

These loanwords provide potent evidence for the ethnolinguistic identity of the Olmecs as speakers of a Mixe-Zoquean language, and they show the impact of this ancient culture and its language on the languages and cultures of the other peoples of the region.

Other Cases

There are many other captivating stories involving linguistic prehistory that unfortunately are not told here for lack of space. Nevertheless, it is worth pointing to a few.

The decipherments of Egyptian hieroglyphics, Linear B (Mycenaean Greek writing), the Maya script (Maya hieroglyphic writing), Epi-Olmec writing, and several other ancient writing systems, and role that the investigation of the languages played in the decipherments are truly stunning intellectual achievements. These decipherments allowed ancient documents written in these languages to be read and interpreted, pushing back known history in both the Old World and the New World by several centuries and even millennia.

The discovery of Hittite documents, their decipherment, and the demonstration that Hittite and related Anatolian languages belong to Indo-European had an enormous impact, rewriting and expanding major chunks of the history of this region. What was discovered in Hittite changed dramatically the reconstruction of the Proto-Indo-European sound system, the internal classification (subgrouping) of the Indo-European language family, and ideas about how languages of the family diversified and spread.

Similar stories can be told about remarkable new knowledge uncovered as scholars discovered and worked out the history and cultural connections involving the languages of other families, including Athabaskan (branch of the more inclusive NaDené family), Austronesian, Bantu (branch of the broader Niger-Congo language family), Sino-Tibetan, Uto-Aztecan, and others. (See Edward Sapir (1916) for a number of striking examples.)

11   Is Linguistic Armageddon Nigh?
What's Ahead for the World's Languages?

> Languages, like organic beings, can be classed in groups under groups; and they can be classed ... naturally according descent ... A language, like a species, when once extinct, never ... reappears. The same language never has two birth-places.
>
> (Charles Darwin, *The Descent of Man*)

Introduction

What's next? Beyond doubt, languages will continue to change. New chapters in the history of languages will be needed. Almost certainly, complaints about language change will go on, as usual. Future changes in languages will beyond doubt be due to already well-known factors, to internal causes that facilitate production/pronunciation and perception/understanding, and to a range of sociocultural factors outside the structure of language per se, including in particular language contact. However, the most shocking changes almost certainly will be in the sharp decline in the world's linguistic diversity, as massive numbers of languages cease to be spoken. Since the catastrophic loss of languages is already upon us, and has been for some time, it is something we know a great deal about. The focus of this chapter is **language endangerment**, why the crisis is so serious, what has brought it about, what can be done about it, and what this means for the future.

"Extinction" vs. "Dormant"

As people representing many language groups have pointed out, there are problems in how we talk about language loss, in particular with calling a language "extinct" or "dead." Sadly, "extinct language" has often been taken to mean that the people whose heritage language it is are also "extinct." However, in most cases the people survive, though they may have shifted to another language. For many Indigenous people it is demoralizing to be wrongfully considered extinct. Many of these groups today are actively trying to revive their heritage language based on whatever documentary materials may be available. Unfortunately, calling their language "extinct" or "dead" can make learning it seem futile. Calling it "dormant" or "sleeping" carries with it the possibility that the work to learn the language can help wake it up and bring it back, hence the many "awakening language" projects now underway to revive and recover these "dormant" languages. For these reasons, best practices recommendations are that "extinct," "extinction," "dead," and "language death" not be used in reference to these languages.

With languages becoming dormant, ceasing to be spoken, at an ever faster and alarming rate, and with so many in threat of imminent loss, it is easy to comprehend the sense of urgency that distresses both Indigenous peoples and scholars alike. It is difficult to overstate the seriousness and severity of the language endangerment crisis. (See Rehg and Campbell 2018 and *The Catalogue of Endangered Languages* at www.endangeredlanguages.com.)

The Myth of the Vanishing American Indian

It may help to begin by exposing the myth of the vanishing American Indian, in order to combat the mistaken conception that a no-longer-spoken language implies the extinction of the people whose heritage language it is. The theme of the "vanishing American Indian" has been intense and enduring since even before the classic novels of James Fenimore Cooper (1789–1851), in which he romanticized Native Americans as a dying race, as portrayed in particular in his *The Last of the Mohicans* (1826). Much has been written about this theme; it has been severely scorned by Native Americans, anthropologists, and others.

The record shows definitively that American Indians are not vanishing, far from it, regardless of the status of the language of any particular group. According to the 2021 US Census Bureau (information released June 2023), some 9 million people in the US identify themselves as American Indian or Alaska Native. According to the census statistics, 2.7 million US residents identified as American Indian and Alaska Native, alone, and 6.3 million as American Indian or Alaska Native in combination with one or more other "races" (i.e. ethnic groups). According to the Canadian Census, in 2021 there were 1.8 million First Nations people in Canada, representing 5 percent of the total Canadian population. That's a total of ca. 11 million in North America. In 2022 the US Bureau of Indian Affairs recognized 574 "tribes" on 326 federal Indian reservations. From US census data, from 2010 to 2020, the American Indian population alone in the US grew 11.6 percent, while that of the American Indians alone and American Indians in combination with other ethnic identities nearly doubled. The Alaska Native population alone grew 10.9 percent and the Alaska Native population alone or in any combination increased a massive 45.6 percent. The Canadian Indigenous population alone grew 20 percent, while the Indigenous population alone or in any combination with other groups skyrocketed by a whopping 390 percent!

So much for the myth of the vanishing American Indian. May this misconception itself vanish.[1] As mentioned, many of these groups, whether or not they currently have native speakers of their heritage languages, are actively working to revive them and strengthen them.

Criteria for Determining Language Endangerment

The main criteria used to determine whether a language is endangered are:

- The absolute number of speakers – the fewer the number of speakers, the less likely the language's long-term survival.
- Intergenerational transmission – if a language is not being learned by children in the traditional way, passed on from one generation to the next, it is essentially doomed unless <u>revitalization</u> efforts prove successful. The greater the intergenerational transmission, the more likely the language's survival.
- Decreasing number of speakers – the more the number of speakers decreases, the more endangered the language becomes.
- Decrease in domains of use – the more the contexts in which the language is used are diminished, the greater its endangerment becomes.

Language Endangerment in Context

Language loss ("extinction") is hardly new.[2] Language loss has been going on throughout human history, with many well-known cases of total loss from antiquity, for example Ancient Egyptian, Sumerian, Hittite, Akkadian, Etruscan, Gothic, and so on. So, some might ask, why the alarm? The alarm is because of the strikingly accelerated rate of language loss currently.

---

[1] See US Census Bureau www.census.gov/newsroom/press-releases/2023/acs-selected-population-aian-tables.html#:~:text=According%20to%20the%20newly%20released, races%20from%202017%20to%202021, and www.census.gov/library/stories/2023/10/2020-census-dhc-a-aian-population.html.

[2] Parts of the sections here about endangered languages and language revitalization follow the discussion in Campbell and Rehg (2018) and Campbell (2022).

The sharp increase in language loss is seen in the fate of languages everywhere. For example, California had some 100 American Indian languages at the time of the Gold Rush, ca. 1850, but only 18 are still spoken by native speakers today. None is being learned by children in the conventional way, via intergenerational transmission. All are highly endangered. Of the some 314 languages once spoken in what is now the US and Canada when Europeans first arrived, 152 no longer have native speakers (48%). Of 280 languages at the time of first European contact in present-day US territory, 168 no longer have native speakers (60%). However, these numbers are very misleading – all of the remaining 112 still-spoken North American Indigenous languages are endangered, most of them critically so, and only about a dozen are still being passed on to children. Many will soon become dormant unless language revitalization efforts prove successful.

The statistics for dormant and critically endangered languages in Australia, Latin America, and across Eurasia are similarly dire. No area of the world is free from language endangerment, except Antarctica. (See Map 11.1.)

The *Catalogue of Endangered Languages* lists 437 languages as "critically endangered"; 302 languages have fewer than ten speakers. Altogether, the *Catalogue of Endangered Languages* lists 3,466 endangered languages.[3] That is 46 percent of the nearly 7,000 living languages in the world.[4]

The loss of whole language families gives a telling perspective on the crisis. Of the world's ca. 399 independent language families (including language isolates; see Chapter 8), 91 are dormant – no language belonging to any of these 91 language families has any remaining native speaker. Nearly a quarter of the linguistic diversity of the world (23%), calculated in terms of language families, has been lost. Of all the millennia in which languages could have disappeared, two-thirds of these language families became dormant in only the last sixty years, dramatically underscoring the accelerating rate of language loss ("extinction") in recent times. Many other languages and language families are on the brink of losing their last native speakers and will soon follow, bringing a drastic change in the linguistic diversity of the world and in the numbers of still-spoken languages.

---

[3] The total number of languages listed in the *Catalogue of Endangered Languages* is 3,466, but this includes 252 dormant or awakening languages, that is, languages with no known native speakers.

[4] *Ethnologue*'s total number of languages is 7,164 (Eberhard et al. 2024). *Ethnologue* considers 42% of them endangered (www.ethnologue.com/insights/how-many-languages-endangered).

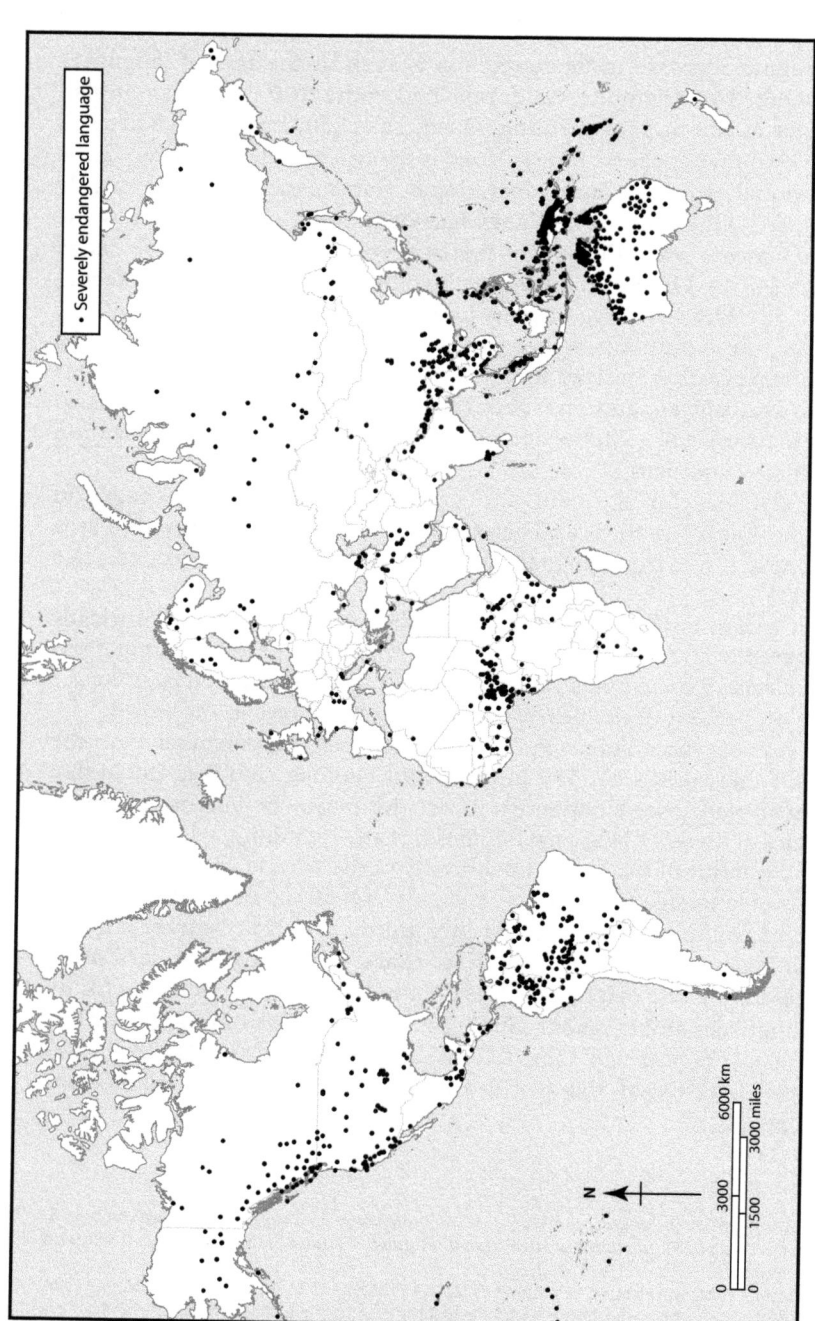

Map 11.1 Map of severely endangered languages
Map by David McCutcheon FBCart.S www.dvdmaps.co.uk.

Endangered Languages Compared to Endangered Species

This loss of languages is often compared with endangered or extinct species. Perhaps the comparison can provide insight on the magnitude of the endangered languages crisis, though languages and biological species are different in many ways. The loss of a specific language is similar in gravity to the loss of a species, say the woolly mammoth, Tasmanian tiger, or the passenger pigeon. However, the extinction of whole families of languages is a tragedy comparable in magnitude to the loss of whole branches of the animal kingdom. Just imagine the distress of biologists attempting to comprehend the animal kingdom with major branches missing. Yet, nearly a quarter of the linguistic diversity of the world has been lost, gone forever.

Comparisons show that loss in the world's linguistic diversity is vastly greater in magnitude than the loss of biological diversity. Figures reported for endangered biological species vary widely, some elevated no doubt in part due to well-meaning attempts to raise public sympathy for the cause and in part due to the fact that little is known about many species. Representative information is provided by the IUCN's (International Union for Conservation of Nature and Natural Resources) Red List of threatened species.[5] The IUCN's Red List counts 157,190 assessed species of which 44,016 are "threatened species," that is, 28 percent. For animals, they give, for example, the following estimates for "threatened species" (critically endangered, endangered, or vulnerable):

birds	12%
reptiles	21%
mammals	26%
amphibians	41%

Not even the amphibians reach a percentage as high as that of endangered languages. Clearly the threat to biological species on the whole is significantly smaller in scale than that of the 46 percent of human languages that are currently endangered (*Catalogue of Endangered Languages*). Bird species, for example, are only a quarter as "threatened" as human languages are "endangered." These figures underscore the seriousness of the endangered language crisis.

---

[5] www.iucn.org/resources/conservation-tool/iucn-red-list-threatened-species.

Causes of Language Endangerment

Nothing about the languages themselves leads to their attrition and loss, though many other factors can contribute to language endangerment. They include the following.

Economic Factors

Economic circumstances are often thought to be the most important. They include: lack of economic opportunity, rapid economic transformation, shifts in work patterns, migration and migrant labor, resource depletion, forced changes in subsistence patterns, communication with outside regions, resettlement, destruction of habitat, and globalization.

Political and Social Factors

The political and social factors that affect language endangerment include discrimination, repression, ethnic cleansing, official language policies, amount of education available, population relocation, among other things.

Attitude

Attitudes of the speakers towards their languages and towards the dominant languages that surround them contribute to a language's attrition, as do the mainstream society's attitudes towards minorities and their languages; the symbolic value of the dominant language (e.g. as a symbol of nation, civilization, progress, affluence, of the future) vs. that of endangered languages (e.g. as symbols of the past, of poverty, etc.); the relative prestige of the language (with notions of being international and urban vs. local and rural), and the stigmatization of local languages (low prestige), among other things.

Lack of Institutional Support

Institutional support is seen in the roles of the languages in education, government, churches, the media, and recreational activities (sports events, popular culture, music, etc.). Absence of institutional support contributes to shift away from minority languages.

Why Should We Care?

Why does it matter that languages are being lost (becoming "extinct")? The answers given for why language loss matters include reference to social justice, human concerns, loss of knowledge, and the scientific understanding of language.

Social Justice and Human Rights

Very often, language loss is not voluntary. Frequently it involves violations of human rights, pushed by political or social repression, oppression, prejudice, violence, and at times by ethnic cleansing and genocide. This is a matter of right and wrong, and that is important to everyone. Globally, the apprehension over language endangerment is intimately intertwined with concern for social injustice.

Several compelling studies show that ongoing language loss leads to damaged communities and dysfunctional behaviors. They argue that a person's psychological, social, and physical well-being is connected with their native language – it shapes a person's values, self-image, identity, relationships, and ultimately success in life. The vital role that language plays in personal identity is affirmed over and over again in reports from Indigenous people. Language loss can have severely negative impacts on one's social identity and well-being. For many Indigenous communities, work towards language revitalization is not only about the language, but combines with broader efforts to combat the negative consequences for personal and societal well-being.

Human Concerns

Languages are treasure houses of information for history, literature, philosophy, art, and the wisdom and knowledge of humankind. Their stories, ideas, and words help us make sense of our own lives and of the world around us – of the human experience, of the human condition in general. When a language goes dormant without documentation, we lose incalculable amounts of human knowledge. This can be seen in many fields of study, but let's just look at literature and history to illustrate it.

Literature

"By studying literature, we learn what it means to be human."[6] The life-enriching value of literature is well understood. This is equally true of the oral literatures of the peoples of the world – they, too, have grappled with the complexities of their world and the problems of life, and the insights and discoveries, and beauty and wisdom represented in their literatures – whether

---

[6] www.cliffsnotes.com/cliffsnotes/subjects/literature/why-should-literature-be-studied.

written or oral – are of no less value to us all. When a language becomes dormant without documentation, taking all its oral literature, oral tradition, and oral history with it into oblivion, all of humanity is diminished.

History

"Understanding the linkages between past and present is absolutely basic for a good understanding of the condition of being human. That, in a nutshell, is why history matters. It is not just 'useful', it is essential."[7] Great reservoirs of historical information are contained in languages (as seen in Chapter 10 and elsewhere in this book). The classification of related languages teaches us about the history of human groups and how they are related to one another. We gain understanding of contacts and migrations, of the original homelands where the languages were spoken, of how they diversified and spread, and of past cultures from the comparison of related languages and the study of language change – all irretrievably lost when a language is lost without adequate documentation.

Because languages encompass the world's knowledge and wisdom, the loss of the literature and historical information and much more when a language is lost means loss in the potential ways of experiencing and understanding the world.

Loss of Knowledge

The world's linguistic diversity is one of humanity's greatest assets. The loss of the hundreds of languages that have already become dormant is a cataclysmic disaster, on many levels. Encoded in each language is knowledge about the natural and cultural world it is used in. This knowledge is often not known outside of the small speech communities where the majority of languages are spoken. When a language dies without adequate documentation it takes with it irreplaceable knowledge. Loss of such knowledge, it is argued, could have devastating consequences for humankind's very survival. Reduction of language diversity diminishes the adaptational strength of the human species because it lowers the pool of knowledge from which we can draw.

A telling example comes from Seri (a language isolate of Sonora, Mexico, with ca. 700 speakers). The Seri use and understand 'eelgrass' (*Zostera marina L.*) and 'eelgrass seed', which they call *xnois*. It is "the only

---

[7] https://archives.history.ac.uk/makinghistory/resources/articles/why_history_matters .html.

known grain from the sea used as a human food source ... eelgrass has considerable potential as a general food source ... Its cultivation would not require fresh water, pesticides, or artificial fertilizer" (Felger and Moser 1973: 355–356). Seri has a whole set of vocabulary items dealing with eelgrass and its use. It is all too plausible to imagine a future in which some natural or human-caused disaster might compromise land-based crops, leaving human survival in jeopardy because of the loss of knowledge of alternative food sources such as the knowledge of eelgrass reflected in the Seri language, if such languages and the knowledge embodied in them are not documented. There is no doubt that documentation of the languages of small-scale societies and of the knowledge they hold has significantly benefitted humanity.

Some more examples come from medicine. It has been reported that 75 percent of plant-derived pharmaceuticals were discovered by examining traditional medicines, where the language of curers often played a key role.[8] If these languages had become "extinct" and knowledge of the medicinal plants and their uses had been lost, all of humanity would be impoverished and human survival would be left less secure.

In principle it should be possible for a society to shift to another language and find ways to talk about the kinds of knowledge they possess in the new language. What we observe, however, in case after case, is that when a language is not passed on to the next generation, the knowledge of the natural and cultural world encoded in that language fails to be transmitted as well.

Consequences for Scientific Understanding of Human Language

A major goal of linguistics is to understand human cognition and human language capacity through the study of what is possible and impossible in human languages. Discovery of previously unknown linguistic features and traits as more languages are described and documented contributes to achieving this goal and advances knowledge of how the human mind works. For achieving this goal, language loss is an unspeakable horror. The following example illustrates this.

The discovery of languages with OVS [Object-Verb-Subject] and OSV [Object-Subject-Verb] basic word orders forced abandonment of a previously postulated language universal. Joseph Greenberg (1978: 2) had proposed that "whenever the object precedes the verb the subject does likewise." However, it was discovered that Hixkaryana (a Cariban

---

[8] See, for example, Bierer et al. (1996).

language of Brazil, with only 350 speakers) has OVS basic word order, seen in the sentence:

> toto   yonoye   kamura
> man   ate   jaguar
> 'The jaguar ate the man.'

It has since been discovered that a few other languages have OVS or OSV basic word order. Most of these languages are spoken in small communities in the Amazon. Discovery of languages with these basic word orders not only forced abandonment of this postulated universal, but also required revision of a number of other theoretical claims about language. It is all too plausible, given what has happened in Brazil to speakers of Indigenous languages at the hands of unscrupulous loggers, miners, and ranchers, that the few languages that have these word orders could have become "extinct" before they were documented, leaving us forever with erroneous assumptions about what is possible and impossible in human language and what that means for understanding human cognition.

Documentation of endangered languages has frequently and repeatedly demonstrated the importance of obtaining adequate descriptions of these languages. The discovery of previously unknown linguistic traits is helping linguists to comprehend the full range of what is possible and impossible in human language.[9]

Peace through Monolingualism?

A final reason for why we should care about language loss involves combatting misinformation about the role of languages in geopolitical conflicts, to avoid wrong-headed policies based on such assumptions. It is often asserted that if we had fewer languages, we would understand each other better and live in greater harmony. That just isn't so. That monolingualism does not guarantee nor even foster greater "understanding" is attested throughout history. "All of the large monolingual countries of the world have had their civil wars," so observed David Crystal (2000: 27). This is seen in the many recent and ongoing armed conflicts among groups speaking the same language, in Colombia, Iraq, Libya, Northern Ireland, Syria, Thailand, and Yemen. In the 1994 genocide in Rwanda involving Hutu and Tutsi, both speakers of the same language, Kinyarwanda, more than 800,000 were killed, primarily Tutsi, but also

---

[9] For numerous examples, see Palosaari and Campbell (2011) and Campbell (2022).

Hutu, and some 2,000,000 fled the country because of the genocide. We could add cases of conflicts among speakers of the same language in the so-called drug wars in several countries, as in the fighting among Mexican drug cartels or between the cartels and federal authorities, all speakers of Spanish.

This contrasts with lack of such conflicts in relatively peaceful, officially multilingual Belgium, Canada, Finland, Luxembourg, Singapore, Switzerland, and Tanzania. Multilingual and multicultural countries need to recognize that national unity and understanding are not fostered by monolingualism or ethnic cleansing, but that recognition of minority languages' rights can bring about mutual trust, peace, and ultimately national stability. We need to expose the erroneous assumption that people and countries cannot be both multilingual and successful, and show, rather, that there are significant benefits from multilingualism. Several recent research publications report that bilingual children tend to grow up to be more tolerant citizens than monolinguals.[10]

In short, there is no evidence that fewer languages might lead to greater harmony.

For those thinking that monolingualism means less conflict, I would say get real. It is variously reported that over 40 percent of the world's population are bilingual and 17 percent are even multilingual, speaking three or more languages. That is, monolingualism is neither a normal nor desirable state for individuals or countries.

You can help. You can call the endangered languages crisis to the attention of your associates and others. You can donate to any of a number of non-profit organizations dedicated to fostering language documentation and supporting language revitalization.

---

[10] See, for example, Dewaele and Wei (2013) and Singh et al. (2020).

Appendix: Language Families of the World (Including Language Isolates)

Africa (42 Language Families)

1. Afro-Asiatic (Afroasiatic)
2. Bangi Me (isolate)
3. Berta
4. Central Sudanic
5. Daju
6. Dizoid
7. Dogon
8. Eastern Jebel
9. Furan
10. Gimojan (Gonga-Gimojan)
11. Hadza (isolate)
12. Heiban
13. Ijoid
14. Jalaa (isolate)
15. Kadu (Kadugli-Krongo)
16. Khoe (Kwadi)
17. Koman
18. Kresh-Aja
19. Kuliak
20. Kunama
21. Kx'a (Ju + ǂHuan)
22. Laal (isolate)
23. Maban
24. Mande
25. Mao
26. Nara (isolate?)
27. Narrow Talodi
28. Niger-Congo
29. Nilotic

30. Nubian (possibly including also Meroitic)
31. Nyimang
32. Rashad
33. Saharan
34. Sandawe (isolate?)
35. Songhay
36. South Omotic (Aroid?)
37. Surmic
38. Ta-Ne-Omotic
39. Tama (Taman)
40. Tegem (Lafofa) (isolate? unclassified?)
41. Temein
42. Tuu

North America (54)

1. Adai (isolate)
2. Algic
3. Alsea (isolate)
4. Atakapa (isolate, small family?)
5. Beothuk (isolate)
6. Caddoan
7. Cayuse (isolate)
8. Chimakuan
9. Chimariko (isolate)
10. Chinookan
11. Chitimacha (isolate)
12. Chumashan
13. Coahuilteco (isolate)
14. Cochimí-Yuman
15. Comecrudan
16. Coosan
17. Cotoname (isolate)
18. Eskimo-Aleut
19. Esselen (isolate)
20. Haida (isolate, possibly a small family?)
21. Iroquoian
22. Kalapuyan
23. Karankawa (isolate)
24. Karuk (isolate)
25. Keresan
26. Kiowa-Tanoan

27. Kootenai (Kutenai) (isolate)
28. Maiduan
29. Muskogean
30. NaDené (Eyak-Athabaskan and Tlingit)
31. Natchez (isolate)
32. Palaihnihan
33. Plateau (Plateau Penutian)
34. Pomoan
35. Salinan
36. Salishan
37. Shastan
38. Siouan-Catawban
39. Siuslaw (isolate)
40. Takelma (isolate)
41. Timucua (isolate)
42. Tonkawa (isolate)
43. Tsimshianic
44. Tunica (isolate)
45. Utian (Miwok-Costanoan)
46. Uto-Aztecan
47. Wakashan
48. Washo (isolate)
49. Wintuan
50. Yana (isolate)
51. Yokutsan
52. Yuchi (isolate)
53. Yukian
54. Zuni (isolate)

Mexico and Mesoamerica (14)

1. Cuitlatec (isolate)
2. Guaicurían
3. Huave (isolate)
4. Jicaquean (Tol)
5. Lencan
6. Mayan
7. Misumalpan
8. Mixe-Zoquean
9. Otomanguean
10. Purépecha (Tarascan) (isolate)
11. Seri (isolate)

12. Tequistlatecan
13. Totonacan
14. Xinkan

South America (100)

1. Aikanã (isolate)
2. Andaqui (isolate)
3. Andoque (isolate)
4. Arara do Rio Branco (isolate)
5. Arawakan
6. Arawan
7. Arutani (Awaké, Uruak) (isolate)
8. Atacameño (Cunza) (isolate)
9. Aymaran
10. Barbacoan
11. Betoi-Jirara (isolate)
12. Boran
13. Bororoan
14. Cahuapanan
15. Cañar-Puruhá
16. Candoshi (isolate)
17. Canichana (isolate)
18. Cariban
19. Cayuvava (isolate)
20. Chapacuran
21. Charrúan
22. Chibchan
23. Chicham (Jivaroan)
24. Chiquitano (isolate)
25. Chocoan
26. Cholonan
27. Chonan (Chon family)
28. Chono (isolate)
29. Cofán (A'ingaé) (isolate)
30. Culle (isolate)
31. Enlhet-Enenlhet
32. Esmeralda (isolate)
33. Guachí (isolate)
34. Guaicurúan
35. Guajiboan
36. Guamo (isolate)

37. Guató (isolate)
38. Harákmbut-Katukinan
39. Huarpean
40. Iatê (Fulniô) (isolate)
41. Irantxe (isolate)
42. Itonama (isolate)
43. Jirajaran
44. Jotí (Yuwana) (isolate)
45. Kakua-Nukak
46. Kamsá (isolate)
47. Kanoê (Kapixaná) (isolate)
48. Karirían
49. Kawesqaran (Qawasqaran, Alacalufan)
50. Kwaza (isolate)
51. Leco (isolate)
52. Lule-Vilelan
53. Macro-Jê Sensu Stricto
54. Máku (Mako) (isolate)
55. Mapudungun
56. Matacoan
57. Matanawí (isolate)
58. Mochica (Yunga, Chimú) (isolate)
59. Mosetén (isolate)
60. Movima (isolate)
61. Munichi (isolate)
62. Nadahup
63. Nambiquaran
64. Omurano (isolate)
65. Otomacoan
66. Paezan (isolate; possibly a small family)
67. Pano-Takanan
68. Payaguá (isolate or unclassified)
69. Pirahã (isolate; possibly a small family)
70. Puinave (Wãnsöhöt) (isolate)
71. Puquina (isolate)
72. Purí-Coroado (isolate)
73. Quechuan
74. Sáliban
75. Sapé (Kaliana) (isolate)
76. Sechura ((isolate or unclassified?)
77. Tallán (isolate or unclassified)
78. Taruma (isolate)

79. Taushiro (isolate)
80. Tequiraca (Auishiri) (isolate)
81. Tikuna-Yurí
82. Timotean
83. Tiniguan
84. Trumai (isolate)
85. Tukanoan
86. Tupían
87. Urarina (isolate)
88. Uru-Chipaya
89. Waorani (isolate)
90. Warao (isolate)
91. Witotoan
92. Xukurúan
93. Yahgan (Yaghan, Yámana) (isolate)
94. Yaguan
95. Yanomaman
96. Yaruro (Pumé) (isolate)
97. Yuracaré (isolate)
98. Yurumanguí (isolate)
99. Zamucoan
100. Zaparoan

Europe and Asia (31)

1. Ainu (isolate)
2. Austroasiatic
3. Basque (isolate)
4. Burushaski (isolate)
5. Chukotko-Kamchatkan
6. Dravidian
7. Elamite (isolate)
8. Hattic (isolate)
9. Hmong-Mien (Miao-Yao)
10. Hruso (Hruso-Aka) (isolate?)
11. Hurrian (Hurro-Urartean)
12. Indo-European
13. Japonic
14. Kassite (isolate)
15. Koreanic
16. Kra-Dai (Tai-Kadai)
17. Kusunda (isolate)

18. Mongolian
19. Nakh-Dagestanian (Northeast Caucasian)
20. Nihali (isolate)
21. Nivkh (isolate, possibly a small family)
22. Northwest Caucasian (Abkhazo-Adyghean)
23. Sino-Tibetan
24. South Caucasian (Kartvelian)
25. Sumerian (isolate)
26. Tungusic
27. Turkic
28. Tyrsenian (Etruscan-Lemnian, possibly includes also Rhaetic)
29. Uralic
30. Yeniseian
31. Yukaghir

Pacific (128)

1. Abinomn (isolate)
2. Abun (isolate)
3. Afra (Usku) (isolate)
4. Amto-Musan
5. Anêm (isolate)
6. Angan
7. Anim
8. Ap Ma (Botin, Kambot, Kambrambo) (isolate)
9. Arafundi
10. Asaba (isolate)
11. Austronesian
12. Awin-Pa
13. Baibai-Fas
14. Baining
15. Baiyamo (isolate)
16. Banaro (isolate)
17. Bayono-Awbono
18. Bilua (isolate)
19. Bogaya (isolate)
20. Border
21. Bosavi
22. Bulaka River
23. Burmeso (isolate)
24. Busa (Odiai) (isolate)
25. Dagan

26. Damal (Uhunduni, Amung) (isolate)
27. Dem (isolate)
28. Dibiyaso (isolate)
29. Doso-Turumsa
30. Duna (isolate)
31. East Bird's Head
32. East Kutubu
33. East Strickland
34. Eastern Trans-Fly
35. Eleman
36. Elseng (Morwap) (isolate)
37. Fasu (isolate)
38. Geelvink Bay (Cenderawasih Bay)
39. Goilalan
40. Great Andamanese
41. Guriaso (isolate)
42. Hatam-Mansim
43. Inanwatan
44. Kaki Ae (isolate)
45. Kamula (isolate)
46. Kapauri (isolate) (Kapori)
47. Karami
48. Kaure-Narau (possibly an isolate)
49. Kayagar
50. Kehu (isolate)
51. Kibiri-Porome (isolate)
52. Kimki (isolate)
53. Kiwaian
54. Koiarian
55. Kol (isolate)
56. Kolopom
57. Konda-Yahadian
58. Kosare (isolate)
59. Kuot (isolate)
60. Kwalean
61. Kwerbic
62. Kwomtari
63. Lakes Plain
64. Lavukaleve (isolate)
65. Left May (Arai)
66. Lepki-Murkim
67. Lower Sepik-Ramu

68. Mailuan
69. Mairasi
70. Manubaran
71. Marori (Moraori)
72. Masep (isolate)
73. Mawes (isolate)
74. Maybrat (isolate)
75. Mombum (family, 2 languages)
76. Monumbo (family, 2 languages)
77. Mor (isolate)
78. Morehead-Wasur
79. Mpur (isolate)
80. Namla-Tofanma
81. Ndu
82. Nimboran
83. North Bougainville
84. North Halmahera
85. Onge-Jarawa (Jarawa-Onge)
86. Pahoturi
87. Pauwasi
88. Pawaia
89. Pele-Ata
90. Piawi
91. Powle-Ma ("Molof") (isolate)
92. Purari ("Namau") (isolate)
93. Pyu (isolate)
94. Sause (isolate)
95. Savosavo (isolate)
96. Senagi
97. Sentani
98. Sepik
99. Sko (Skou)
100. Somahai
101. South Bird's Head
102. South Bougainville
103. Suki-Gogodala
104. Sulka (isolate)
105. Tabo (Waia) (isolate)
106. Taiap (isolate)
107. Tambora (isolate)
108. Tanahmerah (isolate)
109. Taulil-Butam

110. Teberan
111. Timor-Alor-Pantar
112. Tor-Orya
113. Torricelli
114. Touo (isolate)
115. Trans New Guinea
116. Turama-Kikori
117. Ulmapo ("Mongol-Langam")
118. Walio
119. West Bird's Head
120. West Bomberai
121. Wiru (isolate)
122. Yale (Yalë, Nagatman) (isolate)
123. Yareban
124. Yawa
125. Yele (Yélî Dnye) (isolate)
126. Yerakai (isolate)
127. Yetfa-Biksi (isolate)
128. Yuat

Australia (30)

1. Bachamal (isolate, possibly belongs with Northern Daly family)
2. Bunaban
3. Eastern Daly
4. Gaagudju (isolate)
5. Garrwan
6. Giimbiyu
7. Gunwinyguan
8. Iwaidjan
9. Jarrakan
10. Kungarakany (isolate)
11. Limilngan
12. Mangarrayi (isolate)
13. Maningrida
14. Maran
15. Marrku-Wurrugu
16. Mirndi (Mindi)
17. Northeastern Tasmanian
18. Northern Daly
19. Nyulnyulan
20. Oyster Bay

21. Pama-Nyungan
22. Southeastern Tasmanian
23. Southern Daly
24. Tangkic
25. Tiwi (isolate)
26. Umbugarla/Ngurmbur (isolate or small family?)
27. Wagiman (Wageman) (Yangmanic?) (isolate)
28. Wardaman (isolate or small family)
29. Western Daly
30. Worrorran

Glossary

abjad writing A writing system in which only consonants are represented, with the vowels left unrepresented. In contrast, true alphabets have symbols that represent both consonants and vowels. Arabic, Hebrew, and Phoenician writing is abjad.

acronym A word derived from the initial letters of each of the successive parts of a compound term or successive words in a phrase, such as *radar* from 'radio direction and ranging', and *ASAP* from 'as soon as possible'.

affricate A combined consonant that begins with a stop and is released as a fricative. Though complex, an affricate is a single speech sound, as the "ch" sound ([č], IPA [ʧ]) in *chin* or the "dzh" sound ([ǰ], IPA [ʤ]) in *jam*.

amalgamation The fusion of two or more words occurring in a phrase into a single word; for example, English *never the less* > *nevertheless*.

amelioration, see **elevation**

Amerind, Amerind hypothesis Joseph Greenberg's (1987) proposal of a distant genealogical relationship that would group all the Indigenous languages of the Americas, except NaDené and Eskimo-Aleut, into a single, very large "Amerind" mega-family grouping. The Amerind hypothesis has been heavily criticized, rejected by nearly all practicing American Indianists and by most historical linguists. They hold that valid methods do not at present permit classification of the Native American languages into fewer than about 170 independent language families and isolates.

analogical extension A kind of analogical change that extends some already existing alternation to new forms that formerly did not undergo the alternation. For example, the *dive* : *dived* pattern was replaced by *dive* : *dove* in most of North America by analogy that extended the verb pattern in *drive*: *drove, ride* : *rode*, etc.

analogical levelling Reduces the number of variants a form has; it makes paradigms more uniform. Forms that formerly underwent alternations no longer do so after analogical levelling. For example, the earlier comparative and superlative forms of *old* have changed from the *old : elder : eldest* pattern to the non-alternating pattern *old : older : oldest* by analogical levelling.

analogy A process whereby one form in a language becomes more like another with which it is somehow associated. It is a change in which something changes to become more like something else in the language when speakers perceive the changing part as similar to the thing that it changes to become like. For example, earlier English *brethren* 'brothers' changed to *brothers*, by analogy with the more common pattern of nouns with *-s* plurals as in *sister/sisters*, *mother/mothers*, etc.

archaism (also called **relic**) A form or construction characteristic of a past state of a language, a vestige. Archaisms are exceptional or marginal to the languages in which they are found. They are most commonly preserved in special kinds of language such as in proverbs, folk poetry, folk ballads, legal documents, prayers and religious texts, very formal genres or stylistic variants. For example, English archaic *pease* for 'pea', is preserved in the nursery rhyme "pease porridge hot, pease porridge cold," where in former times *pease* was the singular form of the word meaning 'pea'.

aspirated In phonetics, *aspirated* refers to a consonant sound whose articulation is released with a small puff of air, a brief burst of breath when the sound is produced. In English, stops are typically aspirated at the beginning of words, represented in phonetics with a raised "h", as in *pie* [p^{h}ai].

back formation A type of folk etymology in which a word is assumed to have a composition that it did not originally have, usually a root plus some suffix, so that when the assumed but historically inaccurate suffix is removed, a new root is created. For example, in *pea* from earlier *pease* (singular), the *s* that formerly had been part of the root was taken to be the *s* plural, backforming *pease* to *pea* and producing a new plural *peas*.

basic vocabulary Very common words that have counterparts with the same meanings in almost all languages, such as terms for body parts (eye, hand, foot, nose), basic geographical and environmental terms (mountain, river, water, star, rain, hot, cold), common activities (eat, sleep, die), and low numbers (one, two, three). It is assumed that basic vocabulary is more resistant to borrowing and replacement than other kinds of vocabulary.

borrowing The process by which a language takes linguistic elements from another language and makes them part of its own. The borrowed elements are typically loanwords, but borrowing is not restricted just to words taken from one language into another. An example is English *beef* borrowed from French *bœuf* 'beef'. Then later, French borrowed English *beefsteak* as French *bifteck* 'beefsteak'.

boustrophedon Writing from left to right and then right to left on alternate lines.

broadening, see **widening**

branch, see **subgroup**

calque A loan translation or semantic loan, where a word or phrase is "borrowed" from another language by literal word-for-word or part-for-part translation, borrowing the meaning but not the pronunciation from the donor language. For example, several languages have a calque based on English *skyscraper*, as seen in French *gratte-ciel* (literally 'scrape sky') and Spanish *rascacielos* ('scratch skies').

chain shift A set of interrelated sound changes where the change in one speech sound or series of speech sounds is linked with and assumed to cause a change in another sound or series of sounds, maintaining the distinctions between the sounds involved. Either one sound moves into the phonetic space of another, causing that sound to change in order to avoid merging with the encroaching sound, or a sound moves out of its original space, allowing another sound to move into the gap left by the move. The English **Great Vowel Shift** and **Grimm's Law** are well-known examples of chain shifts.

clipping The process of coining new words by shortening longer words, eliding material from them – for example, *lab* from *laboratory*, and *gym* from *gymnasium*.

cognate A word that comes from the same source as a word in a sister language. It is a word in related languages that is inherited from a word in the parent language of the languages that share the cognate. For instance, the Romance languages Spanish, Portuguese, French, and Italian share a cognate meaning 'hand': Spanish *mano*, Portuguese *mão*, French *main*, Italian *mano*. These languages share these words because they were inherited from the original Proto-Romance word **manu* 'hand'. Language change can modify both the sound and meaning of a word, such that cognates may not necessarily be clearly similar. Their cognate status is established by application of the comparative method. Loanwords are not cognates.

comparative method A method for comparing languages that descend from a common ancestor in order to reconstruct that parent language (proto-language). It infers the properties of the ancestor language (the proto-language) by identifying systematic correspondences in the sound systems, vocabulary, and grammar of the related languages. This is called reconstruction. The method is used to reconstruct proto-languages, but it is also used in determining what changes the related descendant languages of a language family have undergone, how they are classified within the language family (their subgrouping), and to determine whether languages are genealogically related to one another.

compound A word formed by combining parts that are (or were) themselves distinct words into a single word. The process is called **compounding**. For example, *rainbow* is formed from *rain* + *bow*; **bookstore** is compounded from *book* + *store*.

creole The traditional definition of a creole is a language descended from a pidgin language that has become the native language of a group of people – a creole is a pidgin that has acquired native speakers. This happens when individuals who have only the pidgin language in common marry and their children grow up with the pidgin as their primary means of communication and in time the language becomes elaborated to fulfill all normal communicative functions.

cuneiform A writing system of wedge-shaped characters impressed in clay tablets used in the writing systems of ancient Mesopotamia to write Akkadian, Assyrian, Babylonian, Elamite, Hattian, Hittite, Hurrian, and Sumerian.

Danelaw After the Scandinavian invasion and conquest of major parts of England in the late 800s, a treaty from 886 established the Danelaw, a large area in England east and north of a line running roughly from Chester to London, where Danish law applied. The term applies to the areas in which English kings allowed the Danes to keep their own laws

daughter language A language descended from an ancestral language. For example, the various related sister languages in a language family are each individually daughter languages of the proto-language, as, for example, English, German, Swedish, and several others are the daughters of Proto-Germanic.

degeneration A kind of semantic change (also called pejoration) in which the sense of a word takes on a less positive evaluation in the minds of language users, an increase in negative value judgement. For example, English *silly* 'foolish, stupid' meant 'blessed, blissful' in Old English times.

devoicing Sound change in which a sound is converted into a voiceless sound. A voiceless sound is one where the vocal cords do not vibrate during its production.

dialect Any regional or social variety of a single language that is mutually intelligible with other dialects of the same language and that differs in some definable features from other varieties of that language. The term "dialect" does not refer to little-known or minority languages, though it has sometimes been used, particularly in the past, in that sense.

diffusion In linguistics *diffusion* refers to the spread of language traits (words, sounds, grammatical entities, etc.) from one language or dialect to another. *Diffusion* is often used as synonymous with borrowing. When diffusion of multiple structural features across the languages of a particular geographical region takes place, we speak of a *linguistic area*.

digraph A combination of two letters representing a single speech sound, such as "ch" in *church*, representing [č] (IPA [ʧ]).

diphthong, diphthongized, diphthongization A diphthong is a combination of two vowel sounds in a single syllable, as for example in *coin, loud, break* ([breik]). *Diphthongization* refers to the change of a single vowel into a diphthong.

distant genetic relationship A genealogical relationship between languages that are only remotely related. Many distant genetic relationships have been postulated among languages not known to be related, where, owing either to the lack of convincing evidence or to doubts about the methods used (or both), the hypotheses are disputed. Some examples of these controversial proposals of distant genetic relationship include Altaic, Amerind, Nostratic, Proto-World, and many others. Distant genetic relationships that are confirmed are just called language families.

donor language The donor language is the source language that contributes a loanword or other linguistic trait to another language in the process of **borrowing**.

elevation (also called amelioration) A kind of semantic change in which the meaning of a word shifts towards a more positive value in the minds of the language's users, with an increased positive value judgement, as for example, in *pretty*, which in its Old English form meant 'crafty, sly'.

etymology The study of the origin or history of words. In another sense, an *etymology* is the origin and history of a specific word.

etymon An earlier form of a word which is the source from which that word comes. For example, since English *foot* comes from Proto-Indo-European *ped-*, the Proto-Indo-European word is the etymon behind the English word. In another sense, an etymon is an entry in an etymological dictionary.

euphemism A word (or phrase) that replaces another that is considered obscene, offensive, taboo or that otherwise causes discomfort. An example is the euphemistic replacement of words for 'toilet' by *lavatory*, *bathroom*, *restroom*, *washroom*, and others. *Euphemism* also refers to the process by which such replacements take place.

extension A mechanism of syntactic change that results in change in the actual form of a grammatical construction but does not involve modification of the interpretation or function of the construction. Extension is found following or in association with reanalysis. For example, after the reanalysis of *will* from 'want' to a new future-tense auxiliary, the change was later extended so that the new 'will' future could occur in situations which formerly were not possible. Earlier, *will* could only occur with subjects capable of wanting – humans and animals – but later it was extended so that it could occur as the future-tense auxiliary with a greater range of subjects, for example, *it will snow tonight*, *the poison will kill him*, and *she will want to sing*.

family, see **language family**

family tree The set of genealogical relationships holding among the languages of a language family, and also the graphic representation of the genealogical classification of the languages of a language family in a tree-like diagram.

fricative A speech sound in the production of which the airstream is not completely blocked, where the vocal tract is constricted to a narrow passage so that friction (turbulence) characterizes the sound, as in English *f, s,* "*sh*" ([š]), *v, z,* "*zh*" ([ž]), and "th" ([θ]) and "*dh*" ([ð]).

folk etymology A kind of analogical change in which the form (pronunciation) or meaning of a word or part of a word is changed as a result of a mistaken assumption about the word's composition or meaning. That is, speakers believe the word to have an etymology or analysis that is false from the perspective of the form's true history. An example is the English word *hamburger*, whose true etymology is from German *Hamburg* + *-er*, 'someone from the city of Hamburg'. Hamburgers are not made of 'ham', but speakers associated *hamburger* with *ham* and on this basis created new words such as *cheeseburger, fishburger*.

genetic relationship (also **genetic affiliation**) The relationship among languages that descend from a shared common ancestor, among languages that are members of the same language family.

gerund A verb form that functions as a noun. The gerund in English usually has the suffix *-ing*, as in ***seeing*** *is **believing*** and in the shocking old example linguists cited to illustrate ambiguity, *the **eating** of children can be messy*.

gloss A short translation of a word, phrase or sentence in one language to give its meaning equivalence in another language. For example, 'dog' is the gloss for the German word *Hund*.

glottal stop The sound made when the vocal cords are briefly closed, as for example the sound in the pause between the two parts of *oh-oh*.

grammaticalization A kind of change in which an ordinary word changes to have a grammatical function.

Great Vowel Shift A set of interrelated vowel changes in Middle English in which long low and long mid vowels were raised, and the long high vowels /i:/ and /u:/ diphthongized to /ai/ and /au/, respectively.

Grimm's Law A set of interrelated sound changes associated with Jacob Grimm (of Grimm Brothers fairytale fame) involving changes in the stop consonants from Proto-Indo-European to Proto-Germanic: voiceless stops > fricatives (p, t, k > f, θ, h, respectively); voiced stops > voiceless stops (b, d, g > p, t, k, respectively); and voiced aspirated stops > plain voiced stops (bh, dh, gh > b, d, g, respectively).

hieroglyphic, hieroglyphic writing A writing system that employs characters that are logograms (in the form of picture images that represent whole words). The individual signs, called **hieroglyphs,** may be read either as symbols that represent objects and concepts, or in some cases as symbols for sounds. Ancient Egyptian and Mayan writing are well-known examples of hieroglyphic writing.

homophony When different words sound the same but have different meanings, as for example *to, too,* and *two*. Such words are said to be homophonous.

hyperbole Semantic change in which the meaning shifts due to exaggeration by overstatement. For example, *starve* now means 'to suffer or perish from hunger', but it is from Old English *steorfan* 'to die'. Saying 'die' when 'suffer hunger' was intended is an exaggeration by overstatement that led to this change in meaning.

hypercorrection A kind of analogical change in which speakers make an attempt to change a word, phrase, or construction in a less prestigious variety to make it conform with how it would be pronounced in a more prestigious variety of the language, but in the process they sometimes overshoot the target so that the result is erroneous from the point of view of the prestige variety being mimicked. For example, saying *you and I* in situations where Standard English requires *you and* ***me*** is a hypercorrection. It is based on stigmatized use of *me* as subject pronoun in sentences such as *You and* ***me*** *ate supper*. Speakers, in attempting to correct instances such as these, sometimes go too far and hypercorrect *me* to *I* even when *me* is required in Standard English when it is an object, not the subject, of the sentence, as in *She saw you and* ***me*** (not *She saw you and* ***I***).

interjection In grammar, an **interjection** is a word or phrase that expresses a sudden emotion or feeling, standing alone or inserted into a sentence, for example, *hey!, ouch, wow.*

isolate, see **language isolate**

language family A group of languages that are related because they developed from a common ancestor language that diversified over time to result in these descendants, called "daughter languages." Some well-known language families are Austronesian, Indo-European, Mayan, Sino-Tibetan, and Uralic.

language isolate A language that has no known relatives, that is, a language family that has only a single member. Some well-known isolates are Ainu, Basque, Burushaski, and Sumerian.

language revitalization Refers to efforts to strengthen an endangered language or sometimes also to efforts to revive a language which has lost all of its native speakers. Language revitalization attempts to reverse language shift, the decline in a language's use as its speakers tend to shift more and more to another language.

lingua franca A language regularly used for communication between people who do not share a native language, sometimes referred to as a bridge language. The name *lingua franca* (literally, 'Frankish tongue') is taken from the medieval Lingua Franca, a Romance-based <u>pidgin</u> used especially by traders in the Mediterranean region from the eleventh to the nineteenth centuries.

linguistic homeland, homeland (also called *Urheimat*) The geographical location where a proto-language was spoken before it diversified into its daughter languages and spread.

litotes A type of semantic change resulting from exaggeration by understatement, as for example, English *kill*, which changed from its original meaning 'to strike, hit' to mean 'kill'. Saying something meaning 'hit' but intending it to mean 'kill' is an exaggeration by understatement.

macro-family A speculative and often controversial proposed grouping of languages hypothesized to be distantly related to one another, often on the basis of inconclusive evidence.

merger A kind of sound change in which two (or more) distinct sounds change into a single sound. The sounds merge into a single indistinguishable sound.

metaphor A semantic change that involves understanding one kind of thing in terms of another kind of thing thought to be similar in some way. Metaphor involves <u>extension</u> in the meaning of a word that suggest a semantic similarity or connection between the new sense and the original one. The extension or transfer of meaning of a word is based on such a similarity coming to bridge the old and new meanings. For example, *grasp* 'to seize' changed to include also 'to understand', seeing physical 'seizing' as somehow similar to mental 'comprehension'.

metathesis Sound change involving the transposition of sounds, in which sounds exchange positions with one another within a word. For example, Old English *brid* 'bird' changed to *bird*, with the metathesis (interchange) of *ri* to *ir*.

metonymy A figure of speech in which a concept is referred to by the name of something closely associated with that thing or concept. It is a kind of semantic change in which a word comes to include additional senses that were not originally present but that are associated with the word's original meaning. Metonymic changes often involve things that are physically or conceptually located near each other, for example, English *cheek* 'fleshy side of the face below the eye' changed from its original meaning in Old English of 'jaw, jawbone'.

mutual intelligibility Ability of individuals speaking different varieties of the same language to understand one another without major difficulty and without prior study. The criterion of mutual intelligibility is often considered diagnostic for distinguishing between varieties of the same language (dialects), which are mutually intelligible, and distinct languages, which are not mutually intelligible.

narrowing Semantic change in which the range of meanings is decreased so that there are fewer contexts in which a word can be used appropriately than before the change. An example is *meat*, which originally meant 'food' in general.

Neogrammarian The Neogrammarians were a group of younger scholars who, beginning in about 1876, antagonized the leaders of the field by attacking older thinking and loudly proclaiming their own views. They were called *Junggrammatiker* 'young grammarians' in German. *Jung-* 'young' had the sense of 'young Turk', originally intended as a term of abuse, although the Neogrammarians adopted it as their own name. Their slogan was "sound laws suffer no exceptions."

Neogrammarian hypothesis, see **regularity of sound change**

neologism A newly formed word that has become accepted into mainstream language.

Nostratic A proposed distant genetic relationship that, as formulated in the 1960s by Vladislav Illich-Svitych, would group Indo-European, Uralic, Altaic, Kartvelian, Dravidian, and Hamito-Semitic (later also Afroasiatic) as members of a single macro-family, though other versions of the hypothesis include several other languages. It is controversial.

onomatopoeia Property of words that mimic the sound associated with their meanings, for example, *bow-wow, peep, buzz, hum.*

palatalization A sound change that makes a sound more palatal, that is, raises the blade of the tongue toward the hard palate (the roof of the mouth). Typically front vowels (*i* and *e*) and *y* can have this effect on consonants.

Penutian A very large putative distant genetic relationship, first proposed to include the Californian language families: Wintuan, Maiduan, Yokutsan, and Miwok-Costanoan. The name is based on words for 'two', of the form something like *pen* in Wintuan, Maiduan, and Yokutsan, and *uti* in Miwok-Costanoan, joined to form *Penutian*. Later proposals have attempted to unite various languages from as far afield as Alaska to Bolivia with Penutian. Today, Penutian, in all of its variations, is controversial, with very few supporters.

philology Philology has several meanings. It means the study of some classical or older language, for example English philology, Germanic philology, Romance philology. It also means historical linguistics as practiced in the nineteenth century. What today is called "historical linguistics" was often referred to earlier as "philology," as in "Indo-European philology." Philology also means the field that attempts to retrieve systematic information about a language from written records, for example, to obtain historical information from documents in order to learn about the culture and history of the people behind the text. And, in a narrower sense, it is investigation to interpret older written attestations with the goal of obtaining information about the history of the language (or languages) in which the documents are written.

phylum A proposed genetic relationship that would group together language families (also isolates) in a larger-scale classification. "Phylum" usually refers to a grouping of languages thought by some to be distantly related to one another, though on the basis of inconclusive evidence, more or less equivalent to macro-family. See also distant genetic relationship.

pidgin A simplified language, typically with a reduced grammar and vocabulary, used for communication between groups speaking different languages who have no other language in common. A pidgin is not spoken as a first or native language. The process by which pidgins arise is referred to as *pidginization*.

PIE, see **Proto-Indo-European**

Proto-Indo-European The parent language from which the languages of the Indo-European language family descend – presumed to have once been an actual spoken language – also the results of attempts to reconstruct this language by means of the comparative method. It is often abbreviated as PIE. Proto-Indo-European diversified into several branches. The main ones are: Anatolian, Tocharian, Greek, Armenian, Albanian, Italic, Celtic, Germanic, Balto-Slavic, and Indo-Iranian. English is an Indo-European language, a member of the Germanic branch.

proto-language (also spelled *proto language* and *protolanguage*) The once-spoken ancestral language from which daughter languages descend, and, in another sense, the language reconstructed by the comparative method that represents the ancestral language from which the compared languages descend.

Proto-World A postulated proto-language from which, according to its supporters, all the world's later languages have developed.

reanalysis A change in which the structure of a linguistic element takes on a different analysis from that which it had before the change, that is, a change in which a linguistic element is assigned a different structure from what it formerly had. Reanalysis is one of only three primary mechanisms of syntactic change, together with extension and syntactic borrowing. Reanalysis changes the underlying structure of a syntactic construction, but does not modify its actual form.

recipient language The language into which a word or other linguistic element is borrowed. The language which does the borrowing from another language is called the recipient language.

reconstruction Postulation of the forms in an ancestor or in an earlier state of a language or of related languages based on the evidence available. The dominant methods for reconstruction in historical linguistics are the comparative method and internal reconstruction. The comparative method aims at recovering aspects of the proto-language, the ancestor from which forms in various daughter languages descend. It compares what the daughter languages inherited from their ancestor and postulates, that is, reconstructs the linguistic traits that the proto-language possessed. Internal reconstruction aims at arriving at a stage of an individual language prior to various conditioned changes the language may have undergone.

rebus In writing systems, representation of words (or parts of words) by pictures of objects or symbols, where regardless of its meaning, the name of the object or symbol depicted sounds like the intended word. Rebuses have been likened to word puns, visual riddles. For example, a picture of the sun together with a picture of a flower is interpretable as meaning 'sunflower'.

reflex A sound or linguistic form in a daughter language that descends from a particular sound or element of the proto-language. An original sound of the proto-language is said to be reflected by the sound which descends from it in a daughter language. Elements other than just sounds, for example words or grammatical constructions, can also reflect the elements of the proto-language from which they descend.

regularity hypothesis, see regularity of sound change

regularity of sound change (regularity hypothesis, Neogrammarian hypothesis) A well-established principle of historical linguistics that holds that sound changes are regular. This means that sounds do not change in unpredictable ways, that a sound changes systematically, regularly, throughout a language everywhere it fits the description of the change, the contexts in which the sound change takes place. For example, every *k* before *n* at the beginning of words in Old English was regularly lost, as seen in the modern-day pronunciation of *knee*, *knife*, *knight*, *knot*, and *know*.

relic, see **archaism**

revitalization, see **language revitalization**

rhotacism Sound change in which *s* or an *s*-like sound becomes *r*.

Romance, Romance language A term referring to languages that descend from a form of Latin often referred to as 'Vulgar Latin' (meaning 'vernacular, popular' or 'people's Latin'), which has been independently reconstructed using the comparative method to give Proto-Romance. This vernacular variety of Latin differs considerably in all regards (words, sounds, and grammar) from elite Classical Latin, which is abundantly attested in the literary texts of Roman antiquity. The popular variety was mostly unwritten but was spoken by the large, illiterate majority. Modern Romance languages include French, Italian, Portuguese, Romanian, Spanish, and a number of others.

sister language A language that is related to another language by virtue of having descended from the same common ancestor (proto-language); a language that belongs to the same language family as another language. (See also daughter language.)

semantic Pertaining to meaning in language. **Semantics** is also the subfield of linguistics that studies meaning.

shared aberrancy (also called "submerged feature") Something shared by languages that is so arbitrary or anomalous that the matching is highly unlikely to be due to borrowing or accident. Such cases are held to be strong evidence that the languages sharing the trait are likely to be genetically related to one another. English *good/better/best* compared with German *gut/besser/best* is considered a solid example of this kind of arbitrary association that shows that these languages are related to each other genealogically.

sound correspondence Sounds that correspond regularly among related languages because they descend from a common ancestral sound inherited in the daughter languages from their common parent. In the comparative method, one seeks regular sound correspondences in sets of cognates in the daughter languages in order to reconstruct the proto-sounds of the ancestral language from which each sound correspondence derives.

sound symbolism A direct association in a language between sounds and meaning, where the meaning typically involves "size" or "shape." The relationship between sound and meaning is assumed to be arbitrary in ordinary words, but it is not arbitrary in instances of sound symbolism. For example, in English, lengthening of a vowel is sometimes associated with larger size or intensity, sometimes represented in writing as, for example, 'it was soooo ugly', 'it was reeeaaally wonderful', 'it was biiig and looong'. Nevertheless, a vowel length opposition is not a formal part of the English sound system, though it is in some languages. In English, there is no contrast between long versus unlengthened vowels; contrasting meanings in words in English cannot be shown by a difference between long and plain vowels, as the difference between high and mid vowels can, as for example, in *bit* versus *bed* or *fill* versus *fell*.

stock A term used sometimes in the past as equivalent to language family or family tree. It is sometimes used also in the sense of a group of genetically related languages that is larger and usually older than ordinary language families, for example as a language family that includes several other (sub)families among its daughters. Unfortunately, *stock* has also frequently been used not just to designate larger-scale, more inclusive language families, but also as a term for a proposed distant genetic relationship among languages whose relatedness has not been demonstrated.

stop (also called *plosive*) A consonant in whose articulation the flow of air in the vocal tract is completely blocked momentarily before it is suddenly released, as in the pronunciation of *p, t, k, b, d*, and *g*.

subfamily, see **subgroup**

subgroup (also called *subfamily, branch*) A group of languages within a language family that are more closely related to one other than to other languages of that family. *Subgrouping* involves the internal classification of language families, determining which sister languages are more closely related to one another within the family, working out the relationships among the related languages of a family tree. Larger-scale language families can include smaller-scale families among their branches, their subgroups. As a proto-language (say, Proto-Indo-European) diversifies, it develops daughter languages (such as, in the case of Indo-European,

Proto-Germanic, Proto-Celtic, and so on). If a daughter (for instance Proto-Germanic) later on splits up and develops daughter languages of its own (such as English, German, and so on), then those descendants (English, German, and others) of that earlier daughter language (Proto-Germanic) constitute members of a subgroup (the Germanic languages), and the original daughter language (Proto-Germanic) becomes in effect an intermediate proto-language in its own right, a parent of its own immediate descendants (its daughters, English, German, and so on), but still at the same time it is a descendant (daughter) itself, a branch of the original proto-language (Proto-Indo-European).

subjunctive A term of traditional grammar for forms of verbs in utterances that express a wish, suggestion, demand, anticipation, or hypothetical situation. Subjunctives do not refer to real events and states but rather to possible events or states, typically viewed emotionally or with a particular attitude on the part of the speaker. Examples of subjunctives in English are: Coyote wishes that he **were** faster. Roadrunner demanded that Coyote **stop** chasing him.

syllabary In writing systems, a syllabary is a kind of script where each character represents a syllable, or often just the first consonant and vowel of a syllable. Some syllabaries are the scripts used to write Cherokee, Japanese, and Linear B for Mycenaean Greek.

synecdoche A kind of semantic change, often considered a kind metonymy, that involves a part-to-whole relationship in which a term with more comprehensive meaning comes to be used for a less comprehensive meaning, or vice versa. In synecdoche a part (or quality) is used to refer to the whole, or the whole is used to refer to a part, for example *hand*, a part, was extended to include also 'hired hand, employed worker', the thing or person that *hand* is a part of.

umlaut A sound change in which a vowel is fronted, that is, pronounced more towards the front of the mouth, under the influence of a following front vowel (*i* or *e*) or *y*, usually in the next syllable. For example, Proto-Germanic **badja* 'bed' became *bedja* by umlaut because the first *a* was fronted to *e* when it was followed in the next syllable by *j* (the symbol used in Germanic to write *y*). Later the **-ja* was lost in most of the Germanic languages, leaving English *bed* and German *Bett*, among others. Umlaut is also the diacritic mark with two dots over certain vowels in Finnish, German, Turkish, and other languages, as for example *ä, ö, ü*.

unclassified language A language which has either no documentation at all or for which the available documentary evidence is so scant that it cannot be shown to be related to any other language. Actually, such languages are unclassifiable, because there is not sufficient evidence upon which to base decisions of classification. Unclassified languages differ from language isolates. Language isolates have sufficient available information on the basis of which to show that they cannot be shown to be related to any other language. For unclassified languages, the available information is insufficient to be able to reach such a conclusion.

Uralic A large, well-known language family that takes its name from the Ural Mountains. Uralic languages extend over a vast area from Siberia to central Europe to the Baltic Sea. Its two major branches are *Finno-Ugric* (some thirty languages) and *Samoyed* (some dozen languages). Finnish, Estonian, Hungarian, and numerous others belong to Finno-Ugric.

variety Any distinct form of language that is sufficiently homogeneous to be analyzed linguistically, particular to some specific region or social group. It includes dialects, registers, or styles of language, as well as both nonstandard and standard forms of a language. Variety is sometimes used as a sort of purposely vague cover term when it is not certain what kind of language is being talked about, whether an independent language, dialect, or anything else.

voiced Sounds with the vocal cords vibrating during their production, as in English *b, d, g, v,* "*zh*" ([ž]), "*dh*" ([ð]), *r, l, m, n,* "*ng*" ([ŋ]), *w, y,* and vowels.

voiceless Sounds produced without the vocal cords vibrating during their production, as with English *p, t, k, f, s,* "*sh*" ([š]), "*th*" ([θ]), etc.

voiced aspirated stop More accurately, voiced aspirated stops are considered breathy stops or murmured stops. These are technical terms. Here, "breathy" or "murmured" means that the vocal cords vibrate as they do for plain voiced stops, *b, d, g,* and *g^w*, but are adjusted to allow more air to escape. The *bh, dh, gh,* and *gwh* of Proto-Indo-European, Sanskrit, and many modern Indic languages sound like a cross between normal voiced stops and a whisper.

widening (also called *broadening*) A kind of semantic change in which the range of meanings of a word increases so that the word can be used in more contexts than were appropriate before the change. For example, in Middle English times, *cupboard* meant 'a table (then a table was called a "board") upon which cups and other vessels were placed, a piece of furniture to display plates', but its meaning was broadened to became 'a closet or cabinet with shelves for keeping cups and dishes', and then finally in America it changed to the even wider meaning of any 'small storage cabinet'.

References

Aarsleff, Hans. 1982. *From Locke to Saussure: Essays on the Study of Language and Intellectual History*. London: The Athlone Press. (Originally published by University of Minnesota Press 1982.)

Anthony, David W. and Don Ringe. 2015. The Indo-European homeland from linguistic and archaeological perspectives. *Annual Review of Linguistics* 1: 199–219. https://doi.org/10.1146/annurev-linguist-030514-124812.

Anttila, Raimo. 1989. *An Introduction to Historical and Comparative Linguistics*, 2nd edition. Amsterdam: John Benjamins.

Bierer, Donald E., Thomas J. Carlson, and Steven R. King. 1996. Shaman pharmaceuticals: Integrating indigenous knowledge, tropical medicinal plants, medicine, modern science, and reciprocity into a novel drug discovery approach. *Retreat Ayahuasca*. http://www.retreatayahuasca.com/Ethnobotaniq ue/feature11.html.

Boas, Franz. 1911. Introduction. *Handbook of American Indian Languages*. (Bureau of American Ethnology, Bulletin 40, part 1: 5–83.) Washington, DC: Government Printing Office.

Brown, Cecil H. and Stanley R. Witkowski. 1979. Aspects of the phonological history of Mayan-Zoquean. *International Journal of American Linguistics* 45: 34–47.

Burnet, James [Lord Monboddo]. 1774. *Of the Origin and Progress of Language*, vol. 2. Edinburgh: J. Balfour.

Campbell, Lyle (ed.). 2018. *Language Isolates*. Abingdon: Routledge.

Campbell, Lyle. 2020. *Historical Linguistics: An Introduction*, 4th edition. Edinburgh: Edinburgh University Press.

Campbell, Lyle. 2022. *Linguist on the Loose: Adventures and Misadventures in Fieldwork*. Edinburgh: Edinburgh University Press.

Campbell, Lyle. 2024. *The Indigenous Languages of the Americas: History and Classification*. Oxford: Oxford University Press.

Campbell, Lyle and Russell Barlow. 2020. Is language change good or bad? *Questions About Language: What Everyone Should Know about Language in the 21st Century*, ed. by Laurie Bauer and Andreea S. Calude, 80–90. Abingdon: Routledge.

Campbell, Lyle and Terrence Kaufman. 1976. A linguistic look at the Olmecs. *American Antiquity* 41: 80–89.

Campbell, Lyle and William J. Poser. 2008. *Language Classification: History and Method*. Cambridge: Cambridge University Press.

Campbell, Lyle and Kenneth Rehg. 2018 Introduction. *Handbook of Endangered Languages*, ed. by Kenneth Rehg and Lyle Campbell, 1–18. Oxford: Oxford University Press.

Cooper, James Fenimore. 1826. *The Last of the Mohicans*. New York: Penguin.

Copping, Jasper. 2011. The 'conTROversy' over changing pronunciations. *The Telegraph*, Feb. 5. www.telegraph.co.uk/news/newstopics/howaboutthat/8305 645/TheconTROversy-over-changing-pronunciations.html.

Crystal, David. 2000. *Language Death*. Cambridge: Cambridge University Press.

Crystal, David. 2005. *The Stories of English*. New York: Abrams.

Crystal, David. 2009. *Just a Phrase I'm Going Through*. London: Routledge.

Darwin, Charles. 1871. *The Descent of Man, and Selection in Relation to Sex*. London: John Murray.

Defoe, Daniel. 1889. *The Compleat English Gentleman*. London: David Nutt.

Dewaele, Jean-Marc and Li Wei. 2013. Is multilingualism linked to a higher tolerance of ambiguity? *Bilingualism: Language and Cognition* 16: 231–240.

Driem, George van. 2001. *Languages of the Himalayas*. 2 vols. Leiden: Brill.

Durkin, Philip. 2014. *Borrowed Words: A History of Loanwords in English*. Oxford: Oxford University Press.

Eberhard, David M., Gary F. Simons, and Charles D. Fennig (eds.). 2024. *Ethnologue: Languages of the World*, 27th edition. Dallas, TX: SIL International. www.ethnologue.com.

Farmer, Steve, Richard Sproat, and Michael Witzel. 2004. The collapse of the Indus-script thesis: The myth of a literate Harappan civilization. *Electronic Journal of Vedic Studies* 11: 19–57.

Farrar, Frederick W. 1873. *Chapters on Language*. London: Longmans, Green & Co.

Felger, Richard and Mary Beck Moser. 1973. Eelgrass (*Zostera marina L.*) in the Gulf of California. *Science* 181.4097: 355–356.

Frazer, Sir James George. 1957 [1922]. *The Golden Bough: A Study in Magic and Religion*, abridged edition. London: Macmillan. (First published in two volumes in 1890, in three volumes in 1900, and in twelve volumes in the third edition, 1906–1915.)

Freud, Sigmund. 1965. *New Introductory Lectures on Psychoanalysis*. (Translated by James Strachey.) New York: Norton.

Greenberg, Joseph H. 1963. *The Languages of Africa*. (Indiana University Research Center in Anthropology, Folklore, and Linguistics, publication 25, *International Journal of American Linguistics* 29.1.II) Bloomington, IN: Indiana University Press. (2nd edition with additions and corrections 1966, Bloomington, IN: Indiana University Press.)

Greenberg, Joseph H. 1978. Introduction. *Universals of Human Language*, ed. by Joseph H. Greenberg, Charles A. Ferguson, and Edith A. Moravcsik, vol. 2, 1–6. Palo Alto, CA: Stanford University Press.

Greenberg, Joseph H. 1987. *Language in the Americas*. Stanford, CA: Stanford University Press.

Grimm, Jacob. 1848. *Geschichte der deutschen Sprache*, vol. 1. Leipzig: Weidmannsche.

Grimm, Jacob and Wilhelm Grimm. 1854. *Deutsches Wörterbuch*, vol. 1. Leipzig: S. Hirzil.

Gurov, Nikita Vladimirovich. 1989. *Kusunda – sinokavkazskie leksicheskie paral-leli. Lingvisticheskaja rekonstrukcija I drevnejshaja istorija vostoka.* Moscow: Izdatel'stvo Nauka.

Harris, Alice C. and Lyle Campbell. 1995. *Historical Syntax in Cross-Linguistic Perspective.* Cambridge: Cambridge University Press.

Haspelmath, Martin and Uri Tadmor. 2009. *Loanwords in the World's Languages: A Comparative Handbook.* Berlin: Mouton de Gruyter.

Hewson, John. 1982. Beothuk and the Algonkian Northeast. *Languages in Newfoundland and Labrador,* ed. by Harrold J. Paddock, 176–187. St. John's, Newfoundland: Department of Linguistics, Memorial University.

Hickey, Raymond. 2000. Models for describing aspect in Irish English. *The Celtic Englishes,* vol. II, ed. by Hildegard Tristram, 97–116. Heidelberg: Winter.

Holmes, Bob. 2013. How many uncontacted tribes are there left in the world? *New Scientist,* August 22. www.newscientist.com/article/dn24090-how-many-uncontacted-tribes-are-left-in-the-world.

Hrozný, Friedrich. 1915. Die Lösung des hethitischen Problems. *Mitteilungen der Deutschen Orient-Gesellschaft* 56: 17–50.

Hrozný, Friedrich. 1917. *Die Sprache der Hethiter.* Leipzig: J. C. Hinrichs.

Igla, Birgit. 1997. Romani. *Contact Linguistics: An International Handbook of Contemporary Research 14,* ed. by Hans Goebl, Peter H. Nelde, Zdenek Stary, and Wolfgang Wölck, 1961–1971. Berlin: Mouton de Gruyter.

Kuhn, Franz Felix Adalbert. 1845. *Zur Ältesten Geschichte der Indogermanischen Völker.* Berlin: Berliner Real-Gymnasium.

Lass, Roger. 1980. *On Explaining Language Change.* Cambridge: Cambridge University Press.

Lass, Roger. 1992. Phonology and morphology. *The Cambridge History of the English Language,* vol. 2: *1066–1476,* ed. by Norman Blake, 23–155. Cambridge: Cambridge University Press.

Lounsbury, Thomas R. 1908. *The Standard of Usage in English.* New York: Harper & Brothers.

Mallory, J. P. and D. Q. Adams. 1997. *Encyclopedia of Indo-European Culture.* London: Fitzroy Dearborn.

Martin, Laura. 1986. "Eskimo words for snow": A case study in the genesis and decay of an anthropological example. *American Anthropologist* 88: 418–423.

Matras, Yaron. 2002. *Romani: A Linguistic Introduction.* Cambridge: Cambridge University Press.

Maugham, W. Somerset. 1949. *A Writer's Notebook.* Garden City, NY: Doubleday & Co.

Meillet, Antoine. 1967[1925]. *La méthode comparative en linguistique historique.* Paris: Champion. (English translation 1967: *The Comparative Method in Historical Linguistics.* Paris: Champion.)

Montaigne, Michel de. 1943. *The Complete Essays of Montaigne.* (Translated by Donald M. Frame.) Stanford, CA: Stanford University Press.

Nash, Ogden. 1960. Laments for a dying language. *The New Yorker,* April 23, p. 43. New York: The New Yorker.

Newman, Edwin. 1974. *Strictly Speaking: Will America Be the Death of English?* Indianapolis: Bobbs-Merrill.

Orrery, Charles Boyle. 1698. *Dr. Bentley's Dissertations on the Epistles of Phalaris, and the fables of Æsop, examin'd by the Honourable Charles Boyle, Esq.* London: Printed for Tho. Bennet.

Palosaari, Naomi and Lyle Campbell. 2011. Structural aspects of language endangerment. *The Cambridge Handbook of Endangered Languages*, ed. by Peter K. Austin and Julia Sallabank, 100–119. Cambridge: Cambridge University Press.

Payne, E. J. 1899. *History of the New World called America*, vol. 2. Oxford: Oxford University Press.

Pereltsvaig, Asya and Martin W. Lewis. 2015. *The Indo-European Controversy: Facts and Fallacies in Historical Linguistics.* Cambridge: Cambridge University Press.

Pfeiffer, Ida Laura. 1852. *A Lady's Voyage Round the World.* London: G. Routledge & Co. (Translated from *Eine Frauenfahrt um die Welt*, 1850.)

Pictet, Adolphe. 1859–1863. *Les Origines indo-européennes, ou, les Aryas primitifs: essai de paléontologie linguistique.* Paris: J. Cherbuliez.

Polenz, Peter von. 1977. *Geschichte der deutschen Sprache.* Berlin: Walter de Gruyter.

Poser, William J. 1992. The Salinan and Yurumanguí data in *Language in the Americas. International Journal of American Linguistics* 58: 202–229.

Pullum, Geoffrey K. 1989. The great Eskimo vocabulary hoax. *Natural Language & Linguistic Theory* 7: 275–281. (Reprinted in Geoffrey K. Pullum, 1991: *The Great Eskimo Vocabulary Hoax and Other Irreverent Essays on the Study of Language.* Chicago: University of Chicago Press.)

Rehg, Kenneth and Lyle Campbell (eds.). 2018. *Handbook of Endangered Languages.* Oxford: Oxford University Press.

Sapir, Edward. 1916. *Time Perspective in Aboriginal American Culture: A Study in Method.* (Canada, Department of Mines, Geological Survey, Memoir no. 90, Anthropological Series no. 13.) Ottawa: Government Printing Bureau. (Reprinted in Mandelbaum, David G. (ed.). 1949. *The Collected Works of Edward Sapir*, 389–467. Berkeley, CA: University of California Press.)

Sapir, Edward. 1933. Language. *Encyclopaedia of the Social Sciences*, vol. 9, pp. 155–169. New York: Macmillan.

Sayce, Archibald Henry. 1875. *The Principles of Comparative Philology.* London: Trübner.

Schrader, Otto. 1883 [1890]. *Sprachvergleichung und Urgeschichte: Linguistisch-historische Beiträge zur Erforschung des indogermanischen Altertums.* Jena: Costenoble. (English translation 1890: *Prehistoric Antiquities of the Aryan Peoples: A Manual of Comparative Philology and the Earliest Culture.* London: C. Griffin.)

Singh, Leher, Paul C. Quinn, Miao Qian, and Kang Lee. 2020. Bilingualism is associated with less racial bias in preschool children. *Developmental Psychology* 56: 888–896.

Swadesh, Morris. 1951. Diffusional cumulation and archaic residue as historical explanation. *Southwestern Journal of Anthropology* 7: 1–21.

Sweet, Henry. 1911. Grimm, Jacob Ludwig Carl. *Encyclopædia Britannica*, vol. 12, pp. 600–602.

Swift, Jonathan. 1711–1712. *A Proposal for Correcting, Improving and Ascertaining the English Tongue: In a Letter to the Most Honourable Robert Earl of Oxford and Mortimer, Lord High Treasurer of Great Britain*, 2nd edition. London: Tooke.

Tolkien, J. R. R. 1963. English and Welsh. *Angles and Britons: O'Donnell Lectures*, ed. by Henry Lewis, 1–41. Cardiff: University of Wales Press.

Twain, Mark. 1935. *Mark Twain's Notebook*. New York: Harper and Brothers.

Tylor, Edward B. 1881. *Anthropology: An Introduction to the Study of Man and Civilisation*. New York: Macmillan.

Watkins, Calvert. 2011. *The American Heritage Dictionary of Indo-European Roots*, 3rd edition. Boston, MA: Houghton Mifflin.

Whorf, Benjamin L. 1956. The relation of habitual thought and behavior to language. *Language, Thought, and Reality: Selected Writings of Benjamin Lee Whorf*, ed. by John Carroll, 134–159. Cambridge, MA: MIT Press.

Zanuttini, Raffaella. 2015. Don't fear our changing language. *Pacific Standard*, February 17. https://psmag.com/social-justice/dont-fear-our-totally-changing-language.

Index

For EU product safety concerns, contact us at Calle de José Abascal, 56–1°, 28003 Madrid, Spain or eugpsr@cambridge.org.

www.ingramcontent.com/pod-product-compliance
Ingram Content Group UK Ltd.
Pitfield, Milton Keynes, MK11 3LW, UK
UKHW021902070626
471968UK00004B/17